DEATH AND BEREAVEMENT AROUND THE WORLD

Volume 1:
Major Religious Traditions

Edited by

John D. Morgan, Ph.D.
London, Ontario, Canada

Pittu Laungani, Ph.D.
London, United Kingdom

Death, Value and Meaning Series
Series Editor: John D. Morgan

Baywood Publishing Company, Inc.
AMITYVILLE, NEW YORK

Library of Congress Catalog Number: 2002020820
ISBN: 0-89503-272-4 (cloth)
ISBN: 0-89503-273-2 (paper)

Library of Congress Cataloging-in-Publication Data

Death and bereavement around the world / edited by John D. Morgan and
Pittu Laungani.
    p. cm. - - (Death, value, and meaning series)
Includes bibliographical references and index.
    ISBN 0-89503-272-4 - - ISBN 0-89503-273-2 (pbk.)
    1. Death- -Religious aspects. 2. Bereavement- -Religious aspects. I.
Morgan, John D., 1933- II. Laungani, Pittu. III. Series.
    BL504 .D335 2002
    306.9'09- -dc21   2002020820

Table of Contents

General Introduction

John D. Morgan
Pittu Laungani

A culture consists of the manners in which groups of persons pursue their interests with one another, and with the material environment. It represents the pattern of values passed from generation to generation; the way of life of the group; material objects; knowledge; customs; beliefs; art; laws; moral ideas; and ideas of success. Briefly, a culture is the set of ideas by which we live [1, p. 70].

Death is a fact. Bereavement is a fact. Dying and grieving, however, are processes in which we engage. As is the case with all processes, we engage in them in the manner in which we have been taught. Robert Kastenbaum has referred to these processes as a "death system" [2, p. 193], the manners in which we have been taught to do our dying and grieving. The death system is a snapshot—a picture of the way we understand, feel about, act with relationship to death and grief.

Death systems are culture specific. They do not indicate some theoretical views of dying or grieving, but the way that real persons die and grieve at particular moments and with particular family and friends. Death systems differ because of four major factors. These factors are: 1) assumed life expectancy; 2) exposure to death and grief; 3) assumed control over the forces of nature; and 4) the perception of what it is to be a person [2, p. 193]. Given the diversity of the peoples of the world, and the diversity even within countries and cultures, one can see that there will be a great variety of views, attitudes, and behaviors about death and grief. It is this great variety of customs that we address in these volumes.

In the industrialized world at the beginning of the 21st century, there are few role models in how to die or how to grieve. One grows up assuming that they, and their loved ones, will live into their 70s, 80s, and even beyond. Since their aged, sick, dying, and dead are cared for by professionals, they have had little personal experience with the end of life. An "out of sight, out of mind" attitude develops. The great benefits produced by strides in sanitation, water purification, food

1

distribution, and improvement of medical care, leaves one thinking that all life-limiting problems can be solved, that control over nature is easily achieved. In addition, we live in a culture which emphasizes the uniqueness of individual persons. While we grow up in families, many believe that they out-grow their families and are fully independent by their early twenties. They do not readily seek support in extended family units or in the larger community. The sum total of these influences leaves one little prepared to face the reality of dying and grieving.

Death is denied in the industrialized world, not in some logical thought but in the sense that ultimate reality is something that one has to think about only rarely and then get back to the "important things of life" as soon as possible. As Goldman has pointed out, whenever there is an emotional event that is likely to happen—a marriage, a child birth, graduation from school, a new job—we think of the event often, perhaps continuously. Even though the death of someone close to us is a highly emotional event that has a 100 percent chance of happening, we never allow ourselves to think of it [3, p. 7]. This is "death denied." Death is a reality, but "not yet." Ours is a "no muss, no fuss" view of death [4, p. 178].

Not everyone in the world handles death and bereavement in the manner of our industrialized societies. Aries postulated that there have been four major orientations to death throughout human history [5]. One we have already seen—the death denied orientation. In other cultures, at other times, death was viewed as a neighbor, a reality who might drop in at any time, welcomed or not. This was the fundamental attitude to death in the long history of humanity until fairly recently. Another view was that death was fundamentally the end of the drama that is each personal life [p. 5]. The death bed was a family (sometimes public) event, last words commonly recorded, the last wishes attended to with devotion. The final orientation that Aries mentions is death as perceived as the end of relationships. This could be found in the death of a life partner or the public execution of a criminal [5, p. 266].

Death of the aged is often still considered "appropriate" ; that is, death comes as an expected neighbor. Grief experiences, as seen in widowhood and at the death of a parent, still show us that death is seen as the ending of a relationship. The fascination with executions, both in the United States and in the rest of the world, indicate our fascination with the death of the other. Each of the "death systems" listed above are still found to some extent in our industrialized societies. But the dominant theme in industrialized societies is that death and grief are realities to be ignored as long as possible. As we will see in the chapters that occur in these volumes, other cultures are closer to the familiarity of death or to the relational aspects of death and grief than are industrialized cultures.

It is not simple however. We live in an increasingly smaller world. The great migrations of peoples which populated North and South America in the last two centuries were exacerbated by the Second World War as well as civil disruptions in the latter half of the 20th century. In addition, the expanded prosperity of the industrialized world has caused a great flow of people from the increasing poverty of the rest of the world. In Canada, for example, in the year 2000, 20 percent of the population was born somewhere else. In the United States, 18 percent. In every case, the immigrant brings with him or her the attitudes and traditions of his or her past.

An understanding of cultural differences is important for everyone today for two fundamental reasons. The first is that cultural traditions and values act as filters through which we, and those we help, understand the world, and through which they hear what is being said to them. We all know how easily we misunderstand what is being said to us, particularly when we are under stress. This normal human behavior is aggravated when we deal with persons of different cultures, especially when we or they are under the stress of death related issues.

A second, but equally important reason to be attentive to the culture of the other is that we make decisions, not simply on the basis of facts—immediate data given to us—but on how those data interface with our fundamental values. If all decisions were logical, we would all have given up smoking, lost weight, and engaged in more physical exercise. We make changes in our lives only when those changes are consistent with our values. By understanding what values and traditions are important to our colleagues, neighbors, patients, students, or clients, we will understand how they arrive at the decisions that they do. This understanding can be an open door to helping them in times of need.

A knowledge of cultures is particularly necessary for health care workers because culture affects: the understanding of the meaning of death; the rituals of coping with the dying process, burial, and commemoration; beliefs about an afterlife; mourning and expressions of grief; roles for men, women, and children; the role of the family in dying, burial, and mourning; the classifications of denied, stigmatized, or traumatic mourning [4, p. 179].

Effective care requires knowledge of the person in their physical, social, educational, and spiritual levels of being. If one is to provide the care needed in moments of crisis, it is imperative to attend to the way that the patient or client views the world. The experience and expression of grief and the needs that emerge, may vary widely from individual to individual. They are subject to many variables, including past experiences, personal beliefs, and relationships. People die and grieve as they live, on the basis of their sense of identity. Our personal identity comes from our sense of personal uniqueness; our sense of solidarity with the group ideals; our sense of continuity from the past, into the present, and thus into the future; and from the culture in which we were raised and/or the culture which we have adopted [6, p. 68].

In these volumes we will look at the values involved in confronting death and bereavement as seen in the "Major Religious Traditions" (Volume 1); "Death and Bereavement in the Americas" (Volume 2); "Death and Bereavement in Europe" (Volume 3); "Death and Bereavement in Asia, Australia, and

New Zealand" (Volume 4); and finally a series of essays reflecting on the discoveries of the earlier volumes (Volume 5).

Works such as these are by their nature incomplete. The world changes daily, and with it the cultures which reflect attitudes to death and dying. The death awareness movement started in the 60s has had a hand in these changes. However incomplete this collection of readings is, we believe that it makes a contribution. Not every religious or national culture is reflected. However, we believe that enough is presented that one can extrapolate for the missing parts.

We have enjoyed gathering these chapters. We hope that you find these volumes useful.

REFERENCES

1. J. Ortega y Gasset, *Mission of the University*, Norton, New York, 1944.
2. R. Kastenbaum and R. Aisenberg, *The Psychology of Death*, Springer, New York, 1972.
3. L. Goldman, *Death and the Creative Life*, Springer, New York, 1981.
4. M. McGoldrick, R. Almeida, P. M. Hines, E. Rosen, N. Garcia-Preto, and E. Lee, Mourning in Different Cultures, in *Living Beyond Loss: Death in the Family*, F. Walsh and M. McGoldrick (eds.), W. W. Norton, New York, pp. 126-206, 1991.
5. P. Ariès, *The Hour of Our Death*, Knopf, New York, 1981.
6. E. G. Pask, Culture, Caring and Curing in the Changing Health Scene, in *Meeting the Needs of Our Clients Creatively*, J. D. Morgan (ed.), Baywood, Amityville, New York, pp. 106-123, 2000.

John D. Morgan, Ph.D.
London, Ontario, Canada

Pittu Laungani, Ph.D.
London, United Kingdom

Introduction to the First Volume

Brian Morgan

As John Morgan points out in the general introduction to this series, "death is a fact." Therefore, it is not difficult to figure out where we will end, only the road we take to get there. This volume indicates the paths that the major religious traditions teach. The paths pointed out by these religions deal little with "known reality," and much more with faith, based "after death" descriptions of those paths' goals. The Christian religions discussed in this book speak of resurrection as the pinnacle moment in a person of faith's life. Yet, resurrection happens after death. Death, the opening to the afterlife, is, therefore, the defining moment in the life of a person who belongs to a Christian faith. We will find that several other belief systems focused at the moment of death as well. For this reason, when life and faith are defined at death, it seems that this would be the time when religion would be most meaningful to a person.

It is at the moment of death that religious people cease to be part of the known and prepare to be part of the unknown. It is here that religion is used as the road map that travels from life to death, to the afterlife, or at least to the unknown. It is by the hopes and expectations of these same religions that grieving families travel through their grief. This book, an in-depth look at the faiths and religions that dying people and grieving families use to travel, is then an appropriate and valuable guide for care givers.

Each of the chapters provide, while discussing death through religion, insights into the people themselves, their history, politics, and hopes. The traditions are strikingly similar and noticeably different. All cultures have developed symbolic systems or religions that incorporate the experience and understanding of death into a larger whole that gives meaning to life [1]. As Gerry Cox writes, "By studying the health practices and the burial and mortuary customs, one can learn much of the philosophy and religion of a people" [2, p. 161]. Pittu Laungani makes this same point, telling us that in researching his chapter about the death rituals of the Hindu faith, how much he learned about the faith of his childhood and culture. These chapters give us insight, not only about the death customs and practices of a particular religion, but also into the people themselves.

Not every religion uses death as the defining event in the life of a person of faith—there are exceptions to this, and these are attended to as well in the book. The notable example of a different approach is that of Buddhism. Dr. Kawamura writes of Buddhist tendencies not as being goal oriented, where "if one can find a response to the question of death and dying, then one can lead a meaningful life in accordance with that response" [3, p. 40]. But Buddhism is, in Kawamura's terms, "an instamatic response to the moment" [p. 40], not concerned about death.

In Judaism and Islam, the rituals of death are focused on life: first of all, a commemoration of the life of the deceased, and secondly practical help with the lives of the bereft. In these traditions, the body is treated minimally and quickly, with a funeral service happening within 24 hours with little fanfare. As Salim Mansur stated simply "the story for this person is over" [4].

The afterlife is not always something wished for, as Cox points out from the perspective of Native American views of death [2, p. 167]. Death and afterlife are not goals to be attained but events to be feared. Large rocks are moved on top of grave sites so that the restless soul cannot come out.

One of the great debates of religious history is the role that the afterlife takes in Judaic thought. Judith Hauptman's chapter on the Jewish rituals of death shows how little the afterlife actually plays in Jewish thought. Ronald Trojcak, however, holds that the Christian belief in an afterlife is based in Jewish philosophy, and afterlife is a large part of the Jewish belief system. Ms. Hauptman's chapter is Talmudic, that is rooted in the first five books of the Bible. Dr. Trojcak takes his thesis from later developments.

The Hebrew Bible begins with an affirmation that the world came from God and is good. At the moment of death, a witness to that death in the Jewish tradition would recite "blessed is the just judge," an affirmation of the goodness of reality. Death rituals in Judaism are created to help the grieving, not the deceased. This would confirm Hauptman's point of "Judaism being a joyful and life-affirming tradition" [5, p. 76].

Christianity has taken a different emphasis. The Christian views discussed in this volume differ greatly from Judaism and Islam. Koop's chapter about the Mennonite tradition, John Chirban's chapter about Greek Orthodox traditions, Edward Jeremy Miller's chapter about Catholic traditions, and Dennis Klass's chapter about Protestant traditions, all emphasize that death is the moment at which a person of faith is defined. That there is an afterlife and a reward for life. As John Chirban states in his opening paragraph, quoting St. Paul, "if Christ had not been raised, then our preaching is in vain and your faith is in vain" [6, p. 103]. Judaism offers practical help to the bereaved; in Islam, excessive grief is a sign of lack of faith; in Christianity, grief is a part of life that must be accepted in the manner of Christianity's source: "Jesus wept" [7].

All cultures have developed ceremonies and rituals that convey these realities to the living and the dying. It is helpful to remember the points Edgar Jackson made some years ago about the value of religion to the dying:

- It helps them control their fears and anxieties by revealing not only the tragedy and sorrow of life, but also its blessings and rich experiences.
- It emphasizes those events in the history and experience of humanity that make life seem more understandable and give more people a sense of change-lessness in the midst of change, of the eternal in the midst of time.
- It helps them to turn their best thoughts and feelings into constructive action.
- Those of faith are inspired to act as they believe, to fulfill their aspirations in life.
- It allows them to transform the tragic events of life through the direction of its hope and the power of its love.
- It leads to deeper sensitivity of the spirit, higher aspirations of service, and a firmer conviction that the cosmic purpose is best understood as creative goodness. Therefore, although grief is painful and disappointing, it does not lead to despair.
- When it contains a belief in immortality, it relieves some of the guilt and sorrow that would be present if it were thought that at no point in time or eternity could wrongs be righted or injustices rectified.
- It highlights tradition, giving people a longer view by allowing them to tie present sufferings to time-honored sources of spiritual strength, and thus transcend current pain.
- It gives courage in the present and direction for the future.
- It moves attention away from death and tragedy, not by denying them, but by fitting them into a larger perspective.
- Through community religious rituals, it provides evidence of group strength and comfort, and recognizes the dignity of life and the validity of feelings prompted by facing death [cited in 1, pp. 316-317].

The religious traditions in this volume have been presented more or less historically. We begin with Hinduism, then move to Buddhism, Judaism, Christianity, Catholicism, Orthodox Christianity, Protestantism, the Mennonite Tradition, Islam, North American Native traditions, and finally Paganism. Paganism probably predates all the others, but it is listed here last because the resurgence of it as a popular religion is new.

The history of religion is fascinating. Ernest Becker states that the confrontation with death is the most important thing that we do. There are, he says, three responses to the knowledge of universal death: denial, neurosis, and heroism. Religion for Ernest Becker is the highest form of heroism. For most people, the urge to immortality is a simple reflex of anxiety about death, but for the religious it is "a reaching out by way of one's whole being toward life" both for the self and for the universe [8, pp. 152-153]. In its ideal form, religion satisfies both of the individual's fundamental needs: It provides affirmation of one's uniqueness since God knows and loves the individual in his uniqueness; and it provides consolation for death in the promise of an eternal life. For Becker, religion is the highest form of creativity, an "outgrowth of genuine life-longing, a reaching out for a plenitude of meaning" [8, p. 153] allowing one to be "open, generous, courageous, to touch others' lives and enrich them and open to them in return" [8, p. 258]. The most remarkable achievement of the great religions has been that persons of all social or economic classes, "slaves, cripples, imbeciles, the simple and the mighty" [8, p. 160], could become heroes. The world may be "a vale of tears, or horrid sufferings, of incommensurateness, of tortuous and humiliating daily pettiness, of sickness and death, a place . . . where man could expect nothing, achieve nothing for himself. Little did it matter, because it served God and so would serve the servant of God" [8, p. 160].

All wars are ultimately religious wars, fighting over the truth that sets one free. It is important that we take this opportunity to learn more about the spiritual roots of those with whom we are privileged to work.

REFERENCES

1. T. Rando, *Grief, Dying and Death,* Research, Champaign, Illinois, 1984.
2. G. Cox, *North American Native Care of the Dying and the Grieving,* this volume.
3. L. Kawamura, *Facing Life and Death: A Buddhist's Understanding of Palliative Care and Bereavement,* this volume.
4. S. Mansur, *Delivering Care to Muslims,* Audio presentation, King's College Conference on Death and Bereavement, 1997.
5. J. Hauptman, *Death and Mourning: A Time for Weeping, A Time for Healing,* this volume.
6. J. Chirban, *Greek Orthodox Understandings of Death: Implications for Living the Easter Faith,* this volume.
7. John, 11, 36. *The Jerusalem Bible,* Doubleday, New York, 1966.
8. E. Becker, *The Denial of Death,* Free Press, New York, 1973.

CHAPTER 1

Hindu Spirituality in Life, Death, and Bereavement

Pittu Laungani

Let me start with a confession.

Right from childhood, I had participated in all the prayers and the religious ceremonies *(samskaras)* related to birth, marriage, and death, both at home and outside. I had performed the daily rites and rituals, imbibed the instructions and the teachings of the gurus and the "swamis," undertaken pilgrimages to the holy cities and shrines, bathed and "cleansed" myself on the banks of the holy river Ganges in Varanasi and Hardwar. Paradoxically, despite my Jesuit upbringing (like many middle class children in Bombay, I too was sent to a Jesuit school), I had studied Sanskrit at school and then in College, and was familiar with a few Hindu scriptures. What more could a person ask?

But when I began to think about the probable contents of the chapter, the number of pages that would need to be written, and the eventual shape and structure it would take, I began to have second thoughts about the project. Doubt, like corrosive acid, began to burn into my soul. I realized that I had made the oldest mistake of all. I had assumed that because I was born into a particular religious and cultural background, and because I could read the scriptures, it was axiomatic that I should have a deep and profound understanding of my own religion and culture. This of course is total nonsense. A merchant seaman may sail round the world a dozen times and know nothing about the countries and the people visited.

I came to the conclusion that experience alone, without genuine scholarship, is a far worse intellectual crime than scholarship without experience. I must confess, the thought of abandoning the chapter and thus "losing face" seemed a desirable death, and I almost succumbed to the temptation; but a few days of reflection convinced me that the actual business of writing the chapter, regardless of the intellectual and emotional costs involved, would be far less painful than "loss of face." I am glad I persevered.

INTRODUCTION

In order to acquire a reasonable understanding of the fundamental ideas related to Hindu spirituality and the unique way in which they manifests themselves in practices related to death and bereavement, it would be necessary to consider the major features of Hinduism. That, however, is not as easy as it sounds, for there is lack of agreement even among scholars of Hindu philosophy on this very issue. It is not clear therefore what the fundamental features of Hinduism are and how they all hang together to form a coherent and comprehensible whole. It is clear that disputations, disagreements, and differences in opinions and interpretations form an integral part of Hindu religion and Indian philosophy. It should be noted that Indian philosophy and Hindu religion are inextricably linked. One cannot study one without studying the other. To wrestle through the various texts, many of which were written in Sanskrit, and arrive at a clear and systematic understanding of the fundamental tenets of Hinduism is akin to trailing through a dense forest in a strange land. One could easily lose one's way.

Even the most fundamental of all questions, viz., the origin of Hinduism does not lend itself to an easy answer. It is riddled with controversy. Let us examine some of the controversies in some depth.

Two opposing views have been offered concerning the origin of Hinduism. At its simplest level, many scholars have argued that Hinduism, like Christianity, Islam, and Judaism, is a revealed religion. There are others who dispute such a formulation, and have argued that Hinduism, like many other religions, has evolved over centuries. Let us consider the two views briefly.

1. Hinduism: A Revealed Religion?

The orthodox Hindus who uphold the revealed nature of Hinduism place their trust in the *Vedas*, which are regarded as the most important sources of Hinduism. The word Veda is derived from the root *vid*, to know. The Vedas, of which there are four, are seen by many scholars as a form of personal communication from God to his chosen *seers* and other holy men. But the more orthodox Hindus maintain that the Veda is not the "Word of God"; it is eternal. It is an embodiment of the eternal law. It transcends the powers of any personal lawgiver.

The Vedic teachings were transmitted orally. The Indian term for this form of oral transmission is *sruti*—that which has been perceived through hearing. Since writing the text was seen by some as a form of desecration, memorization was the only way of acquiring its knowledge. It was only after the Muslim invasion into India that the four Vedas came to be written [1]. They comprise the *Rg Veda, Sama Veda, Yajur Veda,* and the *Atharva Veda.* These, in turn, are sub-divided into three or four categories. The Vedas are considered by the orthodox Hindus to be the holiest of holy books. They consist of hymns, verses, and poems; they are concerned primarily with Vedic ritual, prayers, sacrifices, the chanting of secret *mantras*, and with patterns of worship offered to the pantheon of Vedic gods [2-6].

In addition to the Vedas, there are a large number of books which are considered to be authoritative and sacred to most Hindus. While the Vedas are seen as oral transmissions, or *sruti,* the post-Vedic texts are referred to *smriti* (that which has been remembered; tradition). These books had and continue to have a significant impact on the daily lives of Hindus. Most of the books are concerned with rites, rituals, prayers, ablutions, sacrifices related to rites of passage, birth, marriage, death, and other day-to-day activities of Hindus. They are also concerned with describing the creation of the world, the origin of the four castes, the transmigration of the soul, the notions of birth, death, and rebirth, embodied in the law of karma, the nature of *dharma,* one's duty toward oneself, one's family, and society, and other matters of practical and social significance in the daily lives of Hindus. The *smritis* also have a great deal to say on the very important problem of *moksha,* immortality, or, as a Hindu would put it, liberation from the bondage of birth and rebirth—a theme which holds a cardinal position in Hindu religion. From among the vast number of books comprising the Hindu scriptures, the most popular and the most revered within Hindu culture are the *Ramayana,* the *Mahabharata* and the *Gita,* which comprises an important part of the *Mahabharata.* Stories from the *Ramayana* and the *Mahabharata* have become part of Hindu folklore, and during religious festivals are enacted all over the country, in villages, towns, and large cities—such is the impact of religion on minds, actions, and lives of people in India. Virtuous and noble deeds of valor, sacrifice, and duty by the characters in the two epics are normally held up as archetypal examples for the socialization of children. The stories are told and retold in order to inculcate specific moral values and behaviors in one's sons, daughters, daughters-in-law, friends, relatives, and others.

The influence of religion can also be seen in day-to-day activities which, by all accounts, would be considered mundane, such as washing one's hands, and, in particular, accepting drinking water from others, or offering it to others. Although seemingly trivial, they have deep-rooted religious connotations. To a Westerner, unversed in the day-to-day ritualistic practices of Hindus, such behaviors would seem strange and inexplicable. To a Hindu, however, they fall within the orbit of necessary religious ablutions, which he/she performs automatically. So much of day-to-day Hindu behavior is influenced by religious beliefs that it is virtually impossible to identify behaviors which, from a Hindu perspective, might be seen as secular [7]. In my own case, I can recall very clearly the acute conflicts I experienced when I first came to England. I could not drink a cup of tea in the morning without first having washed, cleaned my teeth, and performed the necessary morning rituals and ablutions. Such obsessive behavior had little to do with hygiene. In Hindu religion, one is in a state of spiritual pollution on waking up in the morning. It is necessary, therefore, to perform all the required rituals in order to regain a state of purification. What I found even more exasperating was the fact that, at a rational level, I could see the silliness of my action, but felt powerless to change it—so strongly had the rituals learned in childhood become internalized! It took several years before I was able to overcome my obsessive, ritualistic behaviors without a feeling of residual guilt. From time to time, it still rankles.

What is not always fully appreciated, even by the most liberal and well-meaning persons, is the extent to which we are all rooted to our own culture. The roots run deep. They extend over several centuries, and are not easily severed. People migrating to another culture bring with them not just their unique skills, qualifications, and experiences; they bring with them their hopes, their dreams, their aspirations, and of course their fears (known and unknown) and their uncertainties. Their own cultural beliefs and values, their traditions, their religious practices, their customs, their rites, rituals, and ceremonies, their dietary practices, their family structures, and equally importantly, their own language(s) which form an integral part of their upbringing, provide them with a haven of safety, security, and a sense of continuity. No immigrant, in that sense, ever travels light. No immigrant ever sheds his or her cultural legacies and acquisitions easily. One can no more jettison one's "cultural baggage" when migrating to another country than a tortoise its shell. In that sense, therefore one is handcuffed to one's culture [8].

Thus, although the rites and rituals might seem trite and ludicrous to others, they provide a source of comfort to those practicing them. Since the theme of rituals has an important bearing on understanding the practices related to death among Hindus, we shall return to it later.

2. Hinduism: An Evolved Religion?

There are several scholars who dispute the claims concerning the revealed nature of Hinduism. They, in turn, have argued that Hinduism, like most other religions, has evolved over the centuries. They have attempted to trace the origins of Hinduism to two sources: the Indus valley civilization which flourished from about 2500 BCE to about 1500 BCE and the Aryan culture which developed soon after. Whether the Aryans were Indo-Europeans who migrated from the Caucasus region into India and South Asia, or whether the Aryan culture was a development from the Indus valley civilization, is still a debated issue.

Several scholars have argued that the fair-skinned Aryans came to India around 1500 BCE as invaders and settlers, and over time established their rule over the dark-skinned Dravidian natives of India. However, the *Rg Veda*, the oldest book of the Hindus, makes no reference to any migrations of their forefathers from outside India [1]. Secondly, the archeological artifacts discovered in Mohenjo-daro and Harrapa in Sind, led to the discovery of the Indus valley civilization, which developed from about 2500 BCE. As Klostermaier points out, the "Indus valley culture did not develop due to the direct influence of external cultural forces from Sumer or Egypt, but was an indigenous development in the Baluchistan and Indus regions, growing out of earlier, local cultures" [1, p. 25]. On the basis of this evidence, it has been suggested that the Aryan culture was a subsequent development from the Indus valley civilization. This view too has not gone unchallenged. Zaehner has no doubts that the Aryans invaded India, but is uncertain as to when such an invasion might have taken place, though the consensus of opinion, according to him, "would now appear to be settling on the second half of the second millennium B.C." [9, p. 14].

While the controversies related to the origins of Hinduism might be of interest to scholars of comparative religion, they are unlikely to arouse similar interest in others. The purpose of introducing the above controversies was to demonstrate the difficulties involved in painting a clear and recognizable picture of Hinduism. It is now obvious that any attempt to explain the nature of Hinduism by discussing its major features is fraught with dangers. While such an approach might be relevant to understanding Hinduism per se, it is not useful for our purposes.

In any case, such an approach is flawed. For what it does, is to explain each important part or feature with the assumption that the sum of all parts will equal the whole. This, as we know, seldom or never happens. The Gestalt psychologists of the 1920s, particularly Kohler and Wertheimer, made it abundantly clear that the whole—the gestalt configuration—is always greater than the sum of its parts. The whole seldom bears any resemblance to its parts. A detailed study of all the parts does not allow us to understand how the whole hangs together. One may read each note of Beethoven's *Pastoral Symphony*, and yet have little understanding and appreciation of its magnificent beauty and structure. In any case, our concern is not with understanding Hinduism per se. Our main object is to understand the nature of Hinduism and Hindu spirituality *in relation to death and bereavement*. This might best be achieved by describing relevant episodes related to death and bereavement among Hindus, and then teasing out from those episodes the relevant features of Hinduism and Hindu spirituality. I have selected two events, the first one real, the second fictitious, which I should like to describe in some detail.

The first event, which took place over 50 years ago, is as follows:

EPISODE 1

A Near-Death Experience or a Return from the Dead?

This happened several years ago. I was about eight years old. We had come for our holidays to Tando Adam, a small, sleepy town, not far from Hyderabad, in Sind, Pakistan. My father had inherited some ancestral property in Tando Adam.

We came there every year from Bombay, which is where we lived. It was nice coming to Tando Adam where I met my cousins, many of whom lived there.

Around four o'clock every afternoon, the familiar and welcome face of Kalia would pass by our house. Kalia was not his real name, but since he was pitch black in complexion, we all called him Kalia, which means black. His real name, as we found out later, was Satyavan. Although Kalia might seem a derogatory term, it is also a term affectionately used when referring to the Hindu God Krishna. He didn't seem to mind—everyone called him Kalia. Kalia was a hawker. He sold hot and spicy Indian savory snacks made from potatoes, chick peas, flour, and onions fried in batter; they were garnished with chutney made with mint, tamarind, chillies, lime, and fresh coriander. No sooner did we hear his familiar cries, than we all—my cousins and I—rushed out of the house to buy the snacks. Each of us clamored for attention, wanting to be served first. By the time Kalia reached the end of our street, our snacks had disappeared and we had started to lick our fingers and bitterly regretted the fact that we did not have any more money on us.

We waited for Kalia every day; and as usual, we waited for Kalia to arrive the next afternoon. But the following morning, we all heard that Kalia had died. We were heart-broken. Not for him, though, but for the snacks which we would never eat again. My cousin, who was the oldest of the kids at home, suggested that we should all attend Kalia's funeral—as a mark of respect for the hawker who had given us such untold joy. My father was pleased and surprised that we all wanted to attend Kalia's funeral. Within our family and our community, no one had any qualms about taking young children to the crematorium. It seemed perfectly natural.

Since Kalia was a well-known and well-liked hawker in our area, virtually everyone in the neighborhood (Muslims and Hindus) turned out for his funeral. By six o'clock in the evening the crematorium was crowded with mourners. Kalia lay in his bier, which was placed on the floor, for all to see. His face was left uncovered, his body wrapped in a white shroud, bedecked with flowers. I had a glimpse of Kalia and was surprised and frightened to see how stiff and waxen he seemed. Like the others, I too bent down before the body to offer my final prayers. I almost jumped out of my skin when I thought I saw his nostrils twitch. But they were flies buzzing around his face.

Presently, the Brahmin priest in charge of the funeral ceremony took over. He recited the sacred texts in Sanskrit, and asked for the body to be lifted onto the pile of logs which had been assembled for the funeral pyre.

Kalia's eldest son, his head shaven, dressed in a white dhoti and kurta, who could not have been much older than me, was expected to perform the final funeral rites. This of course was in keeping with the ancient Hindu traditions, which decree that it is the sacred duty of the eldest son to perform all the funeral rites of his deceased father—for this ensures the peaceful repose of the father's soul. A flame was lit. It was handed to Kalia's son. He was instructed to hold the flame near the logs. The logs took. Smoke began to rise from the logs.

And then, suddenly, to everyone's total astonishment, there was a piercing cry from the logs. Before the people could even gather their wits about them, the Brahmin priest rushed toward the pile of logs, and with his hands and feet, started to dislodge the logs which had been piled on top of Kalia. Others joined in. Within a few seconds, the logs were removed, and Kalia was lifted from the funeral pyre. They placed him on the floor. His chest heaved. He coughed. He choked. He sputtered. It was clear that he was breathing. He was alive! "A miracle! A miracle!" people shouted.

Messengers were sent rushing to Kalia's house to inform his grieving wife, his two daughters, his mother, and all the other female relatives, who custom forbade their coming to the crematorium. The women, as befitting custom, had parted from their departed loved one at the threshold of Kalia's house.

While Kalia was being revived, rumors wilder than the funeral pyre spread through the crematorium. People looked at the dazed Kalia, shook their heads and laughed. Everyone knew—it was common knowledge in their area—that Kalia and his wife did not get on well with each other. In fact, they hated each other. Divorce was a taboo word, unheard of among Hindus. (To a large extent it still is.) Kalia's death had seemed a god-sent deliverance for his wife. They all knew that she would go through the motions of crying and mourning. And now he would be returning home once again. The taunts, the torments, the quarrels, and the fights would continue.

When Kalia had recovered sufficiently and was able to stand and walk, someone suggested that Kalia should once again be placed on the bier and brought home. But the bier had gotten burned. A huge procession of laughing, joking, cheerful "mourners" carried Kalia on their shoulders and brought him home. As children, we were able to enter the house and slip into the quarters where the women who, until a few moments ago, had been wailing and mourning.

Kalia's wife, upon seeing Kalia, burst into genuine tears. She cried, she wailed, she beat her breast, and finally, turned to her husband with fury, "You *shaitaan!* You tormented me while you were alive, and now as a black, evil *shaitaan*, you have returned to torment me after your death." Her screams rang through the house. They were greeted by laughter by all the people who had gathered round the house.

At home, we debated whether Kalia had really died and had returned from the dead. Can people come back from the dead we asked. The only doctor— Dr. Gurudas—who lived in our neighborhood, who would have examined Kalia, had gone to Hyderabad for a few days. It is possible that Kalia may have taken ill and slipped into a coma. Being unable to revive him, his family members and his neighbors may have concluded that he had died. We'd never know. Our neighborhood, however, buzzed with all kinds of fantastic speculations.

We wondered if Kalia would ever return to selling his savory snacks. A week later, Kalia's familiar cries had us all rushing out of the house to buy the snacks which we all craved. But by now we had imbued him with supernatural powers and were not a little frightened of him. We stopped calling him Kalia—as did the rest of the people in our neighborhood—and referred to him by his real name, Satyavan. Different versions of Kalia's supernatural powers began to circulate and gain currency. Some saw Kalia as a person of immense saintly powers, who had seen God and had returned from the dead. Others saw him in more malevolent terms, as though he had been in league with the *shaitaan*, devil. Evil gossip, like poisonous vapor, polluted the atmosphere, affecting all. Kalia had been seen dancing in the crematorium in the middle of the night, Kalia could speak in tongues, Kalia could cast spells, bewitch people; Kalia could summon evil spirits from his nostrils; the rumors were as phantasmagoric as they were absurd. Gradually, people began to avoid him. Kalia, a poor, humble, uneducated peasant, could not cope with the fear, the anger, and the contempt he aroused in the people in the neighborhood. He felt rejected by the very people he had served for several years.

A year later he threw himself into the well outside their house. His bloated body was fished out a few days later by his neighbors.

Hardly anyone—with the exception of his family members—attended his second funeral.

It should be pointed out that although the above event is quite unique, it is not significantly different from many other "near-death" experiences, described by people all over the world. Such fascinating "near-death" and "after-death" experiences have been recorded and discussed at length by Moody [10-11]. Reports of "near-death" and "after-death" experiences contain all the ingredients of high drama. They tended to attract the attention of the media, and soon different versions of the story begin to circulate, each version clamoring for attention, each asserting its own truth. The above incident, which occurred in a small town and took place over 50 years ago, probably went unnoticed.

Several questions come to mind with regard to Kalia's death. Did Kalia actually die? If so, how did he return from the dead? While he remained "dead," so to speak, did he have any experiences? If so, what kind of experiences? Was he actually aware that he had died? (This question of course begs another question: if death means cessation of all awareness, how can one be aware of one's death? The very suggestion that one might be aware of one's death introduces an irreconcilable logical contradiction.) Would he have recovered had his "lifeless" body been brought out into the courtyard and left to warm in the afternoon sun instead of being taken to the crematorium? Would he have recovered had the funeral been delayed by a day? Was Kalia incorrectly diagnosed by his family members and pronounced dead? Would he have been diagnosed correctly had the doctor not gone away from the town on the day of his "death"?

How much credence can one pay to such reported experiences? From an objective, scientific point of view, it is impossible to provide an unequivocal answer. Attempts to test the validity of such claims becomes problematic, to say the least. One might attempt a rational reconstruction of the event which transpired. But this form of post hoc analysis is beset with all kinds of methodological difficulties and is likely to be contaminated by several confounding variables. It does not permit a clear, unambiguous testing of any specific hypotheses. No causal or correlational connections can be made. At any rate, such a task is beyond the scope of the present chapter. Despite the sensational claims of "after-death" experiences which are reported in the popular press from time to time, it is necessary, for the present, to look upon them with a degree of scepticism.

Our main concern here is not whether Kalia died or did not die. Our concern is to tease out the underlying notions of spirituality embedded in the important social customs, the rites, rituals, and the ceremonies which followed Kalia's death and "resurrection." Hindu spirituality can seldom be understood without a close examination of rituals. As Flood points out, "it is ritual action which anchors people in a sense of deeper identity and belonging. While Hindus have questioned the meanings of ritual and interpreted rituals in a variety of ways, ritual has seldom been abandoned within Hindu traditions" [4, p. 198].

Several interesting points emerge from the Kalia episode.

1. Death among Hindus is not a private family affair as it is in the West. Death is a communal event. Any person or persons who knew the deceased in any way may attend the funeral. This became evident at Kalia's death.

2. One does not need an invitation to attend a funeral. Acquaintance with the deceased or the deceased's family is sufficient ground to attend the funeral.

3. To attend a funeral is considered to be holy. It is seen as an act of supreme piety. To miss a funeral is construed as being "sinful."

4. Children are permitted to attend the funeral. They are not shielded either from witnessing death or attending a funeral, as they are likely to be in the West.

5. The funeral is performed swiftly and efficiently, within 24 hours following death. There are two reasons for performing the funeral within 24 hours; the first is related to matters of hygiene. There is a strongly held belief [12-14] that upon death the dead—referred to as *preta*—undertake a voyage, a journey which takes them through several kingdoms of Yama, King of the underworld, until a year later they reach an abode referred to as *pitr-loka*. It is a temporary abode of the ancestors, and it is here that it is decided by Yama, Lord of death, whether the deceased shall go to svarga (heaven) or to narka (hell).

The decision is made on the basis of the nature of actions (*karma*) performed by the deceased during his/her life. To ease the passage of the *preta*, during the year's journey it is expected that the survivors of the deceased will perform all the required ceremonies, *sraddha*, observe all the rites and rituals with zeal and faith. Failure to do so will result in the soul of the deceased, which upon death is painfully torn from the body of the deceased by the *yamadutas*, helpers to Yama, King of the underworld, to remain in a state of acute torment. Lapses—intentional or unintentional—in the faithful performance of these sacred duties may also result in adverse consequences, which befall upon the survivors. The family of the deceased may be tormented, haunted by the presence of *Bhutas,* or malevolent spirits, which manifest themselves soon after the death of the person and the rapid dissolution of the body. These *bhutas,* on occasions, are said to exercise such a malevolent and powerful influence over the lives and fortunes of the survivors that the bereaved may feel compelled to call upon experts to exorcise these evil spirits. However, the zealous performance of all the rites and rituals related to the death of a family member will (so it is believed) lead to the eventual repose of the soul of the departed and ward off the evil influences of the *bhutas.*

It is not always recognized that funeral rites are dedicated to the control, neutralization, and destruction of the *bhutas.* Even cremation does not always guarantee the total destruction of the *bhutas,* or the psychic corpse. It now becomes clear why cremations in India are performed with such speed: first, because of reasons of hygiene; second, because of caste-related factors of "contamination." A corpse in the house has a contaminating influence on the house and on the members of the household. It is, therefore, important for the members of the household to remove the body post-haste so that the bereaved are able to engage in purification rites and ceremonies and wipe out the blot which such contamination brings upon the family. The final function of the cremation is to ensure the destruction of *bhutas* [15].

6. All the rites (samskaras) related to the funeral are ritualistically performed.

7. The Brahmin priest performing the ceremony dominates the ritual process. He guides, the chief mourners follow. The chief mourner, as was already stated in the episode, was Kalia's son. Despite his tender age, it was necessary for him to perform the final funeral rites. This, as was noted earlier, is in keeping with ancient Hindu traditions which decree that it is the sacred duty of the eldest son to perform the funeral rites of his deceased father—for this ensures the peaceful repose of the soul.

8. Failure to perform the funeral rituals in accordance with Vedic teachings is considered to be sinful. Such an action may lead to at least two negative consequences:

a. It does not guarantee the repose of the soul of the deceased
b. The "ghosts" and other malevolent spirits of the tormented soul may haunt the kith and kin of the deceased.

9. Funeral rites, over the last two thousand years, appear not to have changed significantly.

10. Death does not mark the end of life. It signals the beginning of a new one. Belief in the unending cycle of birth and rebirth, expounded in the *Law of Karma,* forms the cornerstone of Hindu spirituality. A strong, unswerving belief in the *Law of Karma,* and its consequences, is an integral part of the Hindu psyche. We shall discuss this point later.

11. Death is not seen as an accidental event, which occurs by "chance." It is determined when and where a person shall die. Destiny plays a hand in one's death.

12. There is a Cartesian dualism concerning the body and soul. The body is perishable. The soul (atman) is immortal.

Several attitudes surrounding the "near-death" or "after-death" experiences emerged from the episode. They eventually led to Kalia's suicide. Let us list a few of them.

1. The initial opinion of the mourners was one of wonder.
2. Kalia's "return" to life was seen as an act of divine providence.
3. Kalia was imbued with benevolent, saintly powers.
4. His "fame" spread. People from all over the town came to see him.
5. There was a gradual split in attitudes among the people in town. What brought that about?
6. Kalia also came to be imbued with malevolent powers. He was seen as being in league with the devil.
7. The malevolent side of Kalia's metamorphosis gained ascendance and people started to avoid him.
8. Finally, Kalia committed suicide.

   a. Could the suicide have been avoided?
   b. Would such attitudes prevail today?

Although the Kalia incident took place over 50 years ago, could such an event occur in India—in the millennium—50 years later? The answer is yes, it could. Why should this be so, particularly in view of the fact that in many respects India is scientifically and technologically as advanced as many of the countries in the West? Moreover, as was established quite recently, India has also joined the "elite" group of countries with potentially destructive nuclear powers at her command. Shouldn't these facts, combined with the recent "invasion" of multi-national enterprises in the mega cities of India such as Bombay, Delhi, and Calcutta, militate against the practices of yester-years?

It should be pointed out that the present population of India hovers around the 1 billion mark. About 70 to 74 percent of Indians (700 to 740 million) still live in rural areas of the country, in villages, where the level of education is low, and where almost 35 to 40 percent of the people subsist below the poverty-line. In many villages, a death certificate is not mandatory for funeral rites to be initiated. It is sufficient that the village panchayat—the elected members of the village council—certify that natural death has occurred.

Illness, disease, and death are not explained in medico-legal terms. They are often construed in terms of sorcery, bewitchment, and evil spirits [16]. Belief in the evil eye—commonly referred to as *najar* or *dishti*—is also quite strong and widespread among Indians. A child who meets with an accident or falls seriously ill or dies might be the victim of an evil eye [7, 17]. Social acceptance of such attributions has served to legitimize the belief in the evil eye, in other evil spirits and their malevolent variants. All over India one finds an army of faith healers, mystics, shamans, *pirs* (holy men), *bhagats* (religious persons), gurus, astrologers, and palmists, who are often accorded greater respect and reverence than the medically trained doctors and psychiatrists.

Beliefs in astrology and the malevolent influence of planets on one's life (and death) are strongly ingrained in the Indian psyche. The belief that one's life is influenced by the nine planets, referred to as *grahas*, headed by the sun, is widely prevalent in India [18]. The heavenly configuration of planets at the moment of birth is seen as a determinant of one's life chances. Such astrological formulations permit explanations and the acceptance of untimely deaths, sudden deaths, including suicides. So too might Kalia's death have been explained by all and sundry: "it was in his stars."

Given that there was little or nothing in Kalia's daily life to suggest that he was "touched" by divinity or saintliness, why did Kalia come to be imbued with divine, saintly powers? Why did the attitudes change? How did the "saint" turn "satan"? What brought about the cruel metamorphosis? Did he jump or was he pushed into committing suicide?

Alas, we shall never know.

EPISODE 2

Death in a South Indian Village

Let us now turn to the second episode. The theme of death is the center-piece of Anantha Murthy's remarkable book *Samskara,* which he wrote in 1976. It is set in a small village in South India. The village is dominated and, for all practical purposes, run by a group of orthodox high caste Brahmin priests who practice and perform all the rites and rituals in their day-to-day lives, in accordance with ancient Vedic teachings. The non-Brahmins who live in the village are dependent on the Brahmins for the performance of all the rites and rituals, the prayers and the sacrifices, related to births, marriages, and deaths, and for all the festive occasions. They are also in fear of the Brahmins and defer to them in all respects. The Brahmins live within their own enclave, and the non-Brahmins live in their own. The low caste Hindus—*Sudras* (untouchables) as they are referred to—live apart. There is very little communication between the Brahmins and the rest of the people in the village, and hardly any between the Brahmins and the *Sudras*. There is peace in the village. This is because each person, regardless of his/her caste and occupation, understands and accepts his/her position within the caste hierarchy as dictated by ancient Vedic traditions.

The peace and equanimity of the village is shattered when one of the high-caste Brahmins dies in the home of a prostitute with whom, it transpires that he formed a sexual relationship. The prostitute, it turns out, comes from the lowest caste, a *Sudra*. His sudden death throws the entire village into a state of turmoil. The Brahmin, while he had been alive, had brought shame and grief upon his family members and upon the elders of the whole village. He had left his wife and had started to live with Chandri, the low caste prostitute. He had taken his wife's jewelry and had given it to the prostitute. He had renounced his own high caste origins. He had started to eat meat. He had started to drink alcohol. He had formed social relations with Muslims and other members of the lowest caste, had visited their homes and had eaten with them. In forming a sexual relationship with a person from the Sudra caste, he had lost his own high caste status, and had forfeited his right to be called a Brahmin. He himself was in danger of being seen an untouchable.

The main problems which the deceased's family members and indeed the entire village and, in particular, the high priest in the village had to resolve were the following: Who would perform the funeral rites? How would the funeral rites be performed? Would the deceased be given a Brahmin funeral?

Ancient Hindu customs, enshrined in the Vedas, make it clear that all the funeral rites are to be performed by the deceased's family members—from the laying out of the corpse, the construction of the bier, the transportation to the crematorium, to the final cremation. Only the family members and the members of one's sub-community are allowed to perform the last funeral rites. No outsiders are ever allowed to perform the last funeral rites. To allow an outsider to touch a corpse would bring the family into a state of spiritual pollution. The entire ceremony, including all the rites and rituals, have to be conducted and overseen by the Brahmin priest.

To initiate the funeral rites, it was of course necessary for the family members of the deceased and the high priest to enter the house of the prostitute. But for a high-caste Hindu Brahmin to enter the home of an untouchable would result in the Brahmin becoming spiritually polluted. Secondly, how could the deceased be accorded the full funeral rites of a Brahmin, considering that as a result of his moral transgressions he had forfeited his right to be regarded as a Brahmin? On the other hand, not to accord the deceased the full Brahmin funeral rites would be to undermine the high status of the family within the community. The corpse, too, could not be left in the house of the prostitute unattended. The longer the corpse remained in the house of the prostitute, the greater the shame and the ignominy that would fall upon the family members and upon the entire village. The Vedic texts, as we noted earlier, make it clear that funerals need to be performed within 24 hours after death.

The high priest, upon whose shoulders rested this gigantic decision, did not know what to do or how to act. When consulting the ancient scriptures and texts there were no precedents he could point to which would safely guide his actions.

Aware that the entire village looked up to him, he consulted all the religious texts and spoke to other priests from neighboring villages, but was unable to find a satisfactory solution. In the meantime of course, the corpse remained in the house of the prostitute. The high priest in the village who was the most revered and respected member of the community felt totally traumatized by this event. He felt he had failed the villagers, and despite his learning and erudition, had been unable to resolve the crises. Without going into further details of what finally happened, suffice it to say that the caste-related moral transgressions of the deceased brought untold misery and sorrow upon all the family members. They also led to devastating consequences for the entire village and for the high priest, who was ultimately destroyed by this event.

This event, despite its rarity, is of immense magnitude when seen within the context of orthodox Hindu society. The tragedy which befalls upon the family members of the deceased and upon the high priest of the village, who was unable to perform the funeral rites, fits into a neat cultural pattern *which can be understood by most members of that culture.* To an outsider, the same event would appear totally bewildering. He/she would be unable to make any sense of it whatever.

When I first discussed this particular episode with some of my European and American friends and colleagues and several of my graduate students, their initial response was one of incredulity. They claimed that there was nothing extraordinary about the event for it to be labeled as a traumatic event. If anything, the event was seen as storm in a "tea-cup." To them the deceased's sexual relationship with the prostitute was a private affair—it was of no concern whatever to others.

To perceive the above event as a "storm in a tea-cup" or as a private affair is in keeping with the philosophy of individualism, which is one of the dominant features of Western society.

Individualism, as Triandis points out, is concerned primarily with giving priority to one's personal goals over the goals of one's group, and where personal choice takes precedence over group considerations [19]. Given their personal adherence to an individualistic philosophy, they failed to understand that the entire structure of Hindu society is centered round caste interdependence and communal norms. They had little awareness of the implacable power which the community wields and is able to exercise over its deviant members. Consequently, they saw the Brahmin's sexual liaison with the prostitute as a private affair and failed to understand why the sexual liaison, combined with other factors, brought about such unimaginable distress and harm to the other Hindus in the village. Nor could they comprehend why the high priest, unable to find an acceptable solution to the crises, was totally traumatized and destroyed by the event.

When they had had time to reflect, they wondered why the funeral arrangements could not have been passed on to undertakers: such an arrangement to them seemed feasible and offered a neat solution to an otherwise insoluble problem. Once again, a Western solution was being offered to a culturally unique Indian problem. Sadly, there was no understanding on their part that Hindus, for a variety of religious, philosophical, and cultural reasons, do not have undertakers. A variety of other plausible explanations and seemingly "rational" solutions were also proposed, but none of them seemed conceivable, let alone acceptable, from the context of Hindu culture.

The discussions related to the above episode which I had with some of my English and American colleagues left me feeling quite sad. In talking to academics and therapists, I had expected to find in them an attitude of Socratic purity: a willingness to suspend judgment and try and understand a problem from a different perspective. Instead of trying to crawl into the psyche of the persons whose tragedy I had described, they were—a few of them certainly were— patronizingly dismissive of the whole event, claiming that they failed to understand what all the "fuss was about."

The point being made is this. It is difficult, if not impossible, for "outsiders" observing a series of events—such as the one described above—to construe accurately the meaning and the significance assigned to those events. To assign an accurate meaning to the event one needs to be either an integral part of that cultural group, or to have acquired a close and intimate knowledge of the culture in question. Otherwise, one is likely to fall into the trap of offering "etic" (universal) explanations of an event which is uniquely "emic" (culture-specific) in its construction.

In recent years, one has noticed that among many Western psychologists there is a tendency to offer universal explanations of behaviors across cultures—to wit, Western explanations. Such explanations, when examined critically, often turn out to be false and without any foundation. If allowed to persist, they ossify into dangerous stereotypes which can lead to untold harm in the long term. It is important to remind oneself again and again that the non-Western world cannot be moulded to fit in with Western notions of universality, Western notions of rationality and irrationality, right and wrong, appropriate and inappropriate, good and bad, etc. Although the search for "universals" in behaviors is a commendable enterprise, and is in keeping with the spirit of science and scientific research, it does not follow that what is right and "true" in Western cultures must necessarily be so in non-Western cultures. As I have stated elsewhere:

There is a widespread Eurocentric belief that all developing countries over time will be influenced by Western science, technology, and know-how, to such an extent that they too, in the process, will become Westernized and indistinguishable from other Western countries. The West sets, so to speak, the gold standard, which developing nations attempt to achieve. If developing nations, and/or members of ethnic minorities living in Western nations are all driven to getting Westernized, there is hardly any point in trying to understand an Indian from his/her own unique cultural perspective. What Westerners find difficult to understand and consequently come to terms with is the fact that the psyche of the members of ethnic minorities (as indeed of every person) is made up of several layers of which the Western persona is the most easily observable one. Such a persona no doubt is desirable. It dilutes, if not conceals, differences, which would otherwise be difficult to accommodate in one's psychological schema. It facilitates inter-cultural relationships at a functional level. But beneath the easily acquired cosmetic Westernized persona, is to be found a psyche whose roots can be traced back to one's own ancestral cultural upbringing, which exercise a profound influence on the individuals in terms of their evaluations of themselves, their identities, and their own unique world views [7, pp. 145-146].

The two episodes, each in its own contrasting way, has given us some insight into the complex problems related to death among Hindus, their familial and social structures, their funeral practices, their religious beliefs, their rites and rituals, and their notions of pollution and purification. Let us now go further and examine some of the major concepts in Hinduism, which have been referred to but have not been examined in any great detail.

THE CASTE SYSTEM

Indian (Hindu) society, not unlike other Eastern societies, is a family-based and community-oriented society [1, 4, 5, 9, 16, 20-26]. Although in many respects it is similar to most other Eastern societies, its unique distinguishing feature lies in its caste system. No other Eastern society has a social structure analogous to the Indian caste system. The earliest reference to the caste system is to be found in the Rg Veda, thus suggesting that the caste system represents a divine, sacred, and natural order of things [1, 9, 26].

Before we move on to describe the structure and the functions of the caste system, there are two terms which need some clarification. They are *varna* and *jati*. The Sanskrit word, Varna, when translated into English, means class and not caste. However, instead of being referred to as class, the term came to be referred to as caste. Anthropological evidence suggests that the term caste (instead of class) came to be used around the 16th century when the Portuguese came to India. *Jati*, on the other hand, is the appropriate word for caste. Through common usage, *varna* has come to be referred to as caste, and *jati* is seen as a sub-caste of a given caste. Within each caste, there exist several hundred *jatis*, or sub-castes. Borrowing terms from zoology, one might suggest that the term caste be seen as the genus, and sub-caste, the species.

From this it is evident that the original class system has been transformed into the caste system, and the original caste system has been turned into a sub-caste system. This was by no means a satisfactory arrangement, but its usage has come to stay. We too shall stick with the term caste and sub-caste, instead of class and caste. Sharma, who is critical of such an arrangement, points out that this has led to considerable difficulties in understanding the exact nature of the relationship between the two terms [26]. In view of the regional and linguistic variations in

India, it is not always clear how members of different groups in different villages define themselves. What adds to the difficulty is the fact that the word *varna* also means color. This would suggest that during the Vedic period, society may also have been classified along the lines of color, with white being attributed to the Brahmins, red to the Kshatriyas, yellow to the Vaishyas, and black to the Sudras.

Lannoy describes the caste system as a form of institutionalized inequality, a social instrument of assimilation, an archaic form of trade unionism, and an extension of the joint family system [22]. None of these descriptions quite captures the essence of what the caste system stands for. The four castes in their hierarchical order are as follows:

Brahmins: the learned and the educated elite; the guardians of the Vedas, the priests,

Kshatriyas: the noble warriors; defenders of the realm,

Vaishyas: the traders, businessmen, farmers, money-lenders,

Sudras: their main function is to serve the needs of the upper three castes.

Members of the upper three castes are known as "twice born" because their male members have undergone an initiation, a rite of passage, which then transforms them into high-caste Hindus. The ceremony which marks their "second birth" is the rite of the sacred thread ceremony, after the completion of which they are allowed to read and learn from the Vedas and participate in all religious ceremonies. It is this extremely important rite that separates the three highest castes from the Sudras, who are not permitted such an initiation.

The Sudras are further sub-divided into touchables and untouchables. The touchable Sudras engage in occupations which are considered by the upper three castes to be demeaning and, to a certain degree, polluting: barber, masseur, cleaner, water carrier, etc. Untouchable Sudras, on the other hand, are obliged to engage in occupations which deal with human and animal waste and refuse, viz., slaughter of animals, working in tanneries, crematorium attendants, etc. Even among the untouchable Sudras, there are gradations, and a crematorium attendant is considered to be the lowliest of the lowly within the caste hierarchy. Although the pattern of caste-related occupations is beginning to undergo a transformation in the urban areas of India, there is little evidence of such changes in the rural areas of the country, which are inhabited by over 70 percent of the Indian population. To come in any form of physical contact with an untouchable leads to a member of the three upper castes becoming polluted. The polluted person would then be expected to perform a series of ritualistic measures to attain a state of purity. In many Indian villages, the untouchables are expected to live a great distance away from the homes of the high caste Hindus so that their presence may not "pollute" the three high caste Hindus.

Untouchability has been banned in India, and India has done its best to eradicate the poisonous social disease. Gandhi, in order to remove the stigma associated with the term Sudra, called them *Harijans*, children of God. But there are pockets of areas in India where an untouchable is literally what the word means—an untouchable—and, despite the Government ban, it is practiced more in its breach than in its observance. However, in recent years, there has been a mass movement, an awakening of consciousness among untouchables, who given the fact that they constitute around 15 percent to 17 percent of the total Indian population are aware of their power as potential vote winners. They have abandoned the old derogatory term Sudra, and now refer to themselves as *Dalits,* the oppressed ones. Their inspiration comes from their deceased leader Dr. Ambedkar, who, despite being an untouchable, rose to eminent position of power soon after the Indian independence in 1947. To grasp the full impact of the caste system on the daily lives of Hindus, it is necessary to understand the fundamental characteristics of the caste system. Let us examine them briefly.

The three fundamental characteristics of the caste system are:

1. Hierarchy
2. Pollution and purification
3. Specialization

1. Hierarchical Nature of Castes

Membership into a given caste is through birth only. One is born into a given caste and is destined to stay in it until death. It is virtually impossible to move from one caste into another, particularly from the lower caste into the higher caste. It is, however, possible to move downwards from a higher caste into a lower caste, as we saw in the last episode where the high caste Brahmin, as a result of consorting with a woman of the lowest caste, stands in danger of losing his high caste status.

The sub-castes within a given caste also operate on a hierarchical model. (Social hierarchies, it should be stressed, are not unique to India; they exist everywhere, even in the reputedly egalitarian societies in the West.) Hierarchy consists of gradations; each sub-caste is graded ranging from the lowest to the highest. Gradations of castes, to a large extent, are organized around degrees of purity and pollution and in accordance with marriage customs. Most marriages tend to be arranged by the elders in the family. An endogamous marriage is the norm to which all members of a sub-caste are expected to conform; to marry outside one's sub-caste is likely to lead to severe stress for the family concerned and for the other members of the sub-caste. Another factor which may also determine the hierarchical status of a sub-caste is concerned with who may receive food and water from whom. As Lannoy points out, "[food and] water is believed to be especially pollution prone, therefore rules are carefully observed and constitute one of the clearest means by which the society represents its status gradations" [22, p. 150].

Communities belonging to a particular sub-caste often attempt to have their own sub-caste upgraded. This may be accomplished in several positive and negative ways: by acts of piety and charity, by the performance of religious ceremonies, and also by ensuring that no member of their sub-caste engages in activities which would bring shame and ignominy upon their sub-caste. The elders of the sub-caste often impose draconian sanctions upon the suspected deviants in an attempt to keep them in line.

A microcosm of such a ranking or hierarchical system is also to be found within each extended family network. Elders are accorded special status within the family and their important role is clearly recognized. Elders, whether they come from rural areas or from large metropolitan cities, are generally deferred to. On important issues—issues which go beyond the concern of the immediate members of the family and may affect the entire community—the elders in the family confer with the elders of their community in an attempt to arrive at a joint decision which would then be binding on the rest of the members of the community. While there is an undeniable sense of security and belongingness in membership to a sub-caste, there is a price to be paid for such comforts. The pressure to conform to familial and communal norms can cause acute stress and anxiety in individual members, leading, in some instances, to psychotic disorders and hysteria [27, 28]. But it would appear that extended family networks and one's sub-caste provide inbuilt safety measures against mental disturbances. The emotional and physical intimacy shared by all members acts as a buffer against the stressors from which the European counterpart is not protected.

2. Pollution and Purification

Pollution and purification play an extremely important role in understanding the day-to-day secular and religious behaviors of Hindus. The elimination of dirt in order to impose a sense of order and control over one's environment is a universal human characteristic. In Western societies the business of eliminating dirt, to a large extent, is a matter of aesthetics and hygiene; to a lesser extent, it has religious connotations, which may be summed up by the phrase, "cleanliness is next to godliness." In Indian society it is the other way round. Although Indians pay lip service to the idea of eliminating dirt, they are more concerned with sacred contagion and pollution. Thus, the concepts pollution and purification need to be understood within a spiritual context and not in terms of hygiene and biology [14, 17, 29]. The status of a person in India, to a certain extent, is determined by the degree of contact with the polluting agent. Proximity to a polluting agent may constitute a permanent pollution. This would mean that certain occupations are permanently polluting—as was mentioned previously, in relation to the untouchables. Such a form of pollution is *collective*—the entire family remains polluted. It is also *hereditary*. In many villages in India—where the strong arm of the law has not made its presence felt—the untouchables are often forced to live away from the high caste Hindus since their very presence is believed to have a polluting effect on others. In certain instances, the high caste Hindus prevent the untouchables from drawing water from the well, claiming that it is for the exclusive use by the high caste Hindus. It is clear that the enactment of law does not guarantee its enforcement.

There are three major ways in which pollution can be categorized. Pollution may be (i) mild and temporary; (ii) severe and temporary; and (iii) severe and permanent.

(i) Mild and Temporary Pollution

This is an everyday affair. One is in a state of impurity or pollution upon waking up in the morning, prior to performing one's morning ablutions, when one has eaten food touched by others, when one has not prayed. Pollution also occurs after a sexual act, during menstruation, after one has had a haircut, pared one's nails, and in the performance of any activity which is considered to be impure. Such mild states of pollution can be overcome by appropriate actions, such as baths, prayers, wearing clean, washed clothes, and engaging in appropriate cleansing and purification rituals.

(ii) Severe Pollution

This comes about when a high caste Hindu comes into physical and/or social contact with persons of the lowest caste, the Sudras, or when a high caste Hindu eats meat (particularly beef). No high caste Hindu is expected to accept (or offer) cooked food from a low caste Hindu. To do so would lead to the high caste Hindu becoming polluted. Nor is it appropriate for a low caste Hindu to receive cooked food from a high caste Hindu. This feature applies not just to inter-caste encounters, but to within caste-encounters. A person of higher grading within a given sub-caste may neither offer nor receive cooked food from a person of lower grading from the same sub-caste. A cobbler, for instance, would be loath to receive food from a crematorium attendant, who occupies a lower grading on the sub-caste hierarchy than the cobbler. A Brahmin engaged in temple duties will not accept hospitality from a Brahmin involved in funeral rites. The latter are regarded as being ritually inferior and even polluting to the former. The privileges of superiority are fiercely protected.

To overcome this form of pollution it is necessary for the polluted individual (in some instances the entire family may get polluted) to perform a series of appropriate propitiation rites, rituals, and religious ceremonies under the guidance of their family priest.

(iii) Permanent Pollution

As was noted above, some forms of pollution are collective, hereditary, and therefore permanent. Permanent pollution may also occur when a Hindu belonging to the highest caste (Brahmin) marries a person from the lowest caste, thereby breaking the principle of endogamy that has always been regarded as one of the cementing factors that has held the caste system together. The person in such a state of pollution may be ostracized by his family members and may be forced to become an outcaste. The children born of a marriage between a Brahmin and a woman of the Sudra caste are referred to as *chandala*—and are seen as being the lowest of the lowly. Since pollution and purification is an everyday affair, Hindus in general have learned to avoid them, or undertake appropriate ritualistic cleansing exercises when avoidance becomes impossible.

Let us now examine the manner in which pollution manifests itself in death and bereavement. When death occurs in a family it leads to severe pollution. This is what happens. The presence of a corpse in the house pollutes the house. The corpse too is in a state of pollution. All members in the house also tend to get polluted. Anyone entering the house also tends to get polluted. The Brahmin priest who performs the last funeral rites is also polluted. The mourners who accompany the deceased to the crematorium get polluted. Entering the crematorium has the effect of polluting the individual. An inappropriate and/or an insincere performance of the cremation rites and rituals of cremation can lead to severe pollution among the family members of the deceased. According to ancient Vedic customs, all the rites related to the preparation of the corpse and the arrangements for the funeral are performed by the family members, although in so doing they themselves enter into a state of pollution. However, such impurity, although serious, is temporary and is considered to be far less serious than the entry of a Sudra into their home [4, 7, 22].

3. Specialization

In early Vedic times, castes were held together by three prime factors: *endogamy, commensality,* and *specialization.*

3.1. Endogamy

Endogamy—marrying within one's own caste and sub-caste—was seen as a desired course of action in India. The Brahmins, in interpreting the Vedas, claimed that it was absolutely necessary for persons to marry *within their own caste.* Such a form of marriage was considered to be sacred. The Brahmins argued that an endogamous marriage enabled the parties involved in matrimony to retain the ritual purity of their caste and avoid any form of inter-caste contamination. It was an ideal form of marriage because it ensured the perpetuation of the caste system. However, endogamous marriages came to be questioned. The early reformers in India were fiercely opposed to such strait jacketed views related to marriage and attempted to break the stronghold exercised by the Brahmins over this problem. But despite their protests, they were unable to overcome the solid resistance offered by the orthodox and conservative forces [30].

It is notable that over the centuries the principle of endogamy has not been swept aside; it has continued to retain its stronghold over the Hindus all over India, particularly in the rural areas of the country. Marriages are still arranged and organized by the parents of prospective spouses. Although the "style" of arranged marriages has undergone a modest change within Indian society— particularly among the affluent members of society in the urban sectors of the country—arranged marriages are still the norm.

3.2. Commensality

Commensality, as we know, is concerned with hospitality, with extending and receiving hospitality. But in Hinduism, it had little to do with inviting people home and accepting invitations to the homes of others. Such a notion of hospitality is a Western notion. It does not have a similar meaning attached to it when seen from a Hindu perspective. Commensality carries a special spiritual meaning within Hindu culture. Since there were strict taboos of ritual purity associated with offering and receiving food, great care had to be taken in terms of who one offered food to and who one received food from. One could not, willy-nilly, invite people home, nor accept invitations from others. One could offer food and, in return, receive it only from those who belonged to one's own caste and sub-caste. To offer food to outsiders resulted in breaking the taboos of ritual purity. One could, of course, offer food (cooked or uncooked) to mendicants, the poor, and the needy—but there were strict rules governing the precise manner in which food could be offered. One also had to be extremely careful in deciding the kind of food that one offered or was offered. As Lannoy points out, among Hindus, ". . . the most important quality of food is the degree to which it is pollution free" [22, p. 150]. There were distinctions, too, between cooked food and uncooked food, and between the relative purity of cooked foods. Uncooked food was said to be less pollution prone than cooked food. Thus, one could receive uncooked food from a lower caste, but not cooked food. Again, the kind of food one offered or received was related to the degree of purity of food.

In addition to food, water was believed to be especially pollution prone. To avoid any form of spiritual contamination, orthodox Hindus always carried with them urns and jugs of water whenever they undertook any long journeys. The practice of carrying water is still prevalent among many sections of Hindu society. My family members, for instance, never undertook a long journey without carrying their own supply of water. Whenever we went on our holidays, which involved a two- or three-day train journey, my father made sure that we carried several urns and jugs and canteens of water with us to see us through the journey. The number of urns and jugs of water often exceeded all other baggage that we carried with us. On one or two occasions, however, the supply of water that he had brought with him ran out. He forbade us all from drinking water from the restaurant car of the train. At the next station, he arranged for all the jugs and urns to be filled with water from the station water pump. The fact that that water may not have been safe from a hygienic point of view was of little concern to him. What mattered to him was that the water from the station tap had not been touched by another human hand! Ritual purity took precedence over hygiene.

It should be noted that the principles of commensality were never strictly adhered to even during Vedic times. They were practically impossible. During times of drought, famine, war, epidemics, and such other calamities, restrictions governing commensality were automatically lifted. To a large extent, although such practices have become a thing of the past, they have not vanished entirely. One might still notice such practices being rigidly adhered to among the very orthodox Brahmins in certain parts of India.

3.3. Specialization

Each village was expected to be a self-contained and a self-sustaining unit which could call upon the services of people with specialist skills and expertise to meet the needs of the village community. A vocational caste group expected its members to stick to its hereditary calling. But this was not always possible. As Desika Char points out, ". . . often enough, the vocation of the caste failed to provide full employment to its members . . ." [30, p. 22]. Gradually, as a result of increased opportunities for diversification, more and more sub-castes based on new vocational alignments were formed. Even among the main castes, there have been instances of Brahmins entering the army, tending cattle, trading, hunting, and even snake charming. Evidence suggests that soldiers, too, came from all castes and sub-castes. Although great stress has been placed on the vocational base of caste, the fact that there was significant diversification has been ignored by the purists who argue for the immutability of vocation based castes. While it is true that many vocations in India are still caste based, and continue to follow a hereditary pattern, the structure of the caste system, insofar as its vocational base is concerned, is undergoing a metamorphosis. The purity of caste-based vocations has turned out to be a myth. It is not uncommon to see uneducated Brahmins working as cooks and waiters in restaurants and in many other humble occupations.

We have seen that the meticulous and precise performance of rites and rituals is seen as being desirable for Hindus. It binds and preserves the caste system, which in turn provides a sense of continuity and belonging. Rites and rituals legitimize social order and uphold social institutions. Rituals also enable Hindus to earn merit, which leads to their own spiritual development. Their importance cannot be overstated. Despite the fact that over the centuries many ancient rituals have lost their functional value and are interpreted in different ways by Hindus in different regions, they have not been abandoned. The question that arises here is this: why do Hindus cling to the performance of rituals with such tenacity? In what ways do ritualistic actions lead to one's spiritual development? For a tentative answer to this question, let us briefly turn to the Law of Karma.

THE LAW OF KARMA

The law of karma, in its simplest form, states that all human actions lead to consequences. Right actions produce good consequences and wrong actions produce bad consequences. At first sight, the law of karma seems to be identical with the law of universal causation, which asserts that every event has a cause, or that nothing is uncaused. Though seemingly identical, there are significant differences between the two laws. Unlike the law of universal causation, the law of karma is not concerned with consequences in general, but with consequences which affect the individual—the doer of the action. Secondly, the law of karma applies specifically to the moral sphere. It is therefore not concerned with the general relation between actions and their consequences but "rather with the moral quality of the actions and their consequences" [31, p. 1]. In his analysis of the law of karma, Hiriyanna explains that the events of our lives are determined by their antecedent causes [32]. Since all actions lead to consequences which are related to the nature and the type of actions, there is absolute *justice* that falls to our lo, in the sense that good actions lead to happiness and bad actions to unhappiness. The doctrine of karma is extremely significant because it offers explanations not only for pain, suffering, and misfortune, but also for pleasure, happiness, and good fortune. Each of us receives the results of our own actions and not another's. Thus, the sins of our fathers are not visited upon us.

Thirdly, what gives the law of karma its supreme moral quality is the assertion that the doer not only deserves the consequences of his/her actions but is unable to avoid experiencing them [33].

It should be made clear that the actions of the doer may have occurred in his/her present life or in his/her past life. Similarly, the consequences of the doer's actions may occur during the person's present life or in his future life. The main point is that it is impossible to avoid the consequences of one's actions.

The law of karma stands out as one of the most unique features of Hinduism. Although there is no basis for establishing its empirical validity, Hindus in general have an unswerving belief in the workings of the law of karma. It has shaped the Indian view of life over centuries. One might even go to the extent of saying that the Hindu psyche is built around the notion of karma [9, 26, 31, 34-37]. The influence of the law of Karma manifests itself at every stage in a Hindu's life: at birth, in childhood, during adolescence and adulthood, in marriage, in illness and health, in good fortune and misfortune, in death and bereavement, and *after death*.

The deterministic belief that one's present life is shaped by one's actions in one's past life (or lives) allows them to explain and accept a variety of misfortunes (and good fortunes) which befall them through the course of their journey through life. It engenders within their psyche a spirit of passive, if not resigned acceptance of misfortunes, ranging from sudden deaths within the family, glaring inequalities of caste and status, disease and illness, poverty and destitution, to exploitation and prejudice. The main disadvantage of determinism—and there are many—lies in the fact that it often leads to a state of existential and in certain instances moral resignation, compounded by a profound sense of inertia. One takes no proactive measures; one merely accepts the vicissitudes of life without qualm. It was fated that such and such should happen, becomes the commonly accepted rationalization.

But the belief in the cycle of birth and rebirth has its positive side too. It creates an aspiration of hope. They "know" that they need to act in a manner which would be considered to be meritorious. In so doing they would reap the rewards of their actions in their present life or in their future life. Many Hindus are also guided by the belief that in performing acts of piety, they are likely to be born into a "better" family and into higher caste in their next birth.

A Westerner, at this point, might be tempted to ask an important question. If human existence, according to Hindu philosophy, consists of unending cycles of birth and rebirth, is there any purpose to human existence? Is there any purpose to remaining bonded to an unending cycle of births, deaths, and rebirths? The answer is simple. In Hindu philosophy, the external world is seen as being illusory. It is *maya* [6]. Because the world of the senses, the empirical world, is constantly changing, it is seen as an inconstant, illusory world.

We have already established that in Hinduism beliefs and conduct, rites, rituals, and ceremonies, authorities and dogma are considered to be of extreme importance. Yet they are assigned a place which is subordinate to the art of conscious, spiritual self-discovery and the contact with the divine [38]. The search for *Brahman,* the Absolute, is the coveted goal in Hinduism. The striving of the soul for the infinite is *Brahman.* Ideally, therefore, the sacred and the secular are kept apart. In practice, however, they tend to get blurred.

The ultimate purpose of human existence is to transcend one's illusory physical existence, renounce the world of material aspirations, attain a heightened state of spiritual awareness, and finally liberate oneself from the bondage of the cycle of birth and rebirth, thereby attaining *moksha.* It is then that one's soul (*atman*) merges with the ultimate *brahman.* Any activity that is likely to promote such a state is to be encouraged. But how is such transcendence—inward seeking spiritual consciousness—to be achieved, which will lead to *moksha*? *Moksha* (or *Nirvana,* according to Buddhist philosophy) cannot be achieved overnight. It can only be achieved through continuous effort, which involves following any one of the three paths which lead to liberation. The three paths to *moksha* are:

1. The *bhakti marg*—the path of devotion and prayer;
2. The *gyan marg*—the path of knowledge; and
3. The *karma marg*—the path of action.

The search for *moksha* is long and arduous. It may involve a series of lives and deaths in the process.

Let us now summarize the main advantages in subscribing to the law of karma. A belief in the unending cycle of birth and rebirth, a belief that one's life does not end at death but leads to a new beginning, and that one's moral actions in one's present life or past lives will lead to consequences in one's future life, may create in the Hindu psyche a set of psychologically protective mechanisms in the face of death. These include:

1. A belief in an afterlife creates conditions that help to reduce the terror of death and the fear of extinction. (Those Westerners subscribing to humanist, secularist, atheistic, or scientific doctrines would forfeit the protective mechanisms open to Hindus.)
2. It also takes away the sting from suffering since suffering is explained by one's individual actions in *karmic* terms. Consequently, no guilt or blame is attached to an individual for any failures or sudden unforeseen illnesses, calamities, or disasters which may befall upon the individual. (Westerners, on the other hand, in adopting the doctrine of *free will* become accountable for their actions, leaving them no choice but to accept blame for their failures and credit for their personal achievements.)
3. The acceptance of the doctrine of *karma* instills in one the idea that, in the final analysis, no one but we ourselves are ultimately responsible for the consequences of our actions. *This brings the notion of individualism to its highest level.*
4. The unshakable belief that upon one's death one's indestructible spirit (*atman*) will survive the body and at some point during the individual's *karmic* cycle of birth and rebirth find abode in another body (hopefully a more pious and august one) makes the acceptance of death less painful. (Since such beliefs are unlikely to be shared by most Westerners, they may be seen as being irrelevant, if not meaningless, to their own individualistic doctrines.)

CONCLUSION

We have traveled a long way. It is now time to pause and take stock. We have seen that death arouses a variety of fears and terrors in the hearts and minds of people all over the world. No group or groups of people appear to be totally exempt from such unexplainable fears. Becker, in his remarkable book *Denial of Death,* argues that people in the West have tried to ignore, deny, and avoid death by resorting to a variety of self-deluding subterfuges [39]. They would rather death died a permanent death! They could then live on forever!

In contradistinction to Becker's thesis, the humanists assert that such fears are meaningless because none of us knows what lies beyond the grave [40]. There is no point in worrying about what we do not know and, by all accounts, will never know. This universal ignorance, they argue, ought to insulate us from these unfounded terrors and make us look upon our impending death and that of our loved ones with a certain sense of equanimity. However, the mistake which humanistic thinking makes is to assume that human beings, having arrived at such conclusions, can rationally will themselves to overcome all the primeval fears which have been part of the human psyche since time immemorial. One does not live by reason alone, as the humanists in their naive arrogance would have us believe. Feelings and emotions form an integral part of being human; they cannot always be brought under rational control. Even if it were possible to do so, imagine the colossal loss of creative contributions in the field of music, the arts, literature, drama, and poetry, which involve an intricate interplay of emotions and rationality. Secondly, in their evangelical enthusiasm to proselytize the desirability of rationality in human affairs, they become guilty of irrationalism themselves by preaching Western rationality as the universal standard against which all forms of discourse ought to be judged. To dismiss vast tracts of anthropological and cross-cultural research literature which clearly points to different conceptions of rationality across cultures, displays either profound ignorance or prejudiced arrogance, or both.

Admittedly, several behaviors are exceedingly rational and functionally autonomous, but to assert that all behaviors—the terrors of death and extinction—can be brought under rational control and become functionally autonomous (such as changing gears when driving a car) is to exceed the bounds of rationality. For any behavior to become functionally autonomous, it needs to be reinforced at regular intervals. Adopting a cognitive behavioral model, the humanists might wish to suggest a careful programming of reinforcement contingencies to train people to accept the fears and terrors of death, so that over time they would all become functionally autonomous.

It is here that Indian philosophical thinking scores a victory.

Let us turn to the *Bhagawad Gita*, a major Hindu religious text whose origins date back to around 1500 BCE. The *Gita* consists of a sermon preached by God Krishna to his disciple Arjuna on the field of a battle which is about to be fought between the Pandavas and the Kuravas, who are cousins. Arjuna, distressed at the thought of having to take arms against his own brethren, which include all his Kaurava cousins, his uncles, and his close relatives, throws down his arms in despair and refuses to fight. Seeing his distress and despondency, Krishna preaches his sermon, which constitutes the *Bhagwad Gita*.

The *Gita* adopts a dualistic approach to body and spirit. The body dies and corrupts; the spirit is immortal and therefore indestructible. The spirit survives the body and after a while resides in another body. The process continues until such time the person who has passed through a series of such stages of birth and death, through effort, dedication, and the scrupulous performance of his/her duties, evolves to ever higher states of transcendence, eventually succeeding in attaining release from the bondage from the cycle of birth and rebirth, and merging his great soul, *maha-atma*, with the imperishable *Brahman*.

Examining this from a psychological perspective, one can see the glittering array of reinforcements on offer:

1. It is a relief to know that we do not die, because our spirit or soul survives our death;
2. It is only the body, or the casing that encloses the spirit, that corrupts and is consigned to the flames;
3. It is gratifying to know that soon after our death we shall once again return to earth;
4. We shall return in a younger, newer, and healthier body;
5. The kind of body that we inhabit and the kind of family we are born into is directly related to the kind of life that we had chosen to live;
6. We are the architects of our own future lives;
7. It is within our means to reach an elevated state of transcendence;
8. Each of us is capable of attaining *moksha* by our own individual effort; and
9. Death is not the end of life, but the beginning of a new one.

Clearly, no culture, no society, has all the answers concerning the ideal way of recovering positively and speedily from the death of one's loved ones. It is only when cultures meet—on equal terms and as equal partners—and display a genuine willingness to share and learn from each other, that one might find tentative answers to questions which concern us all. But for the West to assume that there is little or nothing which they might profitably learn from Eastern cultures, many of which have sustained and perpetuated themselves for over four thousand years, is precisely the kind of attitude which is inimical to the creation of a genuine multicultural society and world.

REFERENCES

1. K. K. Klostermaier, A Short Introduction to Hinduism, One World, Oxford, 1998.
2. J. L. Brockington, *The Sacred Thread: Hinduism in its Continuity and Diversity*, University Press, Edinburgh, 1981.
3. A. De Riencourt, *The Soul of India*, Honeyglen, United Kingdom, 1960.
4. G. Flood, *An Introduction to Hinduism*, Cambridge University Press, Cambridge, 1996.
5. J. Lipner, *Hindus: Their Religious Beliefs and Practices*, Routledge, London, 1994.
6. H. Zimmer, *Philosphies of India*, Bollinger Series XXVI, Princeton University Press, Princeton, 1969/1989.
7. R. Pandey, *Hindu Samskaras: Socio-Religious Study of The Hindu Sacraments*, Motilal Banarasidass Publishers Private Ltd., Delhi, India, 1969.
8. S. Palmer and P. Laungani (eds.), *Counselling in a Multicultural Society*, Sage, London, 1999.

9. R. C. Zaehner, *Hinduism*, Oxford University Press, New Delhi, 1966.
10. R. A. Moody, *Life After Life*. Bantam Books, New York, 1976.
11. R. A. Moody, *Reflections on Life After Life*, Bantam Books, New York, 1977.
12. N. N. Bhattacharyya, *Ancient Indian Rituals and Their Social Contents*, Manohar Book Service, Delhi, India, 1975.
13. W. A. Borman, *The Other Side of Death: Upanishadic Eschatology*, India Book Centre, Delhi, India, 1990.
14. S. G. Filippi, *Mrtyu: Concept of Death in Indian Traditions, Reconstructing Indian History & Culture No. 11*, D. K. Printworld (P) Ltd., New Delhi, India, 1996.
15. H. Aguilar, *The Sacrifice in the Rg Veda*, Bharatiya Vidya Prakashan, Delhi, India, 1976.
16. S. Kakar, *Shamans, Mystics and Doctors*, Mandala Books, Unwin Paperbacks, London, 1982.
17. C. J. Fuller, *The Camphor Flame: Popular Hinduism and Society in India*, Princeton University Press, Princeton, 1992.
18. T. N. Madan, *Non-Renunciation: Themes and Interpretations of Hindu Culture*, Oxford University Press, Delhi, India, 1987.
19. H. C. Triandis, *Culture and Social Behaviour*, McGraw-Hill, New York, 1994.
20. A. L. Basham, *The Wonder that was India*, Rupa & Company, Calcutta, India, 1966.
21. J. M. Koller, *The Indian Way: Perspectives*, Collier Macmillan, London, 1982.
22. R. Lannoy, *The Speaking Tree*, Oxford University Press, Oxford, 1976.
23. P. Laungani, Death in a Hindu Family, in *Death and Bereavement Across Cultures*, C. M. Parkes, P. Laungani, and W. Young (eds.), Routledge, London, 1997.
24. P. Laungani, Coronary Heart Disease in India and England: Conceptual Considertions, *International Journal of Health Promotion and Education, 36*:4, pp. 108-115, 1998.
25. D. G. Mandelbaum, *Society in India*, Vol. 2, University of California Press, Berkeley, California, 1972.
26. A. Sharma, *Classical Hindy Thought: An Introduction*, Oxford University Press, New Delhi, 2000.
27. S. M. Channabasavanna and R. S. Bhatti, A Study on Interactional Patterns and Family Typologies in Families of Mental Patients, in *Readings in Transcultural Psychiatry*, A. Kiev and V. Rao (eds.), Higginsbothams, Madras, India, pp. 149-161, 1982.
28. B. B. Sethi and R. Manchanda, Family Structure and Psychiatric Disorders, *Indian Journal of Psychiatry, 20*, pp. 283-288, 1978.
29. N. Chaudhuri, *Hinduism*, Oxford University Press, Oxford, 1979.
30. S. V. D. Char, *Hinduism and Islam in India: Caste, Religion and Society from Antiquity to Early Modern Times*, Markus Wiener, Princeton, 1997.
31. B. R. Reichenbach, *The Law of Karma: A Philosophical Study*, University of Hawaii Press, Honolulu, 1990.
32. M. Hiriyanna, *The Essentials of Indian Philosophy*, Allan and Unwin, London, 1949.
33. R. C. Prasad, *The Sradha*, Motilal Banarasidass Publishers Private Ltd., Delhi, India, 1995.
34. C. Chapple, *Karma and Creativity*, State University of New York, Albany, 1986.
35. W. D. O'Flaherty, *The Origins of Evil in Hindu Mythology*, University of California Press, Berkeley, California, 1976.

36. W. D. O'Flaherty, *Karma and Rebirth in Classical Indian Traditions*, University of California Press, Berkeley, California, 1980.
37. R. A. Sinari, *The Structure of Indian Thought*, Oxford University Press, Delhi, India, 1984.
38. S. Radhakrishnan, *Indian Philosophy*, Vol. 2, Centenary Edition, Oxford University Press, Delhi, India, 1929/1989.
39. E. Becker, *The Denial of Death*, The Free Press Paperbacks, New York, 1973.
40. T. Walter, Secularization, in *Death and Bereavement Across Cultures*, C. M. Parkes, P. Laungani, and W. Young (eds.), Routledge, London, 1997.

BIBLIOGRAPHY

Dubois, A. J. A., *Hindu Manners, Customs and Ceremonies*, Rupa & Co., Delhi, 1906/1993.

Firth, S., "Approaches to Death in Hindu and Sikh Communities in Britain" and "Cross-Cultural Perspectives on Bereavement," in *Death, Dying and Bereavement*, D. Dickenson and M. Johnson (eds.), Sage, London, 1993.

Firth, S., *Dying, Death and Bereavement in a British Hindu Community*, Peters, Leuven, 1997.

Herman, A. L., *The Problem of Evil and Indian Thought*, Motilal Banarasidass Publishers Private Ltd., Delhi, 1976.

Kübler-Ross, E., *On Death and Dying*, Tavistock Publications, London, 1969.

Laungani, P., Patterns of Bereavement in Indian and British Society, *Bereavement Care*, *14*:1, pp. 5-7, 1995.

Laungani, P., Death and Bereavement in India and England: A Comparative Analysis, *Mortality*, *1*:2, pp. 191-212, 1996.

Laungani, P., Patterns of Bereavement in Indian and English Society, in *Readings in Thanatology*, J. D. Morgan (ed.), Baywood, Amityville, New York, pp. 67-76, 1997.

Weber, M., *The Sociology of Religion* (4th Edition), Allen & Unwin, London, 1963.

Willson, B. R., *Religion in Secular Society*, Watts, London, 1996.

CHAPTER 2
Facing Life and Death: A Buddhist's Understanding of Palliative Care and Bereavement*

Lesley Kawamura

The minister stopped beside the bed of an ailing woman whose leg was giving her much pain. "Pray for me," she whispered. He shook his head. "In my religion, we do not pray," he replied. Then added, "But we do have sutra chanting, would that help?" She shrugged and he chanted a few lines of the sutra, the narrative of the Buddhist religious canon, perhaps from the dialogues of Buddha. "It seemed to help her—even if it wasn't a prayer," marvelled the Rev. Tesshi Aoyama, who is a minister of the Buddhist Church of America. As a matter of fact, he is a 19th-generation Buddhist minister, born in Japan.

"There is no chaplaincy in Buddhism," he said. "I am a pioneer," he laughed [1, p. 69]. The above words, quoted from Dan L. Thrapp's article "Buddhist Helps Solace Sick at L. A. Hospital" in the Sunday, February 23, 1973 edition of the *Los Angeles Times* newspaper, relates perhaps the first ever qualified Buddhist ministerial graduate from a clinical pastoral education program. The information that Reverend Tesshi Aoyama, a Buddhist minister of the Japanese Pure Land tradition, became a qualified counselor is one thing, but the dilemma in which both the minister and patient were placed is more interesting for the contents of the present chapter. The minister faced the dilemma of having to be satisfied with the chanting of a sutra, a practice which was quite foreign to the patient. That the situation ended on a positive note was owing to Rev. Aoyama's "... sensitivity and

---

*This chapter originally appeared in J. D. Morgan (Ed.), *Meeting the Needs of Our Clients Creatively,* Baywood, Amityville, New York, 1999.

awareness of the meaning of the relationships and social structures. From his experience he learn[ed] to help persons resolve personal conflicts, grow in maturity, and search for meaning" [1, pp. 69-70].

In recent times there is a tendency for people to think that if one can find a response to the question of death and dying, then one can lead life in accordance with that response. This way of managing of one's life can be understood as "teleo-centric" which is based on a "theo-centric" religious tradition. By "theo-centric" I mean those religious traditions that prescribe a way of life on the basis of a divine intervention of some kind that governs the manner in which one lives in anticipation of a life hereafter. Thus "theo-centric" religious traditions tend to be "teleo-centric" also. However, not all world religions are "theo-centric" or "teleo-centric." Such traditions represented by some forms of Buddhism and by "existential-Phenomenological" philosophies tend not to ask questions on death but tend to emphasize the importance of participating in the act of living. This participation of living can be understood as an "insta-centric" or "insta-matic," because it focuses upon the importance of the here and now and upon the "loneliness" of being in the world alone by oneself. In contrast to the "theo-centric," which places the responsibility of life and death in the hands of an "other," the "insta-centric" puts the responsibility of life and death upon the individual.[1] The distinction between "theo-centric" and "insta-centric" is an important distinction to keep in mind throughout this chapter, because it will be the foundation upon which the following ideas will rest. Further, without a clear discernment of this distinction, we will have a tendency to conclude that a particular way of dealing with death and dying is the only correct way. This myopic view will prevent us from becoming aware that the view of the majority culture may not be the most appropriate way of responding to the process of death and dying. In the words of Donald Irish, we should realize that:

> The United States and Canadian societies have traditionally been predominantly white in race and Christian in religion. Thus the professional personnel who have daily been involved in the treatment of dying and nurture of the bereaved will most certainly have been related to the white Roman Catholics and mainline Protestant patients and clients. The specialists themselves—physicians, nurses, clergy, social workers, hospice, hospital chaplains, and funeral directors—as trained professionals have usually also been members of the dominant groups. For both reasons, these practitioners have tended to be better acquainted with the beliefs about life and death, related rituals, patterns of emotional response, and attitudes toward that body that prevailed within the majority cultures [2, p. 11].

---

[1] I have coined phrases such as "teleo-centric," "insta-centric," "theo-centric," and "existential-Phenomenological" in order to distinguish ways of thinking that produce a different way of seeing reality, although I am uncertain whether one is justified in coining such phrases.

Inasmuch as these words reflect the situation in the past, perhaps through discussions of the kind that we are holding now the professionals from the "majority cultures" will become more sympathetic observers and listeners to the "minority cultures" within our predominantly Roman Catholic and mainline Protestant society. But a word of caution is in order. Paul C. Rosenblatt has pointed out that we must be attentive to the fact that:

> It is easy, in looking at the emotions and experiences of people from other cultures, to adopt a superficiality helpful but nonetheless, ethnocentric stance that implies, "Of course, our understandings are of the right ones, but we will communicate with you in your own terms while still remaining assured that our way of thinking is correct." We will never understand people whose language or culture is different from ours if we translate what they say into our own terms and assume the transcendent reality of these terms [3, p. 14].

Buddhism is a relatively recent guest of the palliative care scene within Canada, and this means that many religious activities and thoughts that are natural to a Buddhist's way of understanding will undoubtedly strike the "majority culture" as unusual, strange, and odd. Consequently, in discussing the topic "Facing Life and Death: A Buddhist's Understanding of Palliative Care and Bereavement," those religious practices and beliefs common to the "minority culture" must be clearly understood, not as bizarre, eccentric, and strange phenomena, but as meaningful activities within the context of that "minority culture."

With the above as a background, it should be made clear that the term "A Buddhist's Understanding" in the title of this presentation is meant to reflect my own understanding of palliative care and bereavement, and therefore one should not conclude that what I am about to explain is an archetypical, normative, and unequivocal Buddhist stance on the subject. It is my opinion that such a standard Buddhist stance cannot be attained even among Buddhist traditions. But, I must quickly add that this does not exclude the possibility of establishing a common thread among those traditions that call themselves Buddhist. The ideas developed in this chapter have been derived from the research and textual information of a few experts in the field of death and dying which I have consulted and from my own experiences as a retired clergy of the Jodo-shin-shu, that is, the Japanese True Pure Land Buddhist tradition. The reminder of this chapter will be developed through a discussion of the following topics:

1. Foundational teachings of the historical Buddha, Shakyamuni;
2. The Expressions of Death;
3. The way we die, place of death, and timeliness or untimeliness of death;
4. Rituals, Mourning and Funeral Customs; Memorial Service; and
5. Conclusion.

1. FOUNDATIONAL TEACHINGS OF THE HISTORICAL BUDDHA, SHAKYAMUNI

The Buddhist religion began in India with the life of a prince of the Shakya clan, Siddhartha (one who attains one's aim). As a child he was moved by various situations of dis-ease that seemed to strike all living beings.

> . . . He grew up enjoying all the comforts and luxuries, pleasure and amuse-ments proper to His age and class. . . . Eventually he was married, probably to more than one wife, and had a son. Yet despite so deep an enjoyment of worldly happiness he was not satisfied. The problem of existence tormented him. In particular He was obsessed by the pitiableness of the human predic-ament. Was there no way out for beings subjected to the miseries of birth, old age, disease and death [4, p. 12]?

In a quest for a response to the question of release from the miseries of birth, old age, disease, and death, the prince renounced his status and family and departed on his journey to the various religious leaders of his time. None could give a response to how to be released from such miseries. Resolved not to move from his meditation spot beneath a pipal tree until he had understood and gained an answer, he practiced the four contemplative stages by which he was able to reflect on his former activities; was able to see how his actions had their retribution; was able to direct his mind toward the destruction of his biases regarding sensual desires, conditioned existence, and opinionated views; and finally was able to realize that there was no permanency to mundane existence. Having passed through the four contemplative stages, the prince awakened to the reality of life as a process of interdependent arising and decaying. In other words, the prince attained the state of enlightenment—buddahood—and thereby realized that there is no way out of the miseries of birth, old age, disease, and death. Whatever comes into existence is bound to age, to decay, and to die. According to *Sammāditthi Sutta (Right View)* found in *The Middle Length Discourse of the Buddha (Majjima Nikāya)*:

> . . . With the arising of birth there is the arising of ageing and death. With the cessation of birth there is the cessation of ageing and death [5, p. 136].

Because there is no state of existence spared from the reality of imper-manence and change, change or impermanence is foundational to "existence." According to Bhikkhu Bodhi:

> The notion of impermanence (*aniccatā*) forms the bedrock for the Buddha's teaching, having been the initial insight that impelled the Bodhisattva to leave the palace in search of a path to enlightenment. Impermanence, in the Buddhist view, comprises the totality of conditioned existence, raging in scale from the cosmic to the microscopic. At the far end of the spectrum the Buddha's vision reveals a universe of immense dimensions evolving and disintegrating in repetitive cycles throughout beginningless time. . . . In the

middle range the mark impermanence comes to manifestation in our inescapable mortality, our condition of being bound to ageing, sickness, and death (MN 26.5) of possessing a body that is subject to being worn and rubbed away, to dissolution and disintegration (MN 74.9). And at the close end of the spectrum, the Buddha's teaching discloses the radical impermanence uncovered only by sustained attention to experience in its living immediacy: the fact that all the constituents of our being, bodily and mental, are in constant process, arising and passing away in rapid succession from moment to moment without any persistent underlying substance. In the very act of observation they are undergoing "destruction, vanishing, fading away, and ceasing" (MN 74.11) [6, p. 26].

These words indicate that impermanence lies at the basis of existence and that to exist is possible only in the process of birth, decay, and death. Death is a natural outcome of birth and of the decaying process.

The picture which I have portrayed so far is not, however, exclusively Buddhist. It seems that anyone who has pondered seriously over the question of life and death must come to such a conclusion. For example, in the "Introduction" to her book *Death: The Final Stage of Growth*, Elisabeth Kübler-Ross makes the following observation:

Death always has been and always will be with us. It is an integral part of human existence. And because it is, it has always been a subject of deep concern to all of us. Since the dawn of humankind, the human mind has pondered death, searching for the answer to its mysteries, for the key to the question of death unlocks the door of life [7, p. 1].

To question the mystery of death is to question the process of life, and to question the process of life is to ponder about death. Death should not come as a surprise to anyone born and, consequently, death should not be a mystery to any of us here today. However, for example, if I or any one of you should die while reading this chapter, everyone, excepting perhaps the person who died, would be surprised that a death took place. However, death itself should not surprise us, because death is a natural outcome of life, and we are not surprised that we are alive. However, in spite of the Buddhist teaching of impermanence, in an actual life and death situation I would suspect that even a Buddhist will mourn when death occurs and feel a sense of loss and grief just like any other sentient being. It seems absurd, therefore, to conclude that by following the Buddhist teachings a Buddhist adherent will not be disturbed should a death occur to someone close or even to oneself.

2. THE EXPRESSIONS OF DEATH

In more recent times, with the advent of professionals—death counselors, psychiatrists, geriatricians, funeral directors, clergy, and others—whose job it is to conceal the natural process of dying, stigma attached to death has increased and as a result death has become a phenomenon that is encountered at arm's length. Elisabeth Kübler-Ross states:

> Death is a subject that is evaded, ignored, and denied by our youth-worshipping, progress-oriented society. It is almost as if we have taken on death as just another disease to be conquered. But the fact is that death is inevitable. We will all die, it is only a matter of time. Death is as much a part of human existence, of human growth and development, as being born. It is one of the few things in life we can count on, that we can be assured will occur. Death is not an enemy to be conquered or a prison to be escaped. It is an integral part of our lives that gives meaning to human existence. It sets a limit on our time in this life, urging us on to do something productive with time as long as it is ours to use [7, p. x].

What is it that prevents us from examining death as a reality within life? What is it that keeps us from expressing our feelings to ourselves and to others so that we would reveal truly who we are? What is it that brings our emotional life to an end? According to Clark Moustakas:

> In the extreme, the person stops feeling altogether and tries to live solely by rational means and cognitive directions. This is the terrible tragedy of modern life—the alienation of [one][2] from one's own feelings, the desensitization of one to one's own suffering and grief, the fear of one to experience one's own loneliness and pain and the loneliness and misery of others [8, p. 34].

When Moustaka states, ". . . the person . . . tries to live solely by rational means and cognitive directions," I understand that he is referring to the feeling of guilt that arises when one lives in accordance with one's feelings. This ". . . desensitization of one to one's own suffering and grief, the fear of one to experience one's own loneliness and pain" and consequently "the loneliness and misery of others" arises from the need of one to protect what one has rationalized and cognitively determined to be the image of the self.

In my previous discussion on the reality of impermanence as the existential reality of a person, what was implied, but not clearly defined, was the fact that whatever exists does not possess an inherent nature by which its existential status is established. Within the Buddhist tradition this has been known as *an ātman,* which unlike the expected understanding that Buddhists believe in no-self or non-self, means that existence lacks essence. Now, if I should apply this Buddhist view of non-self to the human situation, I would come to realize that what is taken to be the "self" is nothing more than a cognitive reality, that is, an idea. An idea, owing to its reality of being an idea, cannot reveal a substantive existence, because if an idea were able to reveal something substantive, one should be able to carry an

---

[2] I have deliberately changed the words "man" to the neutral form "one" and "his" to "one's" throughout this quotation.

idea around in one's pocket, hand it over to another person, and have that idea take up space and time. As absurd as that may seem, the idea of handing an idea over to another person is not as absurd as it seems, because although we know that ideas are not substantive, we would be mislead if we thought that ideas had no efficacy. Ideas do have efficacy; one needs only to look back at the human history of war to verify that. However, even though ideas have efficacy, we should not conclude therefrom that an idea is substantive. What we should see in reflecting upon human history is that history has taken place to a large extent upon the strength of efficacy of ideas that have resulted from a non-substantive reality. In terms of understanding who we are, this means that the self-image that we imagine to be the real self is nothing more than a projection of our cognitive faculty and consequently the "real self" thus conceived has as much substance as one could expect from a son of a barren woman or the hair-net seen by a person with cataract. The same applies to what we have mentally determined to be the reality of death.

Death is not something distinctly separate from life nor is life something distinctly separate from death.[3] Usually, death and life are seen as if they were unique and distinct from each other, because we are capable of thinking of them in that manner instead of thinking of them as one and the same, a reality, by the way, which can be equally imagined. In his article, "The Death that Ends Death in Hinduism and Buddhism," J. Bruce Long states:

> There are, at least, two images of death which seem to inform a large proportion of contemporary fiction, drama and cinema. On the one hand, death is pictured as an ancient enemy who, after centuries of fruitless struggle, is being brought under submission by man's scientific and technological ingenuity. Second, death is imagined as a chilling wind, blowing wherever it wills to snuff out the flame of life in anyone who gets in its way, leaving for those who remain behind only a sense that life is an inexhaustible draught of ennui or anxiety [9, pp. 52-53].

Thus, to those who see, that is for those who rationalize or conceptualize death as an "enemy" or as "chilling wind," there will arise a feeling that death is a very uncharitable, harsh, and abrupt event. However, those who see, that is those who rationalize or conceptualize death as part and parcel of life, will have a more detached feeling toward this event. This means that, ". . . death does not have to be a catastrophic, destructive thing; indeed, it can be viewed as one of the most constructive, positive, and creative elements of culture and life [7, p. 2]. Because we always have understood death and life as separate realities, we have projected a bleak picture on death which it need not have. "If you can begin to see death as an

---

[3] For an interesting discussion on the question of whether death is a process or an event, see Robert S. Morrison, "Death: Process or Event?" and the response to it by Leon R. Kass in his essay, "Death as an Event," in *Death Inside Out*, P. Steinfels and R. Veatch (eds.), Harper & Row, pp. 63-78, 1975. [Unfortunately, for the presentation, I am unable to incorporate these papers, but these essays must be considered for publication.]

invisible, but friendly, companion on your life's journey—gently reminding you not to wait till tomorrow to do what you mean to do—then you can learn to *live* your life rather than simply passing through it" [7, p. x].

3. THE WAY WE DIE, PLACE OF DEATH, AND TIMELINESS OR UNTIMELINESS OF DEATH

The manner in which one dies, the place where one dies, and when one dies are concerns that occupy most people's minds. However, from a Buddhist perspective, there is no good way, or place, or time to die. For that matter, neither is there a bad way, or place, or time to die. When the causes and condition for death are ripe, death will take place, not otherwise. This principle of causation is known as interdependent origination (*pratī tyasamutpā da*) in Buddhism and this means that whatever takes place (birth, life, or death), or does not take place, can occur if and only if the causes and conditions for its occurrence are present. This principle also holds true for space and time; hence the place where one finds one's self is controlled by the activities one did and does, and the time that any event takes place is controlled by causes and circumstances. This means that terms like "good" or "bad," "timely" or "untimely," "life or death," or "place" are not expressions of reality-as-such, but rather such terms are indicators. By the term "indicator" I am referring to something that gives all the indication of being there, but like the appearance of numbers on a digital clock or letters on a computer screen they are not to be taken as really substantively there. Like the numbers and the letters, the manifestation of death at some time and somewhere is simply an indicator of an occurring change. It is neither good or bad nor timely or untimely.

When death is understood as a natural process, then there is little sense in lamenting about the manner in which one dies or the time when one dies. However, just as it was in the case of impermanence, the manner, the place, and the time that we die are of major concern to us, because as ordinary people who are bound up in the guilt produced by our desire to live in the expectations of others, we are completely attached to the ideology of manners and behavior. Therefore, even though impermanence implies that there is no substantive reality behind any beliefs about reality we may entertain and even though death is simply part and parcel of life, the very fact of impermanence lies at the very foundation for our loneliness and fear of dying.

According to the Buddhist teaching of interdependent origination, birth and death, i.e., the process of living and dying, is nothing more than the consummation or the fruition of causes and conditions and there is no untimely consummation or fruition of causes and conditions. That fact that birth occurs or that death occurs means that birth occurs because its occurrence is timely and that death occurs because its occurrence is timely. Understood in this manner, birth or life or death always take place in their proper time frame. Even though this understanding of causation can be acquired only in the realization of the non-substantiality of reality and of impermanence, still death is a traumatic experience, owing to the fact that we ordinary people are bound up in the delusion produced by our desire to live in the expectations of permanence.

The event of birth, of life, or of death has nothing to do with producing joy or anger, but anyone can be the source of joy if it occurs in a manner that one desires or anyone can be the source of anger if it occurs in a manner that one does not desire. According to this Buddhist principle we can understand anger as arising from the desire to maintain life and not from the fact of death itself. Birth becomes a source of joy, life a source of frustration, and death a source of anger for us, because we are bound up in the ideology of permanence and a substantive reality. That is, we are unwilling to meet the challenge of change, because change implies loneliness and loneliness implies a loss of meaning in life. Hence we speak about the death of a child as untimely, death in isolation in the gutter of the street as a bad place to die, or being involved in a car accident as an unfortunate way of dying.

The discussion thus far may have you thinking that in the Buddhist tradition there is no need for rituals in giving care to the bereaved. Such an understanding probably arises from the matter-of-fact way in which I am presenting the basic teachings of the Buddha. The matter-of-fact presentation of the topics was intentional. It was for the purpose of explicating human experience as the constituent of life just-as-it-is in the manner that an Enlightened being may experience it, that is, to experience reality just-as-it-is. In other words, the matter-of-fact presentation was meant to bring to one's awareness what is just natural. It is as if I am saying to someone who is about to enter a rain storm without an umbrella, "You will get wet if you go out into the rain storm without an umbrella." It is absurd and ridiculous to say something so obvious as "You're going to get wet" to someone who is about to go out into a rainstorm without an umbrella, because under the circumstances, "getting wet" is so obvious. In this case, we have no problem in understanding the obvious, and, in a similar manner, we should also realize the fact that death being the final stage of growth is just as obvious. In the words of Elisabeth Kübler-Ross quoted earlier:

> . . . death is inevitable. We will all die, it is only a matter of time. Death is as much a part of human existence, of human growth and development, as being born. It is one of the few things in life we can count on, that we can be assured will occur [7, p. x].

And further her statement that:

> This, then, is the meaning of DEATH: *The Final Stage of Growth*: All that you are and all that you've done and been is culminated in your death [7, p. x].

All that one is and all that one has done is culminated in death. Consequently, there is probably no other event in life, perhaps aside from birth, that should be taken so seriously. It is obvious to me at least that the whole point behind the historical Siddhārtha becoming an enlightened being was to address specifically the question of death. When one understands the significance of death, one will be in a position to confront dis-ease that characterizes one's existence, to confront desire or attachment that causes the dis-ease, to come to some resolution of one's attachments and desires so that one is in control of one's own life and not tossed about by one's fear and uncertainty, and finally to get on with living fully in the moment so that there will be nothing left undone.

To live fully in the moment does not mean to live life superficially as if life had no pain, no distractions, no feelings of loneliness or grief. On the contrary, to live life fully means to live in the very instant (recall my term "insta-centric") of pain, distraction, loneliness, or grief so that when death is encountered, whether it be one's own or someone close, one will not have the regret of not having fulfilled one's life fully. The wisdom of Elisabeth Kübler-Ross expressed in the following statement must be respected:

> Whether you die at a young age or when you are older is less important than whether you have fully lived the years you have had. One person may live more in eighteen years than another does in eighty. By living, we do not mean frantically accumulating a range and quantity of experience valued in fantasy by others, rather, we mean living each day as if it is the only one you have. We mean finding a sense of peace and strength to deal with life's disappointments and pain while always striving to discover vehicles to make more accessible, increase, and sustain the joys and delights of life. One such vehicle is learning to focus on some of the things you have learned to tune out—to notice and take joy in the budding of new leaves in the spring, to wonder at the beauty of the sun rising each morning and setting each night, to take comfort in the smile or touch of another person, to watch with amazement the growth of a child, and to share in children's wonderfully "uncomplexed," enthusiastic, and trusting approach to living. To live [7, pp. x-xi].

4. RITUALS, MOURNING AND FUNERAL CUSTOMS, MEMORIAL SERVICES

In the Buddhist tradition, the various rituals, periods of mourning, and funeral service are meant to aid someone (be it that the someone is the one who is dying or is the one who is in the actual face-to-face encounter with death) to understand the source of sorrow. In order to have the bereaved understand the source of sorrow, as soon as someone dies, the Buddhist priest, if not already present at the place of death, is called to perform a "pillow service." At this time, the priest recites a short sutra, says words of condolence, and reinforces upon the mind of the bereaved the fact that a loved one has died. It may seem unnecessary to reinforce the fact that a loved one has died, but often the bereaved is unwilling to concede to death. The role of the deceased as an Enlightened Buddha, that is one who teaches others the fact of impermanence, is also emphasized.

After the pillow service, the deceased is sent to the funeral home. After the bereaved family returns home, the members of the Buddhist church come to help the family prepare for the funeral service. The members also help the family with cooking and other household chores so that the family members can attend to the preparation of the funeral service. At the funeral service, sutra is chanted, incense is offered, a sermon on the impermanence of life and the importance of the deceased as an enlightened being who, for the benefit of humankind, teaches the reality of impermanence is given, words of condolence are received, and a representative of the family gives words of thanks to the people who attended. A custom that probably originates in East Asia is a practice of bringing money in an envelope to the funeral. This money is given to the family to help cover the funeral expenses. It is not uncommon for the funeral homes to give a 10 percent discount to Buddhist families, because with the money that people bring, the Buddhist family is able to pay for the funeral in full within a day of the funeral. After the funeral, the body is sent to either the graveyard or to a crematorium. There again, a short service of sutra chanting and sermon on impermanence is given. It is also customary for the Buddhist family to meet every seven days for forty-nine days in order to recollect the life of the deceased and to listen to the Buddha's teachings. These services are attended by many of the people from the community and, consequently, these services serve to help and support the family go through the period of bereavement.

It is the caregiver, usually the Buddhist priest, who must direct the bereaved to the source from which the pain of loneliness and of bereavement arises. In the Buddhist tradition the source is understood to be delusion, attachment, and anger, technically known as the "three poisons."

"Delusion," as indicated above, refers to one's inability to confront the impermanence of life. As a result one is "attached" to the idea that death, for example, is not a part of one's life and also that death does not mean the end of one's existence. If one were to find out that one faces an incurable disease such as cancer or AIDS, one will become very perplexed and angry mainly owing to the fact that one feels deprived of life that properly belongs to one. When one becomes perplexed and angry, then perplexity and anger nourishes the deluded mind, and so the endless cycle of delusion, attachment, and anger continues. In order to stop this samsaric existence of going around in circles, one must realize that life is impermanent, is without any substantive permanency, and consequently is not something to which one should be attached. Because attachment is an emotional state which is very difficult to overcome, the caregiver must try to encourage the bereaved person to see or to appreciate the magnificence of the moment or the instant regardless of how difficult the moment or instant may seem. How is one to accomplish this? A few examples from my work as a clergy may help to clarify this.

During my role as a clergy, there were opportunities to assist some in coping with the daily problems of life and to assist others who were completely at a loss because the mother, father, brother, son, or some other member of the family died or ran away to find a new form of life. There were occasions in which I had the opportunity to console a woman whose husband died in a car accident but whose five-year-old daughter and she survived, the opportunity to sit quietly with a mother of a young man whose dream of being an olympic skier was crushed when he rammed himself into a tree and became paralyzed below his hips, and the opportunity to alleviate the pains of the parents who had to come to terms not only with the unexpected reality of their robust son's unforeseen coma but also with having to give consent to remove the life supports that sustained his breathing. In each case, someone was in need of care and I had to depend upon my understanding of Buddhism to respond to these situations. Although I have not been trained as an expert in the field of giving care and palliative care, I would like to share the following experiences with you. (I have refrained from using the names of individuals in order to protect the identity of the people, the whereabouts of whom I no longer know.)

Case I: Giving Care to Those with Worldly Concerns

To find a bride from Japan for many of the available Japanese bachelors was a recurrent event in the Japanese-Canadian experience. Although these events responded to the needs of the young Japanese bachelors, there was always a problem of the Japanese-Canadian spouse not understanding the historical Japanese background that these women represented. The women quickly adapted and absorbed the way of life in Canada. However, because of the long cultural history of Japan and the terrific technological and scientific advances in Japan, often these ladies were much more cultured, educated, and less old-fashioned than their spouses who were nourished in very ancient Japanese customs. Consequently, although from the Canadian perspective the problems faced in such marriages were seen to originate from the women, I saw my role as someone whose duty it was to point out the mutual interdependence of the two cultures and countries. Consequently, rather than siding with either the husband or the wife, I tried to get both to understand their respective perspectives in the relationship. In clinical terms, I tried not to make one or the other the patient or the savior. Rather, I attempted to bring about an understanding of mutuality. There was, however, one case where, for the sake of the sanity of one of the spouses, I counselled one of them to leave the other.

Case II: Giving Care to the Bereaved

There was an occasion in which I had the opportunity to console a woman whose husband died in a car accident but whose five-year-old daughter survived. This family, on a vacation during the summer, was traveling through Banff National Park. For some reason, the husband had to make a quick decision to avert an oncoming car and turned the steering wheel, out of habit, to the left so that the car slammed head on to another oncoming car. The reaction of turning the steering wheel to the left is a subconscious act that arises naturally in a driver from Japan or any other country, such as England, where the traffic normally flows on the left side of the road. In any event, the husband was killed instantly, and when the wife was brought to the hospital she was still unconscious. The child who was virtually unharmed, was in a state of shock and loneliness. Although the husband was conversant in English, neither the wife nor the child had a complete grasp of the English language.

I was called in to arrange the funeral for the husband, because the company for whom the husband worked happened to have a branch office in Calgary and the manager of that branch happened to know about me. Other than the manager of the Calgary branch, everyone else was a total stranger to me. Fortunately, the time I spent during my graduate studies in Japan enabled me to deal with this case totally in the Japanese language. This was somewhat more comforting to me than the time that I was faced with doing a funeral service for a young Chinese man who was killed by a ricocheting bullet or the time I was called to the hospital to perform a service for a Chinese man who died of old age. The Chinese situation gave me concern because, even though I was somewhat familiar with Chinese culture through my reading, I was unfamiliar with the actual customs of a particular Chinese people.

When the woman regained her consciousness, I introduced myself and tried to get her to understand that she was in safe hands and that her daughter was fine. I felt very strongly that, as well as comforting her, she needed to know that someone who spoke her language was near at hand. Often people who can get along in a foreign country even to the degree of shopping and handling the daily affairs of family are totally at a loss when it comes to an emergency situation. One of the assumptions we make when we visit patients is that because the patient under-stands English, she or he will be comfortable even in a hospital situation. From my own experience of being ill in a foreign country, I know that even the ability to speak the foreign language of that country did not bring comfort to me whose mother tongue was English. The reason for the discomfort, I believe, is that to simply know a language even at native fluency does not nourish the cultural and social assumptions of one's own culture. This is something I have learned to keep in mind when dealing with people whose social-cultural background is not grounded in the Canadian soil. However, because the bereaved needs to be comforted, to speak in that person's mother tongue aids the person to gain a sense of comfort more quickly than otherwise.

Case III: Comforting a Mother and a Young Man Who Became Paralyzed

The departure with his companions of an olympic team workout in Canada must have been an exciting moment for this young man from Japan who looked forward to training for his downhill skiing medal. However, human existence is such that one never knows what is in store. He came to Canada with the dream of becoming an olympic star; however, he was not so fortunate. On his way down the mountain slope he lost control and hit a tree. The impact affected his lower spine so that he could not feel anything in his legs nor could he control them anymore. My meeting with him was after the accident in the trauma room of the hospital. He was unable to speak English. He knew that the impact was severe, but he was not totally aware of the extent of his injury. He was alone until his mother flew in from Japan to be by his side. The mother, of course, knew no English so my role was to make her as comfortable as possible in a foreign environment and in a situation which did not look too promising for her son. Gradually, the son was given physical therapy treatments so that he could move his arms more easily. The mother was worried that when they returned, her son would not get the medical attention that he was receiving in the Canadian hospital. During my discussions with her, I tried to have her understand how the human situation evolves through the dynamics of causes and conditions and that neither she nor her son needed to feel that the accident occurred as a result of some divine intervention intended to condemn an act that either she or he or some member of the family may have done previously. During the weeks that followed, special Japanese food requested by the son was taken to him. When a Japanese becomes ill, there is a certain kind of plum pickle that often perks up the person and that was what he wanted. The pickle was helpful but what was important for the healing process of the son and the mother was for them to realize and to accept the probable condition of the son becoming disabled. Once they were able to accept the fact, they were able to get on with their life. A letter form the son indicated that he was able to get physiotherapy in Japan and that slowly he was finding new ways to mobilize himself.

Case IV: The Unexpected Reality of the Son's Unforeseen Coma

I received a phone call from the trauma unit of the local hospital because a Japanese person was admitted owing to a stroke. When I arrived at the hospital the man was hooked up to various monitors that indicated his heartbeat, his temperature, and the lack of certain kinds of brain waves. The man was very young and of such a great build that it was difficult for me to believe that someone who looked so healthy and strong could meet such a disaster. Still, the reality of a person lying on the bed attached to life support through all kinds of wires and tubes was confronting me in a manner that could not be denied. I asked the nurse about the family and was told that the parents who lived in eastern Canada were informed and that they would probably arrive by air the next day. I requested the nurse to inform me of their arrival and then left.

When the phone rang, I sensed that it would be the nurse informing me of the parent's arrival. I went immediately to the hospital and found the parents in a state of dismay. They were unwilling to accept that their son was in a state of coma and only the life support sustained his life. I was asked by the doctor and the nurse to inform the parents of this situation and to obtain their consent to remove the life support, because the son was brain-dead and there was absolutely no chance of his revival. My task was to alleviate the pains of the parents who could not and would not come to terms with the unexpected reality of their robust son's unforeseen coma and consequently were totally unwilling to give consent to have the life supports removed. The questions that they faced were: How do we truly know that there is no chance for the son to recover? What happens if there should be the slightest chance that the son would have recovered had the life support not been removed? How do we know that the hospital staff had done all that it could to come to such a conclusion?

I could see that the situation was not conducive to a discussion on the removal of the life support. I stayed with the parents in the trauma room for some time and then suggested that perhaps we should retire to another room where we could sit down and relax a bit. We went to the room and sat down. I asked them where they came from, about their life with their son, what kind of a son he was, and so on, so that I could contextualize any comments that I might make at a later time within the comfort of their past experiences with their son. Because they were Buddhist of the Japanese Jodo Shin Shu (True Pure Land Tradition) they were familiar with the teaching of gratitude and appreciation.

It is understandable that to deliver care to someone who has even a negligible understanding of a religious tradition is easier than sharing life's woes with someone who has no religious background at all. But the fact of the matter is that, from a Buddhist perspective, anyone who has an interest in staying alive or an interest in dying already has ample religious background. This means that all sentient beings are already immersed in religion. From this assumption, I began to talk to the parents about the unique occasion of being born as human beings. The uniqueness comes from the fact that it is in human existence that each has the opportunity to reflect upon one's own life and to make of it what one will. I asked whether they found their life enriched by the life of their son. They replied how much joy and meaning their son gave them. I asked them to reflect upon what feelings the son might have if he could see the pain that his parents were undergoing. They responded that he would be tormented if he could see their pain. Gradually, I was able to get the parents to understand that life and death are both conditioned states of being. When the condition for life is present then life will take place. When the condition for illness is present, illness will take place. When the condition for death is present, death will take place. No one is able to escape death. Moreover, when one has not lived in the appreciation of conditioned existence, then each event in life will become a burden and cause pain. Thus, for the parents to truly live in the appreciation of their son, they must live in appreciation of having encountered the life of their son. Further, because each being is in some way a teacher of life's process and because such a teacher can be no other than an enlightened being, i.e., a buddha, they should realize that their son in his state of coma is emanating the reality of impermanence. Gradually through discussions like those that went on for several days, the parents, first the father and then the mother, were able to let go of their desire to keep the son in a constant state of coma. On the fourth day, both parents were able to reach a resolution that allowed their son to rest peacefully. The life supports were removed and within two hours the son took his last breath.

5. CONCLUSION

To die is not easy. To live is not any easier. Both life and death are difficult to accomplish. I believe that Elisabeth Kübler-Ross makes explicit the ideas discussed above when she states:

> . . . it is those who have not really lived—who have left issues unsettled, dreams unfulfilled, hopes shattered, and who have let the real things in life (loving and being loved by others, contributing in a positive way to other people's happiness and welfare, finding out what things are *really you*) pass them by—who are most reluctant to die [7, p. x].

To this statement by Elisabeth Kübler-Ross, I wish only to add one final Buddhistic comment to those in bereavement. "It is those who have not really lived who are most reluctant to let die."

REFERENCES

1. D. L. Thrapp, Buddhist Helps Solace Sick at L. A. Hospital, *Los Angeles Times*, Sunday February 23, 1973. Recorded in Aoyama, Tesshi, OYA-GOKORO KO-GOKORO (Parental Heart, Child's Heart), Nagata Bunshodo, Kyoto, 1984.
2. D. P. Irish, Multiculturalism and the Majority Population, in *Ethnic Variations in Dying, Death, and Grief: Diversity in Universality*, D. P. Irish, F. Lundquist, and V. Jenkins Nelson (eds.), Taylor and Francis, Washington, D.C., 1993.
3. P. C. Rosenblatt, Cross-Cultural Variation in the Experience, Expression, and Understanding of Grief, in *Ethnic Variations in Dying, Death, and Grief: Diversity in Universality*, D. P. Irish, F. Lundquist, and V. Jenkins Nelson (eds.), Taylor and Francis, Washington, D.C., 1993.
4. M. S. Sangharakshita, *The Three Jewels: An Introduction to Buddhism*, Windhorse Publications, Surrey, 1977.
5. B. Ñānmoli and B. Bodhi, Sammāditthi Sutta (Right View), in *The Middle Length Discourses of the Buddha. A New Translation of the Majjima Nikāya*, Wisdom Publications, Boston, 1995.

6. B. Ñānmoli and B. Bodhi, Introduction, in *The Middle Length Discourses of the Buddha. A New Translation of the Majjima Nikāya,* Wisdom Publications, Boston, 1995.
7. E. Kübler-Ross, *Death: The Final Stage of Growth,* Prentice-Hall, Englewood Cliffs, New Jersey, 1975.
8. C. E. Moustakas, *Loneliness,* Prentice-Hall, Englewood Cliffs, New Jersey, 1961.
9. J. B. Long, The Death that Ends Death in Hinduism and Buddhism, in *Death: The Final Stage of Growth,* E. Kübler-Ross (ed.), Prentice-Hall, Englewood Cliffs, New Jersey, 1975.

CHAPTER 3
Death and Mourning: A Time for Weeping, A Time for Healing*

Judith Hauptman

One of the ritual areas about which American Jews are least knowledgeable is death and mourning. Many—perhaps most—Jews celebrate birth, coming of age, and marriage in the context of Jewish tradition. But death is more often observed in the American way than the Jewish way. Not only does this abandoning of Jewish practice diminish the dignity and meaning of the rites of closure, it also denies the mourners rich opportunities for consolation.

With hospice care for the terminally ill becoming more common, many people will find themselves present at the moment of death. Overwhelmed by the loss and sorely in need of expressing both grief and love, persons not schooled in Jewish patterns of behavior will not know what to do when death occurs. But those who are familiar with Jewish attitudes toward death and with the rites of mourning do know what initial steps to take to preserve the dignity of the deceased and ease the pain. They would immediately rend their garment and recite the words *barukh dayyan ha-emet*—blessed is the just judge—a brief statement suggesting that as unjust as the death may seem, Judaism asks one to believe that God has reasons for His actions. They would not leave the corpse alone but remain in the room and begin to recite psalms. For a person who feels confused and bereft upon witnessing the death of a loved one, these time-honored structures serve to comfort.

This chapter presents an overview of the laws of mourning, sketching in the general contours and even some details. These laws come to us from the Bible, the Talmud, and more recent Jewish codes of law, in particular the Shulhan Arukh,

*This chapter originally appeared in *Celebration and Renewal: Rites of Passage in Judaism,* The Jewish Publication Society, Philadelphia, Pennsylvania, and is reprinted with the permission of the publisher.

first published in 1565. As specific and situation-oriented as the laws of mourning in these works are, anyone who is steeped in this literature begins to notice that a number of principles predominate.

The first is *halakhah ke-divrei ha-mekel be-evel*, that is, in matters of mourning we rule according to the more lenient opinion (Mo'ed Katan19b) (all references are to the Babylonian Talmud). From the time that an early talmudic master named Samuel formulated this principle, it was invoked whenever there was a conflict of opinion on how to proceed. What it seems to reflect is a sense on the part of the rabbis that dealing with death is so difficult that whatever accommodation can be made to ease the burden of mourning should be made.

A second general principle that emerges from the Talmudic material is that death is the great leveler. Whereas elsewhere in the Jewish law, particularly in marriage and synagogue ritual, women are treated as subordinate to men, in death they achieve parity. It makes no difference if it was a man or woman, a father or mother, who died or who mourns: the same rules apply to both sexes. Just as a man is buried, so is a woman buried; in the same way that a man observes rites of mourning, so a woman observes rites of mourning. The final acts of kindness performed for the deceased know no gender differentiation.

The third general principle is that the main concept underlying all Jewish laws of mourning is *kevod ha-met*, preserving the dignity and honor of the deceased. Although *shivah*, the week of mourning, tends to be viewed in contemporary society as affording individuals an opportunity to deal with grief in the communal embrace, the main point of a family observing *shivah* is to make others take notice of the death. Were it not for *shivah*, the world would not miss a beat when someone dies. Putting the family in limbo for an entire week and drawing the community into their lives is a powerful way of making the world mark and mourn the death of their precious relative.

The last general principle to point out about the laws of mourning is that Jewish contact with Gentile society has altered the rules. In a number of instances the medieval commentators say that a particular ancient practice referred to in the Talmud, such as overturning couches in the house of mourning or wrapping the head as a sign of grief, should no longer be followed because it will make Jews the laughingstock in the eyes of Gentiles or else create the impression that Jews practice magic [1].

Thus mourning practices, which are in essence a commandment between one person and another person and not between a person and God, are shaped and modified by social standards and occasionally even abandoned with the passage of time. Similarly, new customs can emerge that have no basis in rabbinic or biblical teachings. Because bringing closure to relationships with parents and other close relatives is such a sensitive issue, these added practices, despite their tenuous connection to classical Jewish texts, exert an extraordinarily strong grip on people. The custom of covering mirrors during *shivah*, for example, is obscure in origin and purpose, yet it is scrupulously observed in almost all *shivah* homes. It is rather easy to provide homiletical interpretations for customs like these, as is often done; but it is also important to distinguish between ancient practices rooted in and required by Jewish law and those that somehow attached to the body of Jewish practice over the years.

A final note: Jewish mourning rites have great appeal today because of their ability to meet the emotional needs of mourners, helping them to cope with and adapt to altered life circumstances. Yet one must recognize that the theological approach of those who framed this set of observances differs from that of many people today. The pervasive theme in almost all prayers relating to death is that God decides the length of a person's life and that His decision, always a just one, is determined by the person's morals and religious behavior. As foreign and unacceptable as this idea may be to contemporary sensibilities, it is still possible for the centuries-old prayers and customs to heal the wounds and help the mourners regain balance.

DEATH

Judaism values greatly acts of loving kindness performed for the dying and the deceased. The Shulhan Arukh states that one should not leave the room of someone who is about to die so that she not feel abandoned in the very last moments of life (339:4). If possible, when death is imminent, a person should be encouraged to recite the *viddui* (confession), asking God for forgiveness for past misdeeds and a place with Him after death. If the dying person (*goses*) [3] herself is unable to recite this prayer, it may be recited for her by someone else.

Once death has occurred, those sitting with the deceased close her eyes and mouth and pull a sheet over her face (352:4). If they wish to, even if they are not close relatives, they may rend a garment and recite, *Barukh dayyan ha-emet* (340:5) [4]. The *shomer*, a family member or hired stranger who has been appointed to stay with the corpse, generally sits nearby reciting psalms. The act of guarding the corpse exempts the *shomer* from all positive rituals, such as praying or donning tefillin. The corpse must not be left alone from the time of death to the time of burial; even so, no one, aside from those appointed to remain with it or prepare it for burial, may view it. No eating or drinking is allowed in the same room as the corpse. Should the death occur in a hospital on the Sabbath, the body is taken to the hospital morgue until the Sabbath is over; in such a case it is impossible for the *shomer* to remain with the corpse. Whether the person died in the hospital, a hospice, or at home, a close relative should call a Jewish funeral home to have the corpse removed and prepared for burial [5]. Most families also call their rabbi at this time.

In preparation for burial, the *hevrah kadisha* (holy fellowship), a group of community volunteers or people hired by the funeral home, cleanse the corpse and perform *taharah*. This process is akin to immersion in a *mikvah* (ritual bath), except that instead of putting the body in the water, the water is poured over the corpse. They then dress the corpse in simple white shrouds and a tallit worn during the deceased's lifetime, place the corpse in the casket, and close it (351:2). Men tend the corpses of men, and women the corpses of women (352:3).

THE CASKET

Jewish law stipulates that a casket is to be simple, preferably made of wooden boards and dowels. The principle is to return the body to the earth from which it came. In Israel, no coffin is used, only a bier, so as to hasten decomposition and mingling with the earth. In the United States, burial in a coffin is standard practice.

The reason for a simple coffin and shrouds is found in the Talmud (Mo'ed Katan 27b). The text tells us that in the mishnaic period, because of the great expense involved in preparing fine shrouds, burying the dead was more difficult than the death itself for the mourning family. As a result, people began abandoning their dead without burying them. To remedy this situation, Rabban Gamliel, a leading rabbinic figure, waived the honor due him and requested that he be buried in a simple shroud of linen. As anticipated, simplicity then became standard Jewish burial practice. The same text also mentions several other enactments made for the sake of the poor, such as burial for all in a plain casket [6].

TIMING OF THE FUNERAL

A person is to be buried as soon after death as possible. Postponing burial, *halanat ha-met*, is considered disrespectful to the deceased as well as emotionally trying for the grieving family. Even so, since it is considered an honor for the deceased to have a well-attended funeral, burial usually occurs a day after death, thereby giving sufficient time for the family to make arrangements and notify friends and members of the community of the death (357:1). In certain cases, if family members need to travel from afar, the funeral is held even two days after the death.

A funeral may not be held on the Sabbath, High Holy Days, or the *yom tov* days of Passover, Shavuot, and Sukkot. Although the burial could be performed by non-Jews on the second day of these holidays (*yom tov sheni shel galuyot*), which is of lesser sanctity, this is rarely done. Funerals may take place on the intermediate days of the festival.

Aninut

The state of deep grief, from the time of death until completion of the burial, is called *aninut*. During this time the mourner, the *onen*, is exempt from fulfilling any of the positive observances of Judaism, such as lighting Hanukkah candles or putting on tefillin, because it is assumed that he or she is distracted by death and preoccupied with making funeral arrangements (341:1). Should a person enter *aninut* on the Sabbath, he or she may attend services, since no funeral arrangements can be made on that day.

Funeral Preparations

Most American Jewish funerals take place in a funeral chapel, generally a privately owned facility that provides all the necessary services to mourners, such as transporting the corpse and preparing it for burial. The funeral of a rabbi, cantor or communal leader, however, is often held in the synagogue.

While the family members await the start of the funeral, it has become customary for friends to approach them and offer words of condolence. As well established as this custom is, it deviates from the rabbinic teaching: "Do not comfort him while his death lies unburied before him" (Pirkei Avot 4:18).

Keri'ah

One of the most ancient mourning practices, *keri'ah*, rending one's garment, is referred to in a number of places in the bible. Jacob, upon hearing news of Joseph's death, rips his clothing in grief (Genesis 17:34). Rending the garment is giving physical expression to one's emotions, showing that the sadness, pain, and perhaps anger are so intense that they lead one to find relief in the destruction of material goods.

Keri'ah became a requirement of the mourning process in the rabbinic period and was supposed to be performed immediately upon learning of the death. The Talmud says, "any rending which is not performed at the moment of *hamimut* [wrenching emotion] is not considered rending" (Mo'ed Katan 24a). Today, however, two major changes have occurred in the practice of *keri'ah*. The first is that rending is not usually done upon hearing of the death but either immediately prior to the funeral service or else at the cemetery, just prior to burial. A rabbi or other individual approaches the mourners, asks them to stand up, and, with a blade, cuts the garment the mourner is wearing, such as a tie, shirt, or blouse. The mourner then rends the garment with her own hands, making a rip about three inches long (vertically, near the heart) [7]. As she does so, she recites the blessing: "Barukh atah adonai elohenu melekh ha-olam dayyan ha-'emet" (Blessed is God, Ruler of the Universe, the Just Judge). The mourners wear the rent garment for the entire *shivah* period. After this, there is no longer any reason to wear it.

The second change is that many mourners no longer perform *keri'ah* on a garment they are wearing; instead, the mourner pins on a small black ribbon and then rips the ribbon. This custom probably originated at a time when Jews were embarrassed by public display of their own mourning rituals and felt that it was more dignified to wear a rent black ribbon than a rent garment. Today it seems that such feelings of shame have largely disappeared and a return to traditional practices is called for.

The Funeral Service

A Jewish funeral service is short. It consists of three parts: readings from Psalms, a eulogy, and the Memorial Prayer. A rabbi, relative, or friend recites several appropriate psalms, such as chapters 15, 23, 24, 49, and 90, most of which speak of closeness to God and dwelling with Him as the reward for leading a morally upright life. At the funeral of a woman one often reads chapter 31 of Proverbs, which applauds the accomplishments of the woman of valor. A *hesped* (eulogy) is then delivered, usually by a rabbi but preferably by a son or daughter or other close relative of the deceased. The eulogy, which summarizes the life and achievements of the deceased, is intended to praise him and at the same time express the sadness that is in the hearts of those present (344:1). On certain joyous days of the year, such as Hanukkah, Rosh Hodesh (New Moon), and intermediate days of a festival, when burial is permitted but a eulogy is not allowed, a rabbi will find a way to circumvent this ban, such as by interspersing some brief remarks about the deceased between the verses of the psalms.

The funeral service ends with a Memorial Prayer, *El molei rahamim,* which asks a merciful God to care for the soul of the deceased under the sheltering wings of His presence and help it find peace. The centuries-old mournful melody with which these words are chanted is an appropriately somber end to the service.

Several pallbearers, usually friends and relatives, then carry or roll the casket to the hearse, and the assembled group follows for a block or two out of respect for the dead. The Hebrew word for funeral, *levayah,* means to escort; it is this brief act of escorting the body to burial, as was done in ancient times, that is referred to. The casket is then driven to the cemetery, with family and friends following.

The Graveside Service

When the hearse reaches the cemetery, the family members and friends again carry or roll the casket to the gravesite, pausing several times on the way, probably as a sign of grief. The rabbi usually walks ahead reciting Psalm 91, which speaks of God's sheltering presence; all others follow the casket. After it is lowered into the ground, friends and relatives help shovel earth, either filling the grave completely, or just covering the coffin. At this time, *tzidduk hadin,* a justification of the divine decree, is read. The mourners then recite the "burial kaddish" (376:4). This special kaddish has a long opening paragraph that talks about a time in the future when God will resurrect the dead, rebuild the city of Jerusalem and His Temple, and establish His kingdom in the entire world.

Burial, and particularly the act of shoveling the earth into the grave, brings closure. Up until this point it is hard for a mourner to deal with her feelings because the body has not yet been laid to rest, but from this point on she can confront her emotions. It now becomes possible to extend words of comfort to the bereaved family. Friends form two parallel lines through which the mourners pass and receive condolences as they walk from the gravesite back to the hearse [8]. The family then returns to the place where it will sit *shivah*, usually the home of the deceased. It is customary, before entering the home, to pour water over one's hands (376:4), a practice reminiscent of Temple times when ritual cleanness and uncleanness was a significant factor in Jewish life and water functioned as a cleansing agent for corpse-induced defilement.

Se'udat Havra'ah

While burial is taking place, friends prepare a meal, called *se'udat havra'ah* (meal of consolation), for the mourners to eat upon their return from the cemetery (378:1). The menu usually includes eggs, lentils, and other round foods, which may serve as a reminder of the ongoing cycle of life (378:9). This meal is intended to revive the spirits of the mourners, who now need the care and concern of the community to negotiate the emotional turbulence still ahead of them.

Shivah

Shivah begins upon returning from the cemetery, even if it is already close to sundown, and lasts for seven days. For example, if the burial took place on a Thursday at noon, the seventh and last day of *shivah* is the following Wednesday. This last day of *shivah* is abbreviated (see p. 65).

Probably the best known of all Jewish mourning rites, *shivah* (literally, "seven") requires all members of the immediate family to interrupt the normal flow of their lives for an entire week—not go to work, not even go outside—and spend time in the home of the deceased, receiving visits from those who come to comfort them. All their needs are tended to by others, such as preparing and serving meals or answering the doorbell (although the front door is usually left open and visitors enter on their own) and the telephone. It is an old Jewish custom to bring cooked meals to people in mourning. Cut off from the everyday world, the family is given an opportunity to spend all their emotional energy dealing with the death of a person they loved and absorbing the pain, which is deep even if death was expected. Those who come to visit during this week perform the mitzvah of *nihum avelim*, comforting the mourners and also honoring the dead. The best way of fulfilling this dual goal is to speak of the deceased. An easy way of refocusing a conversation that has strayed far from the topic of death is to ask the mourners a leading question about the deceased.

Anyone who has sat *shivah* knows how comforting and stabilizing—and at the same time grueling—this week is. The gratitude that a mourner feels toward those who take the time to visit during this difficult period is boundless.

Rules of Behavior During Shivah

A seven-day period of mourning is a custom that dates back to the Bible, which says, in reference to the death of Jacob (Genesis 50:10), that he was mourned for seven days. It is the Talmud (Mo'ed Katan 21a), though, that presents *shivah* as a full-fledged set of mourning practices, primarily defined in terms of its restrictions:

And these are the things that a mourner is forbidden to do:
1. go to work,
2. Bathe,
3. anoint the body with oil,
4. engage in sexual relations,
5. wear leather shoes,
6. read Torah, Prophets, Hagiographa, and
7. study Mishnah, Midrash, Halakhot, Aggadot.

This set of rules denies the mourner basic physical pleasures as well as spiritual and intellectual pleasure derived from the study of classical texts [9]. In addition, the fact that ordinary labor is forbidden insulates the mourner from the world-at-large and places him at home with little to do other than talk about the deceased and deal with his grief.

Other Talmudic statements indicate that a mourner may not don tefillin for the first several days of *shivah* (Mo'ed Katan 21a);[10] that mourners are not allowed to greet others, inquire after their well-being, or respond to a greeting by speaking of their own well-being (Mo'ed Katan 21b). This limitation creates awkward moments at the beginning and end of the *shivah* visit but accomplishes the goal of suppressing levity.

A positive act required during *shivah*, according to the Talmud, is to overturn all couches and beds in the house of mourning (Mo'ed Katan 27a). This practice was transformed, in the course of time, into a requirement to sit lower than is customary. Today, funeral homes supply low stools or stool-shaped cartons for the mourner to sit on. Unfortunately, these boxes are both unattractive and uncomfortable. To solve this problem, many synagogue groups provide an alternative kind of seating: a set of standard folding chairs with part of each leg sawed off is brought for the week to the home of the family sitting *shivah*. In this way the mitzvah of sitting low is fulfilled in a comfortable and even aesthetic manner.

Leather shoes may not be worn during *shivah*, but, as holds true for Yom Kippur, which is also a day of mourning and self-affliction, shoes made of fabric or some other material, such as plastic, are perfectly acceptable (382:1). If a mourner must leave home to go to the synagogue for services, he is permitted to wear leather shoes in the street for purposes of social acceptability.

Although bathing is not permitted during *shivah*, many rabbis interpret this rule as referring to bathing for pleasure [11]. Those who are accustomed and feel a need to shower each day are permitted to do so. The Talmud, and later the Shulhan Arukh, state that women should not wear cosmetics during *shivah* (Mo'ed Katan 20b; 381:6).

The first three days of *shivah* are considered to be the ones of deepest and bitterest grief, the time it takes to absorb the fact of death and its irrevocability.

After this period has passed, but only if absolutely necessary, the mourner is allowed to go to work. Similarly, if he owns a business, such as a restaurant, and would suffer significant financial loss by closing for the week, as would his waiters who are dependent on gratuities, he is permitted to leave the restaurant open, with others managing it, while he sits *shivah* (380:5).

End of *Shivah*

The last day of *shivah* is not observed for a full twenty-four hours. The principle laid down in the Talmud is *Miktzat ha-yom kh-khulo*, meaning that on the final day, observance of a small portion of the day counts for observance of the entire day (Mo'ed Katan 19b). Today, the family in mourning gets up from *shivah* after *shaharit* services on the seventh day, or after *musaf* if the seventh day is Sabbath. As it turns out, *shivah* often consists of only three full days and four abbreviated ones; on the day of burial, *shivah* begins after returning from the cemetery; on Friday, *shivah* ends for the day about two hours before sunset; on Saturday, the mourners sit only at night, after *havdalah* is recited; and on the seventh day only a fraction of the day is óbserved. However, if *shivah* begins on a Friday or ends on a Sabbath, four full days will be observed.

Other *Shivah* Practices

It has become common practice for the community to make a *shivah* minyan, to pray daily, morning and evening, in the house of the mourner so that she need not leave her home to go to the synagogue. A *sefer Torah* is even brought in these cases for the Monday- and Thursday-morning readings [12]. Some people light candles during all services held in the home. It is also customary for one of the mourners to serve as *sheliah tzibbur* (prayer leader) for all of the services held in the home. In many homes, during the break between *minhah* and *ma'ariv*, a learned friend is invited to teach Jewish texts, usually Mishnah, in memory of the deceased.

Since mourners sit at home all day, it is a good idea for those who plan to visit them to come at different hours during the day, particularly in the morning, when it is less likely for there to be a crowd. Because *shivah* is not a joyous social occasion, Jewish law frowns on putting out food for the visitors to eat. Baskets of fruit and boxes of candy should not be sent to the mourner or served by them to the visitors. However, as noted above, bringing cooked food for the mourners to eat is encouraged.

Many people believe that it is incorrect to pay a *shivah* visit in the first few days. The unfortunate result of this misconception is that the mourners receive little company at the time when they probably need it the most.

People often wonder whether they should bring their children when going to make a *shivah* call. In most instances the answer is yes, particularly if there are children in the home where *shivah* is being observed. The best way to develop in children a sensitivity toward the importance and kindness of comforting the bereaved, and to demystify mourning for them, is to take them along.

Other customs that have developed over time are to light a candle in the *shivah* home and let it burn for the full seven days, perhaps equating the source of light and warmth with the relationship between the deceased and his family. It has also become standard practice, though not prescribed in the codes of law, to cover all mirrors in the *shivah* home. One explanation is that mirrors encourage one to focus on oneself and mourning should involve attention to the deceased.

When one takes leave of a family in mourning, it is traditional to say to them: "Ha-makom yenahem etkhem be-tokh she'ar avelei tzion veyerushalayim" (May God comfort you among all those who mourn for Zion and Jerusalem). Like the reference in the wedding blessings to the joy of Zion, the grieving mother, upon being reunited with her children, this parting statement uses the occasion of an individual's death to express eschatological yearnings for future comfort for the entire bereaved Jewish people.

Intersection of Sabbath and *Shivah*

The Sabbath that falls during *shivah* counts for one of the seven days even though it is not publicly observed as a day of mourning. On that Sabbath, the mourners are expected to go to the synagogue for prayers, and no condolences are to be extended to them. When the mourner arrives at the synagogue Friday night, he remains outside until the conclusion of *lekhah dodi*. The congregation then turns to him and greets him with the words, "May God comfort you. . . ." A mourner may not serve as prayer leader on that Sabbath, or on any Sabbath in the thirty-day or year-long period of mourning. Otherwise the Sabbath supersedes mourning, suspending all public practices of mourning, such as sitting on low chairs, not wearing leather shoes, and not leaving one's home. Only the private practices of mourning still obtain on the Sabbath during the week of *shivah*, such as the ban on sexual relations and study of classical Jewish texts.

Intersection of Festivals and *Shivah*

Even more remarkable are the rules relating to the intersection of *shivah* and a festival. If the burial takes place several days before a festival, or even before sundown on the eve of a festival, the onset of the festival cancels the remaining days of *shivah* or, in the extreme case, cancels *shivah* altogether, provided a symbolic *shivah* was observed for a few moments. In Judaism, public celebration takes precedence over private mourning. No one is expected to mourn, celebrate, and then resume mourning again. Nevertheless, as perplexing as it may seem, if someone dies on a festival, and is buried on one of the intermediate days, the family observes the remaining days of the festival and then, upon its conclusion, sits nearly a full, albeit delayed, *shivah* (Mo'ed Katan 20a; 399:1) [13]. The logical principle at work here is that a festival can cancel mourning that has already begun, but not mourning that has been postponed.

Relatives for Whom One Sits *Shivah* and Says Kaddish

When the Torah talks about the exacting standards of holiness that apply to *kohanim* (priests) who serve in the Temple, it goes on to say that these rules are relaxed if a *kohen's* close relative dies: he is instructed to defile himself for his mother, father, son, daughter, brother, and unmarried sister (Leviticus 21:2, 3). This short list makes it fairly obvious that the Torah links mourning with flesh-and-blood relatives, whom the text calls *she'ero ha-karov*.

The rabbis of the Talmud took the Torah's short list of relatives, expanded it to include one's spouse, married sisters, and half-siblings [14] and ruled that it is for these relatives and no others that a Jew—*kohen, levi,* or Israelite—sits *shivah* [Mo'ed Katan 20b]. That is, the only people for whom one is obligated to sit *shivah* and observe the other rites of mourning are one's immediate family: parents, siblings, spouse, and children.

Today, given the prevalence of complicated family configurations, attributable in many instances to death, divorce, and remarriage, a variety of questions arises. What if a divorced parent's second spouse dies: are step-children required to sit *shivah*? Does one sit *shivah* for step-siblings? The rule seems to be that the obligation for mourning still falls only on blood relatives. As for siblings, only those who are blood relatives, like half-siblings, are included, but not step-siblings. Similarly, one is not required to observe the mourning rites for step-parents or step-children. The question of adoptive parents and adopted children is trickier, given the deep emotional attachment between them, identical to that of natural parents and children. In all of these cases Jewish law holds that although there is no absolute obligation to sit *shivah* and say kaddish, it certainly is permissible and commendable to do so [15].

If a child dies before it is thirty days old, Jewish law does not prescribe any rites of mourning (Mo'ed Katan 24b; 374:8). As insensitive as this rule may seem, the explanation appears to lie in the fact that *shivah* honors the dead, and the Talmudic rabbis did not deem it appropriate to honor such a young child.

Today, more and more people, in particular women, find it meaningful and emotionally restorative to conduct a rite of mourning for the loss of a fetus. Suggestions have been made to recite a *mi shebeirakh* prayer in the synagogue after the miscarriage and, following her recovery, to invite the mother to recite publicly *birkhat ha-gomel* (a blessing said upon recovery from illness). In this way the community can be called upon to offer the couple emotional support and assistance in coming to terms with their grief [16].

Mourners Who Live in Different Cities

Since it is not unusual today for brothers and sisters to live in different cities, apart from each other and also apart from their parents, the question of where to sit *shivah* for a parent who dies can be difficult to resolve. It is becoming common to sit the first three days in the home of the deceased parent or one of the siblings, together with the other mourners, and then return to one's own home for the latter part of *shivah* [17]. The logic behind this division is that the most effective and meaningful comforting can be offered by one's own friends and neighbors, who will be able to do so only when the mourner returns home.

Children and Mourning

Although children who have not reached the age of mitzvot—twelve for girls and thirteen for boys—are not obligated by any of the mourning rules, the tendency in most instances of a child suffering a loss of a parent or sibling is to involve her to the extent possible in the rites. Although it used to be common practice to shelter children from death and cemeteries, mental health professionals now consider it far better for a child to attend the funeral, watch the burial, rend her garment, sit *shivah*, and even recite kaddish for her parent or sibling. Children, too, need opportunities to express their love and grief openly, and Jewish mourning rites offer that to them.

Kaddish

Together with sitting *shivah*, saying kaddish is the most familiar and widely observed of all Jewish mourning practices. During *shivah* and afterward, at each of the daily services, mourners recite *kaddish yatom* (mourner's kaddish). Many mourners try to attend *shaharit* services in the morning and *minhah/ma'ariv* in the late afternoon in order not to miss an opportunity to recite this prayer, but many rabbis rule that attending one service a day fulfils the mourner's obligation. Kaddish may be recited only when a quorum of ten Jews—a minyan—is present.

Kaddish is a prayer that says nothing about death or any event in the life of human beings. It is a doxology, a prayer extolling God, saying that He surpasses our praises, that we are unable, in this world, using our human faculties, to describe Him and His attributes adequately. Kaddish was not composed for mourners but is a set of paragraphs recited many times during every prayer service as a sort of marker or divider between the main sections of the service. For instance, at *ma'ariv* (evening prayer), *kaddish shalem* (full kaddish with an insertion petitioning God to answer our prayers) is recited after the *Amidah* and immediately before *alenu*. *Kaddish yatom* (a slighty shorter version of kaddish) is recited after *alenu*, marking off that last part of the service. That is, in general, each section of the service, be it a section of psalms or hymns, a Torah reading, or a set of petitions, is followed by the recitation of some form of kaddish. The kaddish that has come to be known as *kaddish yatom,* and is now recited only by mourners, was thus originally a fixed part of the service, totally independent of mourning and mourners. Over time, however, it came to be recited only by those present who were in mourning.

No one knows why this change took place. Statements in the Shulhan Arukh suggest that the reason this particular prayer is reserved for male mourners is to give them the opportunity to honor their deceased fathers (376:4). If the sons recite kaddish and lead services, they show the community that their father properly discharged his obligation to educate them and transmit to them the principles and practices of Judaism.

It is also possible, according to some, to find a message appropriate to mourners in the kaddish prayer. By noting in its opening line that the world was created according to God's will, the prayer suggests that we do not understand why death occurs when it does, particularly when people die young, or why dying in some instances is so painful and prolonged. In a sense, what everyone longs for is *mitah bi-neshikah,* death by a kiss—a fast and painless death, preferably in one's old age. But the kaddish which asserts that the world was created as He wished it to be, meaning that God is in control and has reasons for His actions, may offer comfort to those who challenge God because of the untimely or difficult death of a family member. Kaddish is essentially a prayer that looks to a glorious future, one in which the whole world recognizes one God and, as a result, lives in harmony and peace.

Kaddish derabbanan, recited in the mourning service after reading texts from the Talmud, is also reserved for mourners.

Alternatives to Kaddish

When a person finds it difficult or impossible to say kaddish in the synagogue at least once a day, certain alternatives are available. A mourner may read each day a chapter from the Torah or the Prophets or study a mishnah or a passage from the Talmud [18]. Such study would also reflect well on the person's Jewish upbringing and hence on her parents. It is unfortunate that most people are unaware of this option, so that if they find it impossible to attend services, thinking there is no legitimate substitute they do nothing at all.

Women and Kaddish

The recitation of kaddish for nearly a year is traditionally viewed as an obligation upon the sons of the deceased, not upon the daughters. However, since Jewish laws of mourning in every other area obligate women in the same way that they obligate men, it follows that women should feel the same duty men feel and recite kaddish in a synagogue at least once a day. Even in Orthodox synagogues, where women are not counted for the prayer quorum and where they sit separately from men, a woman may recite kaddish along with the men from her own seat, just as she recites other prayers from her place during the course of the service [19]. A daughter who is Jewishly knowledgeable and committed to regular synagogue attendance honors the memory of the deceased parent just as much as a learned and observant son does. It is interesting to note that in the biblical and Talmudic period women were actively and even formally involved in the mourning rites as keeners (*mekonenot*), composing dirges and leading the responsive recitation of various kinds of lamentations.

Long-Term Effects of Kaddish

In many ways, reciting kaddish on a regular basis for almost a year, let alone honoring the deceased parent, also gives the son or daughter an opportunity to receive communal sympathy for this entire time and even to channel his or her own bereftness into positive action. The need to attend services regularly often gives a new focus to the mourning child and fills a void left by the death of the parent, the community's attention substituting in a certain way for parental attention no longer available to him or her. Many mourners actually forge new bonds to their Jewish community and synagogue minyan as a result of this yearlong experience.

At the time of mourning a parent, which for many people occurs in their forties and fifties, many rediscover what Judaism has to offer and emerge from the year more committed and observant than before. The loss of a parent makes one at once more vulnerable and more open to new experiences or to changing one's way of doing things. Whereas Judaism up until that time may have been experienced vicariously through a parent, at this time a person comes into direct contact with it and struggles to find a new personal meaning in the Jewish faith and community.

Arranging for Someone Else to Say Kaddish

In the past, when a person died leaving no sons or leaving sons who were not observant, a kaddish-sayer was paid to recite kaddish at three synagogue services each day. This person was not related to the deceased but was a Jew whose custom it was to pray three times a day in the synagogue. Many have decried this practice because it engenders disrespect rather than respect. If children of the deceased are not available to say kaddish on a relatively consistent basis for the entire period, rather than hire a kaddish-sayer, some rabbis suggest that relatives and friends divide the responsibility among themselves.

Sheloshim

Following *shivah*, the primary mourning period, there is a secondary period of mourning called *sheloshim*, meaning thirty, because it lasts for thirty days. Like *shivah*, one counts from the day of burial, and also like *shivah*, the last day is not full but ends following *shaharit* services.

Although *sheloshim* is a period of mourning, it is far less intense than *shivah*. The mourners resume normal social and professional duties but are still restricted in certain ways. One does not cut one's hair during this time, a custom dating back to the Bible of letting one's hair grow wild when in mourning (Leviticus 10:6); this rule applies to both men and women. In addition, men are not to shave for the duration of *sheloshim* (390:1). Another restriction observed for thirty days is not attending social events or even religious celebrations (391:1). However, a mourner may attend the ceremony itself, such as a circumcision, as long as he does not stay for the festive meal that follows. Wearing new clothes during this period of time is also considered inappropriate.

This thirty-day period eases the mourner back into normal routines by allowing the resumption of many but not all of one's regular patterns of social behavior. At the conclusion of the thirty days, a *sheloshim* memorial service is often held at which time various Jewish texts are taught in memory of the deceased.

The end of *sheloshim* marks the end of the period of mourning for all relatives except parents. Although many people believe and even behave otherwise, after *sheloshim* kaddish is no longer recited for a spouse, sibling, or child. All mourning restrictions are lifted.

Twelve-Month Period of Mourning

The only relatives for whom one observes rites of mourning for twelve months are parents, both father and mother. A text from the Talmud drives home the point that mourning rites for parents are more demanding than those for other relatives. It lists nine ways in which the two sets of practices differ (Mo'ed Katan 22b). The four that are still relevant today are:

[When mourning] for all the others (siblings, spouse, children), he may cut his hair or shave after thirty days have passed; [when mourning] for his parents, he may not do so until his friends scold him [about his appearance].

[When mourning] for all others, he may attend a celebration after thirty days have passed; [when mourning] for his mother and father, not until twelve months have passed.

[When mourning] for all others, he rends [his garment] a *tefah* (handbreadth); [when mourning] for his father and mother, until he bares his heart.

[When mourning] for all others, he bastes the rip after *shivah* and sews it up after thirty days; [when mourning] for his father and mother, he may baste the rip after thirty days, but may never fully mend it.

What is this lengthy rabbinic statement telling us? That parents are in a different category from everyone else; that just as the Torah singles out parents for special honor in their lifetime, promising long life in exchange for proper performance of this mitzvah and threatening death for anyone who curses or strikes parents, similarly the Talmud requires special respect for parents after their death.

I do not think that the Talmud is suggesting that the grief for one's parents is more intense than the grief for a child who dies but, rather, that parents who have give unconditional love to their children, who have given birth to them, raised, educated, and transmitted Jewish and human values to them, and who have established them as functioning and productive human beings, deserve the most prolonged and intensive period of mourning. Children are the continuation of their parents in the most real sense, and therefore they are asked to mourn for the longest period of time.

Following the death of a parent one does not attend *semahot* (religious celebrations) or parties for one year, or twelve months on the Jewish calendar [20]. According to the strictest rabbinic ruling, a mourner is not allowed to listen to music, turn on the radio, watch television, or go to a movie or a concert for twelve months. Other halakhic approaches allow most leisure activities as long as they are done in the company of only one or two other people so that the mourner does not experience *simhat mere'im*, the pleasure of being together with friends.

The key observance for the extended mourning period is saying kaddish each day in the synagogue [21]. Although one would expect the obligation to last for twelve months, it lasts only for eleven. The explanation for this perplexing rule seems to lie in a tradition which states that the most time a person could possibly spend in the netherworld is twelve months. After that, even the blackest soul has atoned for its evil doings and is permitted to make its way to heaven. The recitation of kaddish helps guarantee safe passage from the lower realms to the upper. Therefore, if a child recited kaddish a full twelve months, he might be suggesting that his parents would not leave the netherworld until the end of this period of time—that is, that they were inveterate sinners. The custom thus arose of reciting kaddish for parents for eleven months only (376:4).

Converts and Mourning

A convert to Judaism, according to Jewish law, no longer has kinship ties to her Gentile family. Therefore, if a parent or other relative for whom Jewish law obligates mourning dies, the convert is under no obligation to sit *shivah*. Jewish law, in fact, discourages *shivah* in a case like this but looks benignly upon a convert who wishes to recite kaddish in memory of the deceased relative.

Mourning and Marriage

Should a bride or groom suffer the loss of a close relative within thirty days of a scheduled wedding, it is postponed until the conclusion of *sheloshim* (392:1). Even if it is a parent who died, a marriage may still take place after *sheloshim*—

that is, during the twelve-month mourning period. No restrictions are placed on the joyousness of the celebration.

The *Kohen* and Death

A *kohen*, who in the past was and even today is subject to more demanding laws of ritual purity than other Jews, is not allowed to come into contact with a corpse or even be under the same roof, unless it is one of the seven family members for whom he is obligated to mourn. Because of this holiness code, *kohanim* may not attend funeral ceremonies of anyone other than close family members if the casket is present, nor may they enter a cemetery. Some *kohanim* remain outside the funeral chapel during the funeral service to show their respect for the deceased [22]. These rules apply only to male *kohanim*.

Charity in Memory of the Deceased

Probably the finest way to commemorate the deceased is to make a contribution to charity in his or her name. In many cases the family will indicate what causes were dear to the person's heart, such as social service and educational institutions in the United States or Israel, or a medical research society for a particular disease. Often these donations take the place of flowers, which are not appropriate at Jewish funerals [23].

Yahrzeit

The *yahrzeit*, a Yiddish word meaning year-day, is the anniversary of the death as determined by the Jewish lunar-solar calendar. Because of differences between the Jewish and general calendrical systems, the secular date of the *yahrzeit* will vary somewhat from year to year. It is customary on this day for the relatives of the deceased—the same ones who observed *shivah*—to attend synagogue services, recite mourners' kaddish, be called for an *aliyah* to the Torah (if the Torah is read on that day), and serve as prayer leader. Many also give charity in memory of the deceased on the *yahrzeit*. A *yahrzeit* candle, which burns for twenty-four hours, is lit at home at sundown, when the *yahrzeit* begins. It is also customary to have an *aliyah* to the Torah on the Shabbat preceding the *yahrzeit*. Some Jews who find it difficult to attend services on the exact day of the *yahrzeit* observe it by saying kaddish on the Sabbath immediately preceding the anniversary.

Tombstone

After about a year has passed it is customary to erect a tombstone at the head of the grave. The Hebrew name and patronym and, more recently, also the matronym, are engraved on the stone, as well as the day of death according to the

Jewish calendar. The English name of the deceased and the dates of birth and death according to the secular calendar are usually also engraved.

Unveiling

It is an American (and also Western European) custom to hold an unveiling of the tombstone about the same time as the date of the first *yahrzeit*. The simple graveside service consists of reading several Psalms and reciting the Memorial Prayer *(El molei rahamim)* and mourners' kaddish. The gathering gives the family an additional opportunity to reminisce about the deceased and thereby honor her. Young children in attendance should be taught to walk around the graves and not on them.

Yizkor

In addition to the yearly remembrance of the deceased on the *yahrzeit*, the ceremony of *hazkharat neshamot*, recalling the souls of the deceased, takes place four times a year in the synagogue—on Yom Kippur, Shemini Azeret (also known as the eighth day of Sukkot), the eighth day of Passover, and the second day of Shavuot. *Yizkor*, the first word of the memorial paragraph and the name by which it is commonly known, means "may God remember [the soul of the deceased and take care of it]." In addition to personal *Yizkor* prayers, in which people name their deceased relatives, collective *Yizkor* prayers are recited for martyrs, victims of the Holocaust and deceased members of the congregation. *Yizkor* is also a call to action: it stipulates that the one who recites the prayer make a donation to charity in memory of the deceased.

It is now almost standard practice that individuals whose parents are still alive and who have not suffered the death of any close relative leave the sanctuary during the recitation of *Yizkor*. Since this custom has no clear rationale and may possibly be rooted in superstition, many rabbis encourage all those present at services to remain in the sanctuary for *Yizkor* and not to separate themselves from the community at its time of remembered, shared grief. In particular, they note, the collective *Yizkor* prayers should be recited by all.

Many people light *yahrzeit* candles on the four days on which *Yizkor* is recited.

Visiting the Cemetery

It is customary to visit the graves of relatives once a year, usually a short time before the High Holy Days (Shulhan Arukh, Orah Hayyim, 581:4). In addition to making sure that the graves are being cared for properly by the cemetery authorities, the reason for this visit is the traditional Jewish belief, called *zekhut avot*, that ancestors intercede on behalf of descendants before the Heavenly tribunal as it decides their fate for the coming year. It is appropriate to recite psalms at the graveside and also the Memorial Prayer *(El molei rahamim)*.

CONCLUSION

Judaism is a life-affirming and joy-affirming religion. At the same time, it recognizes the preciousness of each individual and for this reason prescribes rites of mourning that proclaim to the world the irreparable loss that a single death brings to the family, the community, the Jewish people, and the entire world. The laws of mourning also recognize the difficulty a mourner has in confronting the rupture of a valued relationship, the finality of death, and the emptiness left in its wake. Rites of mourning that take the mourner through the first few days, the first week, the first month, and the first year ease the transition, enabling him or her to come to terms with death and return to life in the real world in a gentle, incremental way.

ACKNOWLEDGMENTS

I would like to dedicate this chapter to Professor Baruch Bosker, my colleague on the Talmud faculty at the Jewish Theological Seminary, whose unfortunate death in the prime of life occurred as I was working on this project. My thanks to Rabbi David C. Kogen, Professor Richard Kalmin, and my friends Terri and Jack Lebewohl for their many insightful comments and suggestions.

SUGGESTIONS FOR FURTHER READING

The First Jewish Catalog, a do-it-yourself kit compiled and edited by Richard Siegel, Michael Strassfeld, and Sharon Strassfeld (Philadelphia: Jewish Publication Society, 1973), pp. 172-181, provides a lucid survey of the main laws of burial and mourning. The authors encourage readers to become active in their community in order to "re-Judaize" the procedures surrounding death, burial, and mourning. Good annotated bibliography.

Maurice Lamm, *The Jewish Way in Death and Mourning* (New York: Jonathan David, 1969), is a comprehensive, detailed guide to laws, rituals, and customs associated with burial and mourning. Easy-to-read presentation with an attempt to explain many of the practices in psychological terms; complete index for easy reference.

Isaac Klein, *A Guide to Jewish Religious Practice* (New York: JTSA, 1979), provides a wide-ranging and complete look at the laws of mourning and burial, including related topics such as autopsies, cremation, suicide, and exhumation. Fully indexed to the traditional sources.

Hyman E. Goldin, *Hamadrikh: The Rabbi's Guide* (New York: Hebrew Publishing Company, 1939), pp. 95-184, gives a full rendering, in Hebrew and English, of the laws of burial and mourning, with the relevant liturgical texts interspersed among the legal ones. Material is drawn from a wide variety of law codes and treatises on the subject.

Leopold (Yekutiel) Greenwald, *Kol bo al avelut* (New York: Phillip Feldheim, 1947), in Hebrew, gives a detailed, updated compendium of most laws of burial and mourning. The author seeks to bring people back to traditional practice for the sake of honoring the dead. Detailed analysis of each issue with full reference to the sources.

Shulhan Arukh, *Yoreh De'ah*, secs. 335-403, in Hebrew, is a complete guide to the rules of burial and mourning. Although first published in the 16th century, most rules are still in effect today.

Jules Harlow, ed., *The Bond of Life* (New York: The Rabbinical Assembly, 1975), is a book for mourners. Contains an overview of the rules of mourning, readings from traditional sources, and reflections on death by a variety of authors. Also contains full text, in both Hebrew and English, of all the prayer services that will be recited in the mourner's home.

Jack Riemer, ed., *Jewish Reflections on Death* (New York: Schocken, 1974), is a collection of responses to death written from philosophical, halakhic, and personal perspectives. Fascinating reading.

NOTES

1. Mo'ed Kata 21a, Tosafot, s. v. *Aylu devarim.*
2. All references of this sort are to the Shulhan Arukh, Yoreh De'ah, section, and paragraph.
3. The Hebrew terms will be presented throughout in masculine form, even though the English translation will render them, on occasion, in feminine form.
4. *Keri'ah* (rending the garment) used to be mandatory for all those present at the moment of death. Since fear of loss of valuable garments discouraged people from remaining with the dying, the ritual of *keri'ah* was moved to the day of burial.
5. From this point on, *shomerim* are provided by the funeral home.
6. The Talmud (Mo'ed Katan 27a–b) does not speak of caskets but of plain and fancy biers.
7. For parents the rip is made on the left, for all others on the right.
8. The customary statement of condolence appears below in the section called "Other *Shivah* Practices."
9. Medieval commentators permitted the study of Job, parts of Jeremiah, Kinot, and the laws of mourning (Mo'ed Katan 21a, Tosafot, s. v. *Ve-asur likrot ba-torah*). Therefore, if one wishes to bring the mourner something, a book on the laws of death and mourning is appropriate.
10. According to the Shulhan Arukh, it is only on the first day of *shivah* that a mourner does not wear tefillin (388:1).
11. See Leopold Greenwald, *Kol bo al avelut,* (New York: Phillip Feldheim, 1947), p. 356.
12. Since one may only move a Torah from one place to another if it will be read three times, every effort should be made to do so, for instance by having a Shabbat afternoon *minhah* service in the *shivah* home, at which time the Torah will be read.
13. The eighth day of the festival counts as the first day of *shivah,* even though the family does not observe that day (399:2).

14. It is more accurate to say that the Torah speaks of both whole and half-siblings on the father's side, and that Talmudic rabbis expanded the Torah's list to include even half-siblings on the mother's side.

15. See Isaac Klein, *A Guide to Jewish Religious Practice* (New York: JTSA, 1979), p. 438.

16. See *Women's League Outlook,* Spring 1992, for three fine articles by Conservative rabbis on a ritual response to miscarriage.

17. The first three days are viewed as more intense than the last four. See above discussion on working during *shivah.*

18. I am indebted to Dr. Walter Gadlin for bringing this point to my attention. See Maurice Lamm, *The Jewish Way in Death and Mourning* (New York: Jonathan David, 1969) p. 174.

19. Some Orthodox synagogues will resist such a practice on the part of women.

20. One counts only twelve months even if the Jewish year was intercalated and had thirteen months.

21. R. Moshe Isserles, in his comments in the Shulhan Arukh, states a preference for the mourner leading services rather than saying kaddish. This reflects better, he says, on the Jewish education given him by his father (376:4).

22. Sometimes special arrangements are made, such as setting up an additional microphone, so that a *kohen* may remain outside yet deliver a eulogy.

23. See Greenwald, *Kol bo al avelut,* pp. 59-60, for a discussion of the rabbinic pronouncements on flowers at a Jewish funeral.

CHAPTER 4

The Jewish Foundation to the Christian Belief in Resurrection

Ronald T. Trojcak

What exactly is meant by resurrection from the dead? We must distinguish it from reincarnation, where human beings reappear on the earth in physical or bodily form, to live again, in another life cycle. And it doesn't have anything to do with the Greek notion of immortality of the soul, which, as the non-material part of humanity, cannot wear out, i.e., die. Finally, we have to distinguish from mere resuscitation, which is reported in the Hebrew Bible and in the New Testament. But this simply means that someone whose biological functions have stopped, have received a new vital impulse, that is, they continue the same biological life, in the same way, before they die.

We can usefully seek the meaning of resurrection by examining its history. Belief in resurrection arose fairly late in Jewish history. You can trace it pretty specifically to the decade of 160-150 years before Christ (BCE). It might be useful to pause at this point to see what in fact Jews believed about death prior to that period. The easiest way to do that is to look at Psalm 88. It is an important passage because the Psalms are prayers, and prayers are the fullest expression of lived religion. Prayer is the time and gesture whereby what one believes is enacted, realized. In that Psalm we have the situation of a just person who is suffering gravely, so gravely that they feel they are near death. And we can see the description of the condition of the dead in that Psalm. The Psalmist writes: "do you work wonders for the dead, can shadows rise up to praise you? Do they speak in the grave of your steadfast love? or your constancy in the place of rendition? Are your wonders known in the darkness? Your saving justice in the land of oblivion?" What the psalmist is not talking about is God as being incapacitated, rendered helpless, after people are dead, or that the dead simply forget their religious responsibility. This is the Jewish way of saying that after death, there is no survival of any sort. So God can't act on behalf of the people who have died, because they no longer exist as people. The dead have a shadowy, shade-like existence, because personality and everything that is humanly identifiable has been obliterated.

Reasons for this belief are to be found in the Jewish view of the way humans are constituted. The Jews had a unitary view of the human person as opposed to the view of many of the later Greek thinkers, who would say that the human being is made up of two parts, a body and a soul. The soul will always survive the body because, having no parts, it is indestructible. However, for the Jews, to be a human being was simply to be, as we read in the book of Genesis, a kind of clay dummy into which God has breathed life (the word breath is the same word for spirit or wind). So when there is no longer breath, there is no longer a human person. Again the human person for the Jews is simply a breathing body, an inspired clay figure, to take the image from Genesis. And so, necessarily, once that last breath has gone, once the human being has expired and does not breath in again, they simply disappear as people. (The Jews only word for "body" meant a corpse, and clearly a corpse is not a person.)

But after that period in the 160s, some of the Jews began to believe that there might be something after death. First we need to see what was going on in that period to understand why that belief originated. This was the period of the Maccabean Wars. Palestine, as it had been for most of its history, was occupied by foreigners, by pagans. The occupier in the 160s was a Syrian General named Antiochus Epiphanes who, for reasons that are not entirely clear, despised all things Jewish and systematically attempted to extripate Judaism in Palestine. To this end, he devised a number of strategies: for example, he forced people to eat forbidden food, i.e., pork; he burned copies of the Torah, the first five books of the Bible. He even desecrated the temple by setting up in its inmost and most holy place, a statue, either of himself or the Greek God Zeus. In other words, his was a thoroughly laid-out scheme to destroy, to eliminate Judaism altogether.

Not surprisingly, a number of Jews resisted this and they resisted militarily. A family by the name of Maccabee engaged in guerilla warfare for a number of years against Antiochus and, astonishingly for the Jews, they won. (Now for most of their history they had been conquered, but in this instance they won.) In the wake of this victory a religious problem arose for the Jews and the problem gave grounds for reshaping their view of what happened to people after death.

The background for this is that there was one, dominant way of talking about God that was absolutely consistent throughout Jewish history. It described God as "steadfastly loving." The Hebrew word for God's steadfast love is "hesed" as spelled in Roman letters. This was the absolute, central characteristic of the Jewish God. The problem, therefore, was this. If God is steadfastly loving, what happened to the people who died for the sake of God, whose death itself was evidence of the Jews' own steadfast love of God? *Out of this came the inspiration that, if God is truly steadfastly loving and above all steadfastly loving to those who are steadfastly loving to God, then God would not be deterred, even by death.* That is to say, that God would love, continue to love even after the death of these faithful Jews. But then the question is: whom is God to love? God can only love a person, which means to say, a bodied, breathing human being. So the resurrection is necessarily for the Jews, the resurrection of the body, not the resuscitation of the corpse. Here "body" is simply their way of speaking of a human being. As we saw earlier, a breathing body is a person. So the Maccabean Wars were the occasion for the origin of belief in the resurrection of the body.

But we need to look more closely to see what else is entailed in this belief. We must ask, what do people mean when they say they believe in the resurrection of the body? First of all, as we've just seen, it means that God is steadfastly loving, even after the physical death of the people who are faithful to him. Secondly, the evil human beings can suffer, namely, death as an act of fidelity to God, is overcome by God's steadfast love. Evil is not triumphant, in other words. To say that evil is not triumphant is to say that God's intention, namely, that good prevail, that love prevail, that steadfast love be the essence of the divine-human connection, is fulfilled, not frustrated. Resurrection, then, is the completion of God's intention.

To put it another way, the resurrection of the dead is God's final act or to use the Greek term, God's eschatological act. The Greek word *eschaton* simply means the end, and in this context it means the conclusion, the fulfillment, the completion of God's will. (We will come to see this realized, in the case of the belief that God had raised Jesus from the dead.) In other words, when God raises the dead, the assumption is that God will raise *all* of the dead, that is going to be the final act of human history and the completion of God's intention. So we have the origin of the idea of resurrection and why and what it means.

Now the single instance of resurrection is found in the belief of Jesus' friends, that God has raised him from the dead. So we need to examine that. And as with the case of the Hebrew Bible, we have to go to Biblical texts of the New Testament to discover the meaning of the proclamation that God has raised Jesus from the dead.

Our primary guide here will be the Apostle Paul, who made the earliest, the most extensive, and most profound attempt to understand the resurrection of Jesus. His belief that God had raised Jesus from the dead was the absolutely pivotal event in Paul's own life. As he will state in I Corinthians: "that if Christ is proclaimed as raised from the dead how can some of you be saying that there is no resurrection. If there is no resurrection of the dead then Christ cannot have been raised. And if Christ has not been raised then our preaching is without substance and so is our faith." In other words, Paul looks to the resurrection of Jesus as the crucial point of the whole religious enterprise.

In order to understand why the resurrection was crucial for Paul, we need to look at Paul's own religious background. Paul was a Jew living in Tarsus, a non-Jewish city. And yet he was raised in the most intense form of Jewishness, which was Pharisaic Judaism. Who were the Pharisees? To answer this, we must return to Maccabean Wars, because it was during that period that the Pharisees emerged as a distinct kind of Jew. The pious Jews were really and justifiably afraid that they would be overcome by the efforts of Antiochus and that their religion would be eradicated. They attempted, by a series of means, to deepen their own Judaism, and out of this came what are called the 613 precepts of the law. These were regulations devised by the Pharisees to mark virtually everything in their lives in order to remind them of their Jewishness. Thus we have, at this point, the appearance of the dietary laws. With every mouth of food that they took, the Pharisees were reminded that they were Jews. The laws of the Sabbath observance were created, so that on every Sabbath, one's behavior would be determined by one's Jewishness. It is essential to note that for the Pharisees, the observance of the dietary laws and the Sabbath laws was not a way of winning God's favor, but simply a way of manifesting their own piety, manifesting their fidelity to God.

The effect of the Pharisee observances was to separate the pious Jew from other Jews who were not as pious, or from the pagans. So the Pharisaic Jew did not eat with people who did not observe Pharisaic regulations, because eating with others was literally a sharing of life. A Pharisaic Jew would be very careful to separate themselves from people who were ritually impure—lepers, for example—and for the same purpose, to exclude anything not purely Jewish.

Now we look to the figure of Jesus from within this context. What was remarkable about Jesus, a Jew, was his radical openness to everyone, to women, to the poor, to public sinners, to handicapped people, to lepers, who as we saw were considered ritually impure. He manifested this openness in quite a striking way, namely by what is called totally open table fellowship. If you recall, it became a byword of criticism of Jesus, in the New Testament, that "this man eats with sinners." This is a way of saying this man eats with everyone. Now, again recall this eating, in the first century Mediterranean world, was an act of greatest possible intimacy and acceptance of one person by another.

As things worked out, Jesus' friends came to believe that God had raised this Jew from the dead. In other words, Jesus' mode of behavior came to be understood as being the absolute prototype of what it was to be steadfastly loving toward God. And the claim that God had raised Jesus from the dead was simply the assertion of God's steadfastly loving response to this perfect, steadfast love of Jesus for the Father. But note that Jesus' steadfast love was a violation of all sorts of Pharisaic notions of piety and religious fidelity.

You may remember that Paul is introduced in the New Testament as persecuting the followers of Jesus, precisely because he believed they ignored what Paul thought was proper Jewish behavior. Then there was Jesus' open table fellowship, and the subordination of the dietary and the Sabbath laws to people's immediate needs. This was the pattern of Jesus' behavior. When Paul came to believe that God had raised Jesus from the dead, he came to believe that now Pharisaic Judaism had now been superseded as the proper kind of Jewishness, and here we see Paul at his most inventive and most brilliant. His effort is now bent toward developing his understanding of Jesus in terms of their own Paul's and Jesus', Jewish past.

For the Pharisaic Jew, it is not surprising that Moses, the great mediator of the *law*, was the central hero. But if the law had been seriously relativized by Jesus' own behavior. And if God had raised this Jew, Jesus, then Paul would go even further back in Jewish history to try to make sense of the proclamation of the resurrection. And he would do this by reappropriating the figure of the father of all believers, namely, Abraham. Abraham existed long before Moses, and long before Judaism had been marked by any kind of legislative forms. The call of Abraham, as we get it from the book of Genesis, had this effect: that Abraham was called by God to be the source of God's blessing for all the nations; everybody. Through Abraham, God's saving will was going to be extended to all peoples. And herein we see the fundamental point of the election of the Jews, their most fundamental destiny: to be God's agents in bringing humanity to God. They were to be, as we find in the phrase in the Psalms, the Prophets, the New Testament, "a light of revelation to the gentiles." Now the normal tendency for humans is to form cliques, i.e., separate and exclusive groupings, and religion is a powerful instrument in this effort. But the Jews' vocation was to break down the tribalizing tendency we see in all human communities. The Jews are to be God's agent, in showing that a tribalized, a proprietary, privatized notion of God—than God is a God of my color, of my gender, of my ethnic group—that this is not the true God. The real God is the God who makes the sun shine on the just and the unjust, the rain fall on the just and the unjust. Paul interpreted Jesus and Jesus' open table fellowship as the absolute completion of the destiny of the Jews, the absolute fulfillment of the promises of God made to Abraham, namely, that through the Jews, the universally saving will of God would be both manifested and effected. It is the resurrection of Jesus, the Jew, that is the crucial issue. As a good Jew, Paul was also aware of what I have adverted to earlier, the normal human tendency to close in on oneself, to exclusivity, to the exclusion of other people. And this opens onto the other great theme that Paul picked up from the Hebrew scriptures, in the Fall story of Genesis. And this is what we need to look at now.

In the creation story, the Jews presented a picture of God as intending to make human beings who are radically open to each other. This is expressed in a number of ways. "It is not good for human beings to be alone," as the second creation story in Genesis II, has it. So God makes another human being for the first human being. ("Adam" simply means human being). Paul uses the Fall story as a crucial element in his attempt to interpret the meaning of the resurrection of Jesus. So now we have to go to that.

What's entailed in the Fall story? It has been trivialized and depicted in superficial ways so often, it's difficult to retrieve what the writer was really after. The crucial issue is to be found in the temptation. "If you do this, if you eat this fruit you will become like God." What does that mean? It is an appeal to every human being's normal desire to radically control everything and everyone, to be radically independent and self-sufficient and above all, and perhaps most importantly, to be able to master the future by eliminating the laborious process of learning step-by-step, of making mistakes, of growing in other words. Finally, to pretend that one has already fully achieved one's own reality, which is the essence of God's reality, is the great temptation. In other words, Adam and Eve are tempted to lie to themselves, pretend to themselves that they are other than they are: to deny their own humanity. The eating of the fruit of course is simply a metaphor of Adam and Eve seriously buying into that lie.

The consequences of that lie are very clear. Earlier in the creation story, when Adam and Eve came from the hands of God, they were described as being naked and unashamed with each other. Here we must be very careful. We are not talking about little children. We are talking about responsible adults, because this is the same Adam and Eve who are given charge of the world, who were told to raise children. You don't give that kind of mandate to children. So Adam's and Eve's choice to lie to themselves, was the action of adults, not of children. The writer in this book of Genesis will say that immediately after they bought into that lie, they saw that they were naked. But now, instead of being able to stand radically open to each other, which was what the nakedness was a metaphor for, they hid themselves, not just from each other, but from God. They were ashamed. They were naked and ashamed, and the response, of course was a further distancing of themselves from each other and from God.

And because God had made them for each other, to the extent that they distance themselves from each other and from God, they also distance themselves from their own authentic selves. The text puts it out very clearly. God asked Adam, what had he done? What does Adam do? He blames God. "It's this woman that you gave me who made me do it." And that woman blames the snake, also fleeing from her own responsibility, and thereby destroying the bonds between them. It's not surprising that Paul will take, as his preferred metaphor for understanding who Jesus was, to speak of Jesus as the "new Adam." So here is this man, Jesus, who was in fact naked and unashamed before everyone and in whose presence everyone who chose to respond to him, could be naked and unashamed as well.

Jesus' open table fellowship was not only the realization of his destiny and the Jews' election. It was also the fulfillment of the promise made to Abraham and the radical reversal of the effect of the first sin, the first lie. If you recall, the beginning of Jesus' preaching ran this way, "repent for the Kingdom of God is at hand." What he's referring to, of course, is the total community of the human race. That is the community of God, where everyone can stand naked and unashamed before each other. To repent means to acknowledge those things in ourselves which obstruct that kind of openness.

If you read all of Paul's letters, the thing that most exercises him, the thing that distresses him more than anything else, is the breakdown of the human family. This failure to follow the openness of Jesus with each other is the source of the most famous passage in the first letter to the Corinthians. In the 13th chapter, you may recall, we find the great hymn of love "if I speak with the tongues of men and angels that do not love. I am useless." What Paul was addressing in the church in Corinth is the fact that some members of that church thought that they had the gift of the spirit of God which enabled them to speak in mysterious languages. But they used that gift of God to distance themselves, to see themselves as superior to others, to exclude others. And so Paul will precisely begin by showing the wrongness, the radical wrongness of their move. The great hymn to love, and all the Pauline letters, can be read as a response to people's normal tendency to curl in on themselves, to exclude others, to promote themselves before others.

Because of this, Jesus, the risen Jesus, is now seen as the founder of a whole new kind of humanity. Jesus is the new Adam who is naked and unashamed before everyone and before God. And therefore in his presence everyone can become naked and unashamed as well. This is why the resurrection of Jesus was the absolutely pivotal, illuminating event for Paul who came to be called "the apostle to the gentiles." In other words, the call of Abraham was realized in Jesus and in Paul's missionary activity.

We find resonances of this faith in the resurrection of the dead, in the liturgy as well. Celebration of death in the Christian church, in the Roman church particularly, is always done in that great ritual which is supposed to have as its purpose the constitution of the human community. This is the Mass, the commemoration of Jesus' last supper. Mass is the place where we human beings are supposed to move beyond our narrowness, by first of all recognizing that narrowness of our own lives and visions so we can open ourselves to the God of Jesus and to each other. But the liturgy also expresses a belief in the resurrection in yet another way. The coffin is sprinkled with water, recalling the baptism of the dead person. In other words, the bodilyness of the dead person, the bodily human, the bodily reality is very much focused on in liturgy of the mass.

Finally, every mass is supposed to be an anticipation of the end, the eschaton, the great anticipation of the human community, and not just the human community who have gathered to celebrate together, but that great vast body that we speak of as the communion of saints. Here too, we're all gathered together to be honestly present to each other, so allowing the other to be present to us. And the source of this is, it is believed, God's hesed operating in Jesus' resurrection.

CHAPTER 5

A Roman Catholic View of Death*

Edward Jeremy Miller

The most startling Roman Catholic view on death, which is also the view shared by Christians generally, is that God experienced death. Jesus of Nazareth, confessed by Catholics as being fully human and fully divine, actually died. In fact Jesus died a horrible and scandalous death, crucifixion at the hands of Roman soldiers. Although Christians also believe that Jesus rose from the dead and so entered into his glory [Luke 24:26], nevertheless the awesome fact must not be minimized that Jesus really and truly underwent death. This conviction shapes everything that Roman Catholics understand about human death. Moreover, it influences how a Catholic views his or her own impending death and how the Catholic community (e.g., a parish) gathers together on the occasion of the death of one of its members.

   This chapter, which is intended for bereavement counselors, will treat three major topics. It is first necessary to consider how Roman Catholics, from a biblical perspective, understand the death of Jesus Christ. A biblical picture is simply fundamental to anything else that can be said about death from a believer's point of view. For this topic a caution is in order. It would be impossible to summarize the various exegetical and theological studies within the Catholic community concerning the death of Jesus Christ. Not only are they seemingly innumerable, they would involve us in nuanced arguments and issues which would deflect from the pastoral and pragmatic intentions of this essay and its usefulness for counselors [1]. Our approach, rather, is to summarize in a somewhat pastoral

---

*This is a revision of a chapter which originally appeared in *Death and Spirituality*, K. A. Doka and J. D. Morgan (eds.), Baywood, Amityville, New York, 1997.

manner the biblical teaching on the death of Jesus Christ, much as one would find it in catechetical materials prepared for Catholic laity .

The second major topic deals with the Catholic medieval tradition. Many non-Catholics view Catholic teaching through this prism, as if Catholic thought reached an apex at that period and forever remained frozen. Many of Catholicism's achievements from its medieval legacy remain part of its current teachings, but not all do. To take one example germane to our topic, the medieval teaching on purgatory shaped Catholic devotional practices for centuries, but the situation is changed today. Thus it is instructive to situate the medieval period of Catholicism in a proper prospective [2].

Finally, it remains to consider contemporary developments in Roman Catholicism as these come to expression in liturgical and theological writings. These developments, in large part associated with the Second Vatican Council (1962-1965), reflect understandings and practices of Catholics today. If one were to be at the bedside of a dying Catholic, or to attend a Catholic wake or funeral service, one would encounter these understandings in actual practice.

JESUS CHRIST DIED AND RISEN:
A BIBLICAL PORTRAIT

Concerning the death of Jesus Christ there are two temptations that must be resolutely resisted if one is to appreciate the biblical portrait. First of all, some are tempted to think that Jesus fully and clearly knew he was about to die "into his resurrection" as if it was to be a placid passage from earthly life into heavenly life and without the attendant anxiety of the "unknown." If this were so, not only would this impression be difficult to harmonize with many scriptural texts, it would also make Jesus' experience with impending death so unlike that which his followers would have to face. The Bible describes Jesus' death vigil in the garden as genuine anxiety and fear [Matthew 26:38; Mark 14:33; Luke 22:44], and it describes his experience on the cross as abandonment [Matthew 27:46; Mark 15:34].[1] An early Christian fringe movement, Docetism, was so protective of Jesus' divinity in the face of his death that it "washed out" such fear and anxiety from Jesus' portrait, even to the point of denying that there was any bodily suffering; however, the wider Christian church branded Docetism a heresy and distanced itself from it. Earliest Christianity thus maintained the "scandalous fact" that its Lord genuinely feared death and actually suffered agony unto death.

The second temptation involves how we think of Jesus' disciples during the events leading up to and including his crucifixion. Some would like to think that

---

[1] The Johannine texts remove these elements of fear and abandonment for "theological purposes." Such "redaction theology" of the Fourth Gospel is explained in the standard commentaries. See, for example [3].

the disciples somehow knew all along Jesus was meant to die and meant to rise again. After all, do not the scriptural texts speak of prophecies about such matters, prophecies made by Jesus during his lifetime for his disciples' instruction? We are here involved in the complex question of how the New Testament scriptures came to be written. The Gospels were composed several decades after the disciples experienced the death and resurrection of Jesus. These disciples came to grasp, *after the fact*, that God's hand had been involved in what happened to Jesus; they were able to understand many Old Testament passages in the light of what Jesus experienced in undergoing death. As a result they preached the crucifixion of Jesus with "God's meaning and intention" already embedded into the events, and our scriptures reflect such decades-later preaching. But in their actual experience of their Lord being taken from them and hung on a cross, they were crushed, scandalized, filled with fear, and cast adrift. That is how *they* experienced this particular death at the moment it occurred.

If we resist these two temptations, we are able to establish some very important "Christian experiences" of death, anyone's death. On the part of Jesus himself, dying was a fearful experience. This was natural; it was only human to fear death. But over and above such natural fear, impending death evoked from Jesus the element that will come to characterize, or rather ought to characterize, what a dying person can say in the teeth of death: "Father, into your hands I commit my spirit" [Luke 23:46]. Jesus died in faith and in hope, and into the relationship he called His Heavenly Father. It is left to theologians to explain how Jesus, ever remaining divine, nevertheless as human, lived in faith and by faith, for Jesus surely was dying in faith and by faith. Yet an element of natural apprehension in the face of death must always remain. On the part of Jesus' disciples, his death caused grief, and in their grief they fled that awful crucifixion scene and likely fled Jerusalem itself.[2] Thus if someone were to say that a genuine Christian, a "really believing Christian," ought never to grieve over a death, it is asking an unnatural response and a response that those who "walked with Jesus from the beginning" [Acts 1:21] could not them-selves muster.

With these temptations, then, put to the side, how is the death of Jesus biblically understood by Catholics?[3] It is grasped first and foremost as a death that involves them, his followers, in its deepest meanings. To appreciate the personal implications for Christians of Jesus' death, let us briefly consider what is understood to have happened to Jesus.

---

[2] The resurrection appearances to the disciples are complex. Did Jesus first appear to the disciples in Jerusalem [Mark, Luke, John 20] or in Galilee [Matthew, John 21]? For a clear account of the problem, see [4, pp. 96-113].

[3] Three catechetical sources of a conservative, moderate, and progressive orientation respectively would be [5-7].

Although fearful of what was to transpire, Jesus freely and willingly accepted his death in obedience to the mission given to him by God, by the one whom he addressed as *Abba* (Father). This is clear in the accounts of Jesus' last meal with his followers [Matthew 26; Mark 14; Luke 22]. There is, furthermore, the sense that this death culminates and brings to fulfilment many Old Testament realities, thus leading the earliest Christian preaching to say it was "in accordance with the Scriptures" [Acts 2:23, 3:18]. It is noteworthy that Jesus' death scene echoes Old Testament themes: the offer of wine [Psalm 69], dividing the garments [Psalm 22], the presence of two robbers [Isaiah 53], the mocking words [Psalm 22; Wisdom 2], the vinegar [Psalm 69], the death cry [Psalm 31], and the torn Temple veil [Exodus 26] [8, p. 154].

His is a death that brings forgiveness of human sinfulness [1 Corinthians 15:3] and redemption from all bondages. The very fact that the title "servant" is used to describe the crucified Jesus [Acts 3:13; 4:27;1 Peter 2:22] alludes to the four redemptive "servant passages" in Isaiah 42, 49, 50, and 52. Jesus' spilled blood becomes another vehicle to depict the significance of this awesome death. The blood describes a new fellowship (of those believing in its power), a new covenant that harkens to the animal blood shed in establishing an older covenant [Exodus 24], and the "description by blood" is recalled whenever Christians repeat Jesus' words at his supper on the eve of his death: "This is my blood which is shed for you" [Matthew 26:28; Mark 14:24]. For a Gentile audience not familiar with Old Testament allusions, early Christian preaching described Jesus' death as a ransoming from bondages [Mark 10:45] and as a liberation [Romans 5, 6]. It was not understood as a ransom paid to an avenging God, for God "so loved the world" as to offer his own beloved [John 3:10]. Thus in Catholic thinking the death of Jesus is not a divinely inflicted punishment on him in any sense.

Given such biblical teaching on what the death of Jesus involved and meant, Catholics see themselves in solidarity with all humankind both as the sinners who occasioned the tragedy and as the beneficiaries of its forgiveness and liberation. Catholics participate in Jesus' death, that is to say, they come into contact with its significance and benefits through their experience of Baptism and Eucharist (= Lord's Supper = Mass). Of these two sacraments, and of the sacrament called the "Anointing of the Sick," more will be said later, when death and grief are considered in contemporary liturgical and pastoral practice. It suffices now only to situate those sacramental activities in their proper Christological context: the death of Jesus of Nazareth, as its liberating power is made present to Catholics in these sacraments. Furthermore, the understanding of Jesus' death as somehow "foreseen" by God, which is one way of translating "according to the Scriptures," has riveted the conviction in Catholic minds that all deaths, Jesus' included, are part of God's overall providence. Death is not mere fate or happenstance or without deeper meaning. This "providential view" has implications for how Catholics view anyone's death.

The fuller understanding of Jesus' death requires a further consideration. Jesus was raised (or as some texts say, Jesus rose) from the dead.[4] Good Friday lacks meaning without Easter. And Easter cannot be reached without passing through Good Friday, for the primary symbol of Christians is not the Easter lily but the cross. The New Testament presents Jesus' resurrection as an integral dimension of the death, and this is clearest in John's gospel where the lifting up on the cross is depicted as an exaltation into heavenly glory. Resurrection is not a mere sequel to the death, not simply the thing that happened next in time; nor is it the "award" given to Jesus by his Abba (Father) as if it were a stamp of approval bestowed upon a noble and heroic life's work. Rather, his death is the very entry into kingdom life, and in Jesus' case, entry into the Lordship of that kingdom. The earliest texts are clear: through his resurrection Jesus *becomes* both "Lord" and "Christ" [Messiah] [Acts 2:36; Philippians 2:11],[5] and the Greek word used to describe his Lordship, *Kyrios*, was the very word used by the then current Greek rendition of the Old Testament to translate God's hallowed Hebrew name, *Yahweh*. Accordingly, the risen Jesus is to all of creation what the God of Genesis is: creation's sovereign, the Lord of heaven and earth. In entering resurrected life through death, Jesus dominates the power of death [Romans 6:8-14] and extinguishes its apparent finality and meaninglessness for those who, in Paul's words, believe in him. In John's account, Jesus' resurrection returns him to where he had originated [John 6:62], within God's very being.

All these descriptive words reach for the reality of what Jesus became in dying, and of course the words can never render full justice to it. Jesus lives on the other side of death, and the disciples who describe their experience of him as resurrected live on this side. However, it is important to realize what they said Jesus is not. He was not a resuscitated corpse, for he passed in and out of their midst by another set of laws, as it were. Nor was he there to be "seen" by everyone, but only by those to whom he "revealed" himself, and "insight" was required by them. Such ability to "see into" divine realities is what the New Testament calls *faith*. The disciples' resurrection faith enabled them to "see into death" and to perceive that it was the entry into life with God.

The death-resurrection of Jesus becomes for Catholics, as for all Christians, the pledge (or "first fruits" to use the Biblical term) of their destiny in death. By living through Jesus' power (i.e., by faith, by being baptized, through his grace, by living lovingly, and other such biblical expressions), Christians can die "in Christ"

---

[4] The Greek verb *egerthe* normally means "was raised" but such aorist passive forms can also carry an active sense. When St. Jerome translated the Koine Greek into the Latin bible, he rendered this verb into Latin by the active sense *surrexit*, thus the meaning that Jesus raised (himself) from the dead. Still, many New Testament texts state that God the Father raised Jesus from the dead. For the biblical and theological significance, see [4, p. 79].

[5] When the Gospels describe these titles being accorded Jesus even during his lifetime, it is a recognition by the post-resurrection Church, which composed the Scriptures, that Jesus always was what they, in experiencing Jesus as resurrected, came to appreciate and hence call him.

and thus be raised to glory "in Christ." One does not die into emptiness or become nothing; one passes through the "temple veil" into the true Holy of Holies—note the allusion to the Jerusalem Temple—where God lives because Jesus sundered the veil [Hebrews 8-9]. Accordingly, the New Testament [Revelations 21:2, 10-14] and later Church tradition calls heaven the New Jerusalem.

I have been stressing that Jesus' resurrection is the immediate implication of his death and not its mere sequel or next-in-succession distinct action. The Gospels, however, describe it as if later, i.e., "on the third day," both for the reasons of what that biblical phrase means [9, p. 41] and because gospels are a story, a narrative [Luke 1:1]; narratives require "before and after" segments. The narrative genre, however, has led many Catholics, indeed many Christians, to insert "time" between death and resurrected life with God on the other side of death. In subsequent centuries this led to conceptions of purgatory as a kind of "waiting time" between death and kingdom life. Let us consider some such developments, which came to full expression by the time of the Middle Ages.

MEDIEVAL VIEWS ON DEATH AND DYING

Contrary to many popular depictions of it as well as the current connotation of the word itself, the "medieval" Christian world was heterogeneous and insightful, though it had its myopias and exaggerations. Even when the Protestant Reformation, at the epoch's end, called for a "return to the Bible," those reformers were medievalists; their agendas were shaped by the period, and the *return*, as now recognized by scholars, never fully left the environment. Medieval Christianity, willy-nilly, has shaped the present views of all Christians, especially on death.

Popular medieval piety was preoccupied with the "state of one's soul," that is to say, there was rigorous self-examination of one's moral condition against the background of God's Final Judgment.[6] Whether conditioned by millennial movements expecting Jesus' Second Coming at any moment or by the harshness of social life (e.g., the recurring plagues) or from other factors too complex to identify, many were possessed by a fear of death and hell. Dante Alighieri's *Divine Comedy* (cir. 1313) with its vivid cantos depicting Inferno and Purgatorio, the frequent medieval penitential processions, the emphasis on gaining indulgences, even Martin Luther's "Tower experience,"[7] were expressions of the general anxiety about one's eternal salvation.

The funeral liturgy of the period, the Requiem Mass, fostered this anxiety. The liturgical vestments were black and somber. The prayers called on God to

[6] For one of the best sources on the topic, see [10].

[7] Luther's *Turmerlebnis* became for him a personal revelation that faith in the word of Jesus Christ removed the anxiety of one's possible condemnation.

have mercy on the sinner. The famous hymn, "Dies Irae,"[8] its Gregorian melody mournful and searching, its words sober and fearful, reminded worshippers of their accountability before God's judgment throne. The liturgy reminded everyone that in death their bodies "return to dust."

Prior to the individual's death, the ancient Christian sacrament of anointing the sick had, by the Middle Ages, become restricted to "the Last Rites"; the anointing was offered only to those in danger of death. Thus, the visit by the priest with the anointing oils harbingered one's exit from life; it did not auger bodily and spiritual renewal. The priest also brought final communion, called Viaticum, which was the sacramental body of Jesus to aid passage into death. These sacramental supports, to be sure, assuaged anxieties about the fear of death, but the emotional context was that of the sinner departing this world to face one's demanding Judge. In the concluding section I will report on recent liturgical renewals which place these sacramental actions in a wholly different context and emotional tone.

The *theological* enterprise of the Middle Ages could be characterized as a systematizing of the theological writers of all preceding centuries (e.g., the Latin and Greek Fathers of the early Church, various Church synods, more recent writers, etc.)[9] along with an effort to frame questions from multiple aspects. Let us take one such theological development, the doctrine on purgatory, since it relates to our theme.

In its treatment of sin, medieval theology distinguished those sins which were so heinous as to separate one completely from God's love (mortal sin) from those lesser sins which only weakened one's relationship with God (venial sin). To die with unforgiven mortal sin brought eternal damnation. Regarding any sin, furthermore, medieval theologians distinguished the sin's debt of *guilt* from its debt of *punishment*. God's forgiveness removed guilt but a debt of punishment could remain, and acts of reparation in this life amortized the owed punishment. Prayer, fasting, almsgiving, conversion of life style, etc., are such acts of reparation. Even though all analogies limp in describing spiritual realities, a useful analogy for guilt/residual punishment might be a viral illness. When the *virus* of chicken pox is fully eradicated (= God's forgiveness of guilt), vesicles remain temporarily on the skin awaiting a full reparation of the disease's *remnants* (= sin's debt of punishment).[10]

---

[8] This "Day of Wrath" hymn was composed in the XIII Century and was part of Requiem Masses by the end of the following century.

[9] The personal and original insights of the systematizers must not be overlooked, e.g., Peter Lombard, Thomas Aquinas, Bonaventure, Duns Scotus.

[10] In explaining spiritual realities, it is important to note where analogies "break down." Sin is not a virus except by a stretch of the imagination. Another analogy for understanding sin would be the civil crime of embezzlement. A governor or president could issue a pardon to the felon, thereby eradicating the felony from the record, yet an obligation of monetary restitution remains.

Medieval Christianity, furthermore, was extremely sensitive to the teaching, grounded in the Scriptures and developed by early Church writers, that only the "pure of heart," only the completely sinless who have fully repented for past transgressions, could see the face of God. If a Christian died who had received forgiveness of all (mortal) sins, it was still possible that his or her already forgiven past sins carried a debt of punishment that had not been fully expiated in this life. Thus, in death it would have to be so satisfied before one could enter God's all holy presence. Purgatory is the situation on the other side of death, but before entry into the Kingdom, in which the "soul" undergoes final purification.[11] For those in purgatory, who were known only to God, the Church prayed and commended them to God's loving mercy. Without entering the debate whether purgatory is scripturally warranted, this view certainly answered to a Christian instinct from the very beginning—see Paul's prayer for Onesiphorus (in 2 Timothy 1:18)—to pray for the dead.[12]

Thus construed, purgatory shaped Catholic attitudes toward death and grief which have endured until recent times. In its best features the thought of purgatory chastened moral behavior (conversion) and kept one's eyes focused on death's ultimate issue: the possibility of kingdom life with God. In its worst features it extended suffering beyond this life and drove people to "gain indulgences" with a passion. (Indulgences are spiritual actions that remitted some or all of the punishment owed to forgiven sins; thus indulgences could shorten or eliminate purgatory.)[13] Not only was death terrifying but those who grieved for the dead had also to cope with the thought that the deceased was in a "purifying" torment.

The following remarks apropos purgatory are added to my originally published essay and share in the newness of the present volume. What was then only implied is elaborated upon now for purposes of clarity. The teaching about purgatory continues to be a doctrine of the Roman Catholic church, and it makes sense if understood properly. What has been left behind in contemporary Catholic preaching and catechetical books is the notion of purgatory as a locale or antechamber where something of a punishing nature unfolds over a period of time, as if one lingered at a kind of stop light on the other side of death before the green light announcing heavenly entry shines. The medieval imagination focused on the time dimension of life in purgatory, and the purifying sufferings to be endured were assuaged only by the thought that it all came to an end sometime and heaven awaited.

---

[11]For an English account of Purgatory, see [11]. The fullest account remains the French dictionary article [12].

[12]In post-exilic Judaism, Judas Maccabeus prayed for the forgiveness of his dead soldiers [2 Macc. 12:39-45]. The instinct to pray for the dead, to effect their betterment, crosses religious lines.

[13]It has always been Catholic teaching that the seeker of an indulgence required a contrite and "converted" heart. Yet indulgence-seeking could easily invite less than spiritual dispositions, as when indulgences were bought and sold. Luther rightly objected to this aberration. See [5, pp. 487-488].

The notion of the passage of time on the other side of death does not make sense. On this side of our deaths we live as temporal beings, affected by the passage of time and events, and of course we live as mortal, able to die and expecting it. On the other side of death is eternity, not temporality and not simply perpetuity, which is only time ticking endlessly. Eternity is the absence of time. There is also immortality for human beings on the other side of death. We won't die again. We will exist eternally with God, which is heaven, or we exist eternally alienated from God, which is hell. Whether anyone is in hell is unknown, and Catholics pray and hope that no one is.

I must focus on the passage through death to heaven, and not to hell, because a proper understanding of purgatory is my concern at this moment. What we know about being with God, which is heaven, and as existing as God exists, which is to exist in eternity and not in an environment of time that unfolds in perpetuity, is that we must be "clean of heart" [Matt. 5:8] to be in the company of God. God is the all holy, and nothing of unholiness and imperfection exists in God's world of heaven.

Now consider the person who dies and who is meant for, gifted for, salvation. Are all such persons perfect at the moment of their death? Yes, they are lovers of God but not perfect lovers. They bear into death their faults. Ingredient to the same gift from God that is the resurrection of the body—whether it be thought of as divine creation or divine transformation does not matter for the point to be made—is the perfecting act of God that makes all the saints of heaven to be people clean of heart through and through. In death we are, who pass through it in saving faith, made perfect by God, made into heirs of heaven.

But, you must wonder, why the langauge of purgation, of purgatory as a suffering reality? Our language of God's awesome actions is always drawn from our own earthly experience by way of analogy. What is my own experience of how I grow in holiness and cleanness of heart in this life? It it through a purging of my sinful inclinations, a freely undertaken self-discipline that chastises what is ungodly in me. It is almost a law of our spiritual lives in this world as we know it that growth in holiness invokes a kind of purgation, not all the time perhaps, but not always to be avoided, either. Thus, we are accustomed to associate growth toward perfection with purgation. And thus it is by further extension of our imaginations and use of language that we describe the perfecting action of God, as we pass through death to eternal life, as a purgation. Why not so describe it? In reality we are being gifted with being perfected. The doctrine of purgatory, removed of temporal antechamber images, describes a wonderous action and certainly not something to be feared or by which to be cowed.

CONTEMPORARY CATHOLIC VIEWS
ON DEATH AND DYING

To a non-Catholic observer the most striking feature of a Catholic funeral today is probably its emphasis on *risen life*. The music is joyous and hopeful, the vestments are white (no longer black), the scriptural readings are about resurrection and promise, the Easter Candle burns, the preaching is anything but morbid, and all of this occurs in the presence of honest and healthy tears. 1 Corinthians 15:54 seems pervasive: "Death is swallowed up; victory is won."

What had happened to cause this transformation? The causes are surely too many and too complicated to enumerate, but a few may be signaled: 1) The centrality of Jesus' resurrection had been reclaimed in Catholic theology, over-coming the one-sided emphasis on the Cross which was inherited from medieval Christianity;[14] even Luther and much classical Protestant thought shared the somewhat exclusive medieval emphasis on crucifixion-theology. 2) The Second Vatican Council, which ended in 1965, launched a reform of Catholic liturgical practices which affected all the sacraments (the Mass, Baptism, etc.) and, more germane to this essay, led to a revised *Rite of Funerals* in 1969.[15] 3) Various theologians had been writing on the "theology of death," such as Karl Rahner [15] and Edward Schillebeeckx [16], and such writings influenced catechetical materials and parish preaching. 4) The "mind" of the Catholic laity moved from a preoccupation with sin and death toward an orientation to the blessings of a Christian life, i.e., God's love for the individual, the Gospel promises, the hope for resurrection, etc. One might simply say that a healthy biblicism and pastoral practice, rooted in a sounder psychology, took hold.[16]

The Catholic funeral rite is an instructive source for the "Catholic view" of death. Not only is the rite an official document from the Vatican; the rite also gives expression to and further shapes the Catholic *mentality*. The introductory notes to the liturgical document capture the spirit animating the prescribed rituals so evident in a Catholic "death setting" today, i.e., the prayers for the dying person, the wake service which may or may not be in a funeral parlor, the funeral mass in the church, and the final cemetery rituals. That underlying spirit rather than the rituals themselves merits description.[17]

The Introduction's very first words, *Paschale Christie mysterium* [the paschal mystery of Christ], set the basic Catholic vision. Paschal, from the Aramaic word for Passover, simply means the death-resurrection of Jesus considered as a single interconnected event; in dying Jesus passed over into risen life. As the life of a Christian began with incorporation into Jesus' personal Passover (baptized into his death that one might be born or raised up anew) and was nourished by paschal food (the sacred elements of the Mass are for Catholics

---

[14]One notes the seminal study by F. X. Durrwell [13], with the important introduction to the English translation by C. Davis.

[15]See [14] for the best study in English of the funeral rite.

[16]For literature on death from psychological and other scientific perspectives, see [17]; for a treatment of death and the cultural aspects of "sin" from a gerontological perspective, see [18, pp. 320-324].

[17]My descriptions are indebted to Rutherford [14].

the food of Jesus' risen body), the death of a Christian is his or her consummate contact with the paschal mystery. The Christian follows Jesus into the mystery of death in order to find life like his own. For this reason the tone of the funeral is thanksgiving and consolation rather than morbidity, and the bereaved receive Holy Communion since the Eucharist is the sacrament *par excellence* of Jesus' paschal mystery. It had been the "food of hope" of the deceased during his or her active life as a Catholic. Celebrating Eucharist within a funeral rite is a specifically Catholic practice.[18]

Richard Rutherford detects in this Introduction to the 1969 *Rite of Funerals* two attitudes toward the funeral Mass which shape the pieties of ordinary Catholics. In one attitude the Mass is a prayer proclaiming that Jesus' death-resurrection has reconciled the Christian with God. The other attitude, which was the prevailing one in the recent past, underscores the funeral Mass "being *offered* on behalf of the deceased." The benefits of the Mass[19] are felt to apply to the deceased, even to the point of aiding him or her on the other side of death in a propitiatory way. Rutherford rightly argues that the former attitude is primary in the document, and that the latter attitude can too easily slip into quantitative calculations and a quasi-magical view of prayer in popular pieties. Nevertheless, the ancient practice of prayer on behalf of the dead, prayer that is beneficial to the deceased and not mere trappings or just therapy for the bereaved, is clearly affirmed in the Catholic rite.

The bereaved, however, do benefit directly from the funeral rite. Their personal faith expressed during the prayerful services for the deceased gives them "the consolation of hope" in the words of the document. Their hope is in Jesus' promise of victory over death, at once a hope for the deceased and a hope for *themselves* when they die. The funeral rites put them into an environment where the priorities of Catholic faith are expressed. "I believe in the resurrection of the dead and the life of the world to come" [14, p. 126].

The official funeral ritual, furthermore, recognizes the local customs and family traditions which might prevail. It cautions against any customs, especially those from the funeral industry, which might obscure the paschal mystery by an attempt to cosmetically mask death. As Rutherford notes, "the Christian funeral proclaims life through death and not through the appearance of life" [14, p. 131]. Contrariwise, it affirms those customs which enhance the paschal mystery. The priest who conducts the rites can better accentuate an Easter faith if he had been with the deceased and the bereaved during the dying process; in this case genuine grief is part of the shared experience that also prays in hope of God's promises. The custom, also, of friends and parish community coming to the wake and to the

---

[18]Within "high church" parishes of the Protestant Episcopal Church one also meets this practice.

[19]An older theology spoke of the "fruits of the Mass." See [14, pp. 122-123]. As the reader will note, the reality of post-death purgation is not denied in contemporary Catholicism but it no longer is an emotional focus.

funeral Mass provides the social supports to the bereaved to begin the process of healing, of adapting to the loss of the deceased. "The *Rite* is founded on the principle of Christian community" [14, p. 132]. While the Risen Christ is the support of any Christian in a death, both of the deceased and the bereaved, the assembled community of believers provides the "social vehicle" through which Christ especially supports the bereaved.

From the liturgical practice of Catholics a further observation may be made about the Sacrament of the Anointing of the Sick and Dying. This ritual anointing, popularly called in the past "the Last Rites," has been restored by the Vatican to its ancient and fuller usage. It is meant for the seriously ill, who may or may not be in danger of death. From medieval times until recently it had been restricted to the death bed situation, and the arrival of the priest at the home or hospital presaged final leave-taking. In its healthier present context of being a sacramental support during serious illness, the rite is administered at the onset of a serious illness, whether that illness leads or does not lead to death.

Priest, family, and friends, and most often with the ill person consciously participating, gather in special prayer at the bedside. The prayer is for healing to occur, but if in God's providence it should not, the deeper purpose of the prayer and the anointing is that this illness will not cause the faith of the ill person to waiver. When a dying process does ensue, such emboldened faith casts an entirely salutary aura over "dying and grief." Christ is already accompanying the dying person on the final steps of a "gospel life" toward the rewards of the kingdom. The effects of this sacramental anointing as well as the renewed funeral rites cannot be overestimated on the salutary attitudes of Catholics to dying, death, and grief.

Contemporary Catholic theology has also contributed to salutary attitudes toward death, and with one such vision from Edward Schillebeeckx [16] this essay concludes.[20] Considered from a purely natural perspective, death is unintelligible and even absurd. Whatever one has formed of relationships and however much one has accumulated in this life, all these things pass from grasp. Death snatches everything away. The Judeo-Christian community perceives in this absurdity the power of sin [Genesis, Romans 5:12]. Because sin is absurd, destroying piece by piece the humanity of the sinner who freely chooses to sin, death is the visibly absurd appearance within human existence of a corporate sinfulness afflicting all who are born.[21] This religious insight, which is not meant to compete with biological or medical explanations of death that view the same reality from a different vantage, affirms that death (in its absurdity) is something that we humans have invented; for "God did not make death, neither has he pleasure in the destruction of the living" [Wisdom 1:13].

---

[20]In addition to Schillebeeckx, see also the work of Rahner [15, 19].

[21]The Judeo-Christian understanding of the "Fall," as related in *Genesis*, must not be equated with its mythological description of Adam/Eve/fruit of the tree. The deeper truth is the rebellious spirit of humanity before the all-holy God, and of the consequences which ensue.

This absurdity within human existence touched the being of God when God "dared to become man. Nevertheless, when this happened, death itself entered in the kingdom of God. The last absurd scandal of the tyranny of death, the death of the man Jesus who is God, in fact brought life back to humanity, because whatever the living God touches becomes itself alive, even though it be very death" [16, pp. 69-70]. Humanity can offer God many things which are God's already. Death alone, humanity's doing, was the only thing God did not possess. Death itself having been experienced by God (in Jesus), death can now offer "possibilities" of a way of reaching toward life with God, and these become for the dying Christian an alternative to death's hitherto absurdity. The solitary confinements of death when viewed naturally, i.e., the loss of all contact with what lives and had surrounded the dead person, can give way to contact with the One who truly and forever lives, God.

With the above religious view of death, Professor Schillebeeckx proposes that "dying is not an act; but the attitude of mind in which we accept death can give it the value of an act [of faith in God]" [16, pp. 74-75]. Dying is not an action a person does; it is something that happens or overcomes one. In its absurdity, death *alienates* a person from the only existence he or she has ever known, one's own life and the lives of loved ones. "Death can therefore only have a positive, Christian and salutary significance when we freely accept this alienation from self" out of love for God [16, pp. 74-75]. Only one who loves God above all things, with one's whole heart and soul, who loves in the face of the absurd, can inherit the Kingdom of God, as the Gospels teach.

Such an act of "accepting" death has certain features, all Gospel grounded. It is an attitude of *obedient* love, an acceptance of God's intervention in our life, as and when God wills. It is an act of *contrite* sorrow for the sins of our life, for it is the experience of a sinner who feels the near approach of the holy God who can only be approached by the "pure of heart." It is an attitude that *affirms* the one true priority of a religious life, God. "Death is our most lonely moment: a dying man is cut off, uprooted, the great solitary who knows time and earth, loved ones and friends, fame, prestige and success, all things and everybody to be slipping away, and who comes at last before the one thing necessary, the One who judges all. 'My God and my all': this is the frame of mind in which a Christian ought to die" [16, p. 76]. Accepting death in this fashion can be so complete and intense that it expels every last vestige of self-love. Self-love is used here in its religious sense to mean selfish love, the detrimental love of self that is sin, the very self-centering love that *caused* death to be.

Such an attitude toward death cannot be constructed at a life's last moments. It is an attitude resulting from one's life as a whole. "Whatever during his life a man has made of the whole of his life, that he is at the moment of death. . . . The attitude finally achieved is decisive, but this itself depends to a large extent on earlier attitudes which prepare the way for the final one" [16, pp. 80-81]. One could have pretended and "acted a part" during a life of actually chosen priorities, but in the moment of death all pretense is stilled. The convictions of obedience, contrition, and the felt sovereignty of God, were they not one's true self in life, can unlikely be constructed in one's dying moments. If Jesus is the model for the dying Christian, then it must be recollected that his statement on the Cross, "not my will but Yours be done," was an attitude Jesus had possessed and lived out long before.

COUNSELING POSTSCRIPTS

For the counselor working with Catholic people who either have experienced the death of a loved one or who are dealing with an impending death, some suggestions are offered. Catholics, like members of other faiths, may or may not be active congregants. For active and committed members of Roman Catholicism, the counselor Catholics seek is likely to be a priest, either a friend of the family or someone staffing the local parish. Since Vatican Council II, the parish staff member might also be a deacon, a brother, or nun from a religious order, and in some cases a Catholic layperson suitably trained for this "ministry," as this assistance is now termed.

In the above situation the Catholic person or party looks to the parish for counseling support. It is also true that Catholics utilize other professional counselors for support in "dying and death" situations. Whatever the counseling supports, the following observations are offered as helpful and suggestive. Catholics with an active and strong faith should be urged to call upon the central sensitivities suggested above in the essay. These sensitivities involve recollection that Jesus himself experienced grief, suffering, and death itself. Thus, the God to whom Catholics pray for support is poignantly aware of the pain that is being endured. Furthermore, their Church through its sacraments and funeral rites intends and is meant to be a "community of support" for Catholics in times of grief. For the benefit of counselors I have attempted to elaborate what these community supports are and how Catholics understand them.

Even when a counselor is dealing with a so-called "lapsed" or inactive Catholic, it must be remembered that such a person likely bears "Catholic instincts" at a deeply subconscious level. While the Catholic viewpoints about dying and death, which I have described earlier, primarily had in mind those views of active and participating Roman Catholics, I was attempting a description of the social *ethos* of Catholicism at a more fundamental level. Inactive Catholics were socialized at an earlier time into such an ethos, and it is never fully eradicated, even by those who have ceased participating in the Catholic community. When such Catholics unburden themselves to the counselor, it is unlikely that the language will be exclusively "secular."

The professional counsellor whose own background is not Catholic may encounter issues in a Catholic client that are rooted in misconceptions or exaggerations of Catholic teaching or rituals. For example, the bereaved may be experiencing anxiety about the deceased person "suffering in purgatory." The above essay was not intended as a theological primer to handle such delicate issues then and there but only to give the reader an orientation to Catholic viewpoints and to give the further sense that developments have occurred within the Catholic community. When confronted with such issues, the non-Catholic counselor could profitably refer the client to someone conversant with those aspects of Catholic teaching and practice.

Death and dying pose a fundamental question to human existence, perhaps the most poignant and fundamental question that can be posed. Such a question does not tolerate an "answer" since the question deals with an unfathomable mystery, and mysteries are never answered. They are lived through and endured. To the mystery of death, Catholics juxtapose another mystery: Jesus Christ and their faith in him. Catholic sacraments are also mysteries, not in the English denotation of mysterious, but in the Greek biblical sense of *mysterion*,[22] which connotes that the reality of God has expressed itself in and through visible things like bread and wine, the anointing oils, the words and gestures of the priest, etc. These, too, are brought to bear on the mystery of death, not as answers, not as placebos, but as prayerful experiences of the mystery of the Risen Jesus, who endured death and unmasked it as the entry to where He is.

REFERENCES

1. E. Schillebeeckx, *Jezus: Het Verhaal van een Levende*, Nelissen, Bloemendaal, Netherlands, 1974, ET *Jesus: An Experiment in Christology*, Seabury, New York, 1979.
2. J. Gonzales, *A History of Christian Thought* (Vol. 3), Abingdon, Nashville, Tennessee, 1975.
3. R. E. Brown, *The Gospel According to John*, Doubleday, Garden City, New York, 1966.
4. R. E. Brown, *The Virginal Conception and Bodily Resurrection of Jesus*, Paulist Press, New York, 1973.
5. R. Lawler, D. Wuerl, and T. Comerford (eds.), *The Teaching of Christ*, Our Sunday Visitor, Huntington, Indiana, 1976.
6. R. P. McBrien, *Catholicism*, Winston Press, Minneapolis, Minnesota, 1980.
7. Catechetical Institute of Nijmegen (ed.), *A New Catechism*, Herder and Herder, New York, 1967.
8. D. Senior, *Jesus: A Gospel Portrait*, Pflaum Press, Dayton, Ohio, 1975.
9. B. Vawter, *This Man Jesus*, Doubleday, Garden City, New York, 1973.
10. L. Bouyer, *History of Christian Spirituality*, Desclee, New York and Paris, 1963.
11. J. Ryan, Purgatory, *The New Catholic Encyclopaedia*, *11*:cols., pp. 1034-1039, 1967.

---

[22]The Latin translation of the biblical Greek *mysterion* is *sacramentum*, from which source the word "sacrament" is derived.

12. A. Michel, Purgatoire, *Disctionnaire de Théologie Catholique, 13*:cols., pp. 1164-1326, 1936.
13. F. X. Durrwell, *The Resurrection: A Biblical Study*, Sheed and Ward, New York, 1960.
14. R. Rutherford, *The Death of a Christian: The Rite of Funerals*, Pueblo, New York, 1980.
15. K. Rahner, *On the Theology of Death*, Seabury, New York, 1961.
16. E. Schillebeeckx, The Death of a Christian, *The Layman in the Church*, Alba House, Staten Island, New York, 1963.
17. A. J. Miller and M. J. Acri, *Death: A Bibliographical Guide*, Scarecrow Press, Metuchen, New Jersey, 1977.
18. T. H. Holmes and E. David (eds.), *Life Change, Live Events, and Illness*, Praeger, New York, 1989.
19. K. Rahner, Tod, *Lexikon Fur Theologie und Kirche, 10*:cols., pp. 22-26 and *Eschatologie, 3*:cols., pp. 1094-1098, 1965.

CHAPTER 6

Greek Orthodox Understandings of Death: Implications for Living the Easter Faith

John T. Chirban

> . . . if Christ had not been raised, then our preaching is in vain and your faith is in vain.
>
> I Corinthians 15:14

Understanding death is central to the message of the Orthodox Christian faith. Approaches toward death in the Greek Orthodox tradition explain the direct relationship between a community of believers and the life, death, and Resurrection of Jesus Christ.

> Christ has risen from the dead; by death trampling upon death; and has bestowed life to those in the tomb [1, p. 450].
>
> The Resurrection Hymn

Orthodoxy's teachings about death point to fundamental beliefs and practices of the faith: by participating in the life of Jesus Christ one participates in the conquest of death and "put[s] on immortality," following the example of Christ Himself [I Corinthians 15:53]. As St. Paul explains,

> For this perishable nature must put on the imperishable, and this mortal nature must put on immortality. When the perishable puts on the imperishable and the mortal puts on the immortal, then shall come to pass the saying that is written: "Death is swallowed up in victory." "O Hades, where is thy victory?" "O Death, where is thy sting?" The sting of death is sin, and the power of sin is the law. But thanks be to God, who gives us the victory through our Lord Jesus Christ [I Corinthians 15:54-57].

While the true believer has the promise of emerging victorious from dying, into the eternal life, death remains a mystery. As a "mystery" (with a lower case *m*, meaning "beyond understanding"), death is one of the most challenging and significant issues with which each of us must wrestle. While we will all have our turn at death, the reality of living and our natural fears of mortality render the concept both incomprehensible and painfully mysterious. The unknown nature of death confronts us with a series of paradoxical questions: Does death nullify all we have experienced? Does God await us after death? Should death be preferred over life with all of its trials and uncertainties? Should we resist our natural inclinations to develop attachments to life, since ultimately they must all be relinquished? How does death give meaning to life?

The Orthodox faith attempts to solve this "mystery" through its Mystical Tradition, with an uppercase "M," meaning mystery as a spiritual encounter— a *knowledge of God made possible through a paradoxically unknowing, ever-increasing, and continuously enhancing experience.* Within the Mystical Tradition, the faithful understand the depth of God's love through their relation-ship with Him. By cultivating this relationship over a lifetime, the believer learns that he or she is loved ultimately by Him, whose affection is eternal and transcendent, immune to the temporal constraints and conditions that bind and limit our own lives. By experiencing and expressing this love, one promptly understands that this is the same love that motivated Christ's enormous sacrifice, of which it is written: "God so loved the world that he gave his only Son, that whoever believes in him should not perish, but have eternal life" [John 3:16]. Jesus Himself addresses death, giving counsel and hope to a law-bound lawyer in pursuit of eternal life in the Gospel of Luke. Jesus gently steers the man to a better understanding, asking him: . . . What is written in the law? How do you read? And he (the lawyer) answered, "You shall love the Lord your God with all your heart, and with all your soul, and with all your strength, and with all your mind: and your neighbor as yourself." And he said to him, "You have answered right; do this and you will live" [Luke 10:26-28].

For Orthodox Christians, then, the key to eternal life and overcoming the dread of death is to be found in following Christ's commandments to love God, oneself, and others. Implicit in this lesson is the choice of life over death. The Gospel of John records Christ's words: "Truly, truly I say to you, he who hears my word and believes him who sent me, has eternal life; he does not come into judgment, but has passed from death to life" [John 5:24]. Elsewhere in the Gospel, ". . . if anyone keeps my word, he will never see death" [John 8:51]. Therefore, by living a life in concert with Jesus Christ, the mystery of death is solved through the promise of eternal life. Thus, the understanding and practices of Orthodox Christians concerning death stem directly from the experiences of Jesus Christ. Furthermore, to explicate its understanding of death, the Church has established theological teachings that link the traditions of the Orthodox faith with its practices and rituals.

THEOLOGICAL FOUNDATIONS OF DEATH

What is the Relationship between Sin and Death?

Orthodox Christianity teaches that sin introduced death into the universe [2]. Sin (from the Greek *amartia*, which literally means "missing the mark") results from following what the early Church treatise *The Didache* calls choosing the Way of Death over the Way of Life [3]. Adam and Eve's original transgression exemplifies the way in which sin severs humanity's relationship with God because it separated them from God. St. Maximos the Confessor says, "Death in the true sense is separation from God . . . and this [is] necessarily followed by the body's death" [4, p. 81]. At the root of death lies one's separation from God and the source of sin.

Sin, and thus death, are freely chosen. Orthodox teachings assert that God created man neither mortal nor immortal but, as preached by St. Gregory of Nazianzos, capable of attaining either outcome through his or her own exercise of free will (*aftexousion*) [5]. Death occurs because of our misuse of free will. While God permits free will out of His love for humanity, enabling us to make choices that shape our lives; at the same time He also places a limit on sin through death: ". . . the wages of sin is death" [Romans 6:23]. Yet, hope and salvation are also offered by God. Orthodox theology emphasizes that sin is not overcome by human effort alone but that one ultimately is saved through God's grace.

Christ is the vehicle of that grace. In his treatise, *On the Incarnation of the Word,* St. Athanasios explains that Christ

> took a body like ours, because all our bodies were liable to the corruption of death, He surrendered His body to death in place of all . . . so that in His death all might die . . . and the law of death (could be) . . . fulfilled [6, Chapter II, Section 7, p. 33].

St. Athanasios goes on to explain that Christ's supreme purpose in taking on mortal life was the lesson of the Resurrection: "This was His victory over death . . . which is as assurance to all that He had Himself conquered corruption" [6, Chapter II, Section 22, p. 52]. Christ's coming enabled a godless, fallen humanity to return to God, achieve renewal, and reflect again God's image, restoring the original creation [6, Chapter III, Section 14, 16, pp. 41-45].

For Orthodox Christians, deification and salvation occur when one overcomes sin through living in light of the Message of the Resurrection. Moreover, salvation, renewal, resurrection, and *theosis* (deification) begin already in this life through faith in Jesus Christ, whose Resurrection inaugurated the Age of New Creation. The Resurrection of Christ is a triumph over sin and death. Christ's Resurrection inspires His followers to overcome new sin by embracing the love that is experienced through communion, a "healthy connection," with one's self, one's neighbors, and God Himself. Christ's personal sacrifice and His Message of love transform the cross, a visual emblem of his death, into a symbol of eternal life. Furthermore, Christ's return will herald the dawning of a "new earth," a "new heaven" where we will undergo a spiritual transformation, our bodies will become permanently incorruptible. That is, the body will not be simply material but transfigured. This transformation relies on a natural, biological event and is not to be understood as magical or mechanical [7]. Conversely, for those not engaged with the life of Christ, death and hell are already present spiritual realities in this world.

How Do We Know What Occurs After Death?

The consummation or redemption will occur with Christ's glorious return, the resurrection of the dead, and the final Judgment. Because many details concerning death and the process of the resurrection of the dead have not been revealed by God, theologians and scholars offer teachings and opinions based in Holy Tradition that are not doctrinal, called *theologoumena*. So, for example, while the resurrection of the dead is a doctrinal belief of Orthodox Christians, *theologoumena* are offered to expand on aspects of the afterlife that have not been revealed by God.

Orthodox Christians maintain that the human soul never dies. What then happens to the soul after death? What will become of the soul is determined by one's faith. In the case of the faithful, the soul lives on with Christ, while the faithless, non-believer forfeits the security of this immortal bond. For the nonbeliever, the loss of physical life essentially constitutes "the second death" [8, p. 45]. Throughout the Bible we are instructed that the soul remains conscious after death [see references in Luke 16:27-28; Hebrews 2:23; Philippians 1:22; I Peter 3:19; and Revelation 6:9-10]. Therefore, once mortal life ends, it is not the soul which sleeps, but the body. In keeping with this belief, The Gospel of Matthew reports on the Resurrection of Christ:

> the tombs also were opened, and many bodies of the saints who had fallen asleep were raised, and coming out of the tombs after his resurrection they went into the holy city and appeared to many [Matthew 28:52-53].

An example of differing views regarding *theologoumena* presents itself regarding the subject of the final judgment and the significance of praying for those deceased. According to theologian Metropolitan Maximos, partial judgment follows physical death, ushering the righteous into an *intermediate stage* of partial blessedness [9]. In contrast, Professor Christos Androutsos offers a less generous perspective, arguing that "moral progress" and the eventual redemption of the soul is not possible once it has been separated from the body [10, p. 409].

Memorial services are typically held in the Orthodox Church at intervals of 40 days, one year, and ten years, and may be arranged at the discretion of the family of the deceased at other times. While these opportunities primarily support pastoral needs of the family, some theologians emphasize that such services enhance the fate of the souls of the deceased in gaining forgiveness, while others, again, argue that the fate of the soul is sealed at death, with no possibility of repentance [11]. Not subscribing to the Roman Catholic belief in purgatory, in which the soul must await purification before entering heaven, many Orthodox Christians believe that "change" remains possible in the intermediate stage after death. For some, then, the prayers of living (as part of the *militant Church)* and the prayers of the dead (as part of the *triumphant Church*) can influence one another. This belief explains the importance of prayer for the deceased in Orthodox practice. Additionally, almsgiving will be given on behalf of the departed as a similar support for family and in support of the deceased; but, as with prayer, there is no suggestion that those who do so are buying salvation through the purchase of the indulgences or the remission of sins.

Will There Be a Bodily Resurrection at the Second Coming?

In his vision recorded in the Book of Revelation, St John the Theologian describes what the Kingdom of God will be like when Christ returns:

> Then I saw a new heaven and a new earth, the first heaven and the first earth had passed away and the sea was no more. And I saw the holy city, new Jerusalem, coming down out of heaven from God, prepared as a bride adorned for her husband; and I heard a great voice from the throne saying, "Behold, the dwelling of God is with men. He will dwell with them, and they shall be his people, and God himself with be with them; he will wipe away every tear from their eyes; and death shall be no more death, neither shall there be mourning or crying nor pain any more, for the former things have passed away." And he who sat upon the throne said: "Behold, I make all things new . . ." [Revelation 21:1-5].

This passage serves as a cornerstone to what Orthodox Christians believe about the Second Coming. Bodily death is viewed in Orthodoxy in light of the historical fact that the Kingdom of God has come through Christ but is not fully manifest on earth. The final judgment is a fundamental belief of the Orthodox faith, as recorded in the Nicene Creed, in which the faithful profess: ". . . I await for the resurrection of the dead. . . ." This resurrection marks the beginning of a "new creation" [9]. Just as the body of Jesus Christ was resurrected, so, too, will all physical bodies rise up and be restored to a spiritualized existence. The final judgment will occur after everyone's resurrection. Orthodox Christians believe that Jesus Christ will judge us based not only on our sins, but also on our deeds and works of love. Describing the glory of eternal salvation, the Bible counsels us to ". . . wait for new heavens and a new earth, in which righteousness dwells" [II Corinthians 5:10 and II Peter 3:13]. At this moment of reckoning, the so-called "end-time," a permanent separation, will occur between good and evil, between those who will be awarded an eternal life of happiness in heaven and those who will be condemned to the fires of eternal damnation. The condemned will experience a state of eternal remorse for having rejected God and authentic life in Him [9]. Orthodox believers await Christ's return. Scripture states that upon His return, "the Son himself will also be subjected to him who put all things under him, that God may be everything to every one" [1 Corinthians 15:28].

As noted earlier, the bodily resurrection of the dead is a basic tenet of the Orthodox faith as outlined by the Nicene Creed. Christ's Resurrection and the bodily resurrection of all humankind is so central to the beliefs of Orthodox Christians as to discourage debate or contradiction. In fact, this perspective on the Resurrection embodies so much of the Christian faith that St. Paul is led to assert that:

> If Christ has not been raised, your faith is futile and you are still in your sins [I Corinthians 15:17].

> If in this life we who are in Christ have only hope, we are of all men most to be pitied [I Corinthians 15:19].

Therefore, Christ's Resurrection and the bodily resurrection reflect more than a wish, miracle, or incidental report. An event that exceeds and surpasses our human comprehension, the bodily resurrection testifies to our union with God, our victory over death, and our hope for eternal life.

Discussing the importance of maintaining one's faith in the face of doubts and skepticism, St. John Chrysostom discusses the consequences of faltering trust in the resurrection at the Second Coming:

> For if we were persuaded that there is no resurrection of bodies, he ("the Devil") would have gradually persuaded them that neither was Christ raised. And thereupon he would also introduce this in due course, that He had not come nor had done what He did [12, p. 266].

Consequently, faith in the promise of the general resurrection of the dead becomes inseparable from faith in Christ Himself. The one both implies and necessitates the other.

But while Orthodox doctrine insists on Christ's and our own bodily resurrection, the Orthodox teachings, again, offer little physical or logistical information on the latter process. This had not been revealed. Yet the bodily Resurrection of Christ is described in the Gospels (from the Greek word *evangelion*, literally the "Good News" or "Announcement," that is the announcement of the Resurrection is the essence of Christ's story). His appearance was like lightning, and the rainment white as snow . . . for he has risen. . . . Then go quickly and tell his disciples that he has risen from the dead . . . [Matthew 28: 3-7].

The importance of codifying such doctrine is illustrated by the relationships that social values and customs have with theology, and the fact that theological teachings may otherwise be influenced by changes in the social climate. For instance, a religious tradition which denies eternal life or dismisses the significance of the body of the dead is less likely to emphasize rites of burial and prayer for the dead. At the same time, a rejection of the immortal soul seems to be in open conflict with those religious and spiritual practices that "scientifically" study life after death experiences and seek to prove, empirically, the existence of an afterlife [13]. For Orthodox Christians, theological foundations rooted in the earliest Christian community set the tone for beliefs which take expression in liturgical practice, which directly confronts the experience of the dying and bereaved.

LITURGICAL PRACTICE

The liturgical practices in Orthodoxy, speak to the holistic nature of our experience of death—engaging through ritual, body, mind, and soul, and activating all our senses. The hymns express gratitude to God for the blessed opportunities of life, focusing particularly on the gift of Christ's sacrifice. Traditional Byzantine chant, drawing from eight tonal variations, effectively and powerfully conveys the range of human emotions experienced at death, moving audibly from the depths of sadness (resonated in the lowest, dissonant notes) to the jubilant heights of transcendent joy (captured in the highest notes). Equally symbolic, the burning of incense visually represents the direction of our prayers in honor of the departed—ascending to the heaven—in addition to the image incense conjures up of transporting us to Heaven above. Candles symbolize liberation from darkness as the departed embarks on the path to true light. With solemnity and respect, the faithful approach to touch and kiss the body, in reverent expression of love for the deceased. The final kiss underscores the community and communion of the faithful—living and dead [14]. Finally, the mourners join in a traditional meal of fish, bread, and wine, demonstrating their communal love and grief, and recreating the symbolic power of Christ's last supper.

The Funeral Service

In an exhaustive treatise about death, Nicholas Vassiliadis [14] summarizes the goals of the Orthodox Christian funeral service as: 1) utilizing the opportunity of death to help participants develop a more profound understanding of the meaning and purpose of life; 2) helping the bereaved deal with their emotions at a time of great loss; 3) identifying the powerful, eschatological hope of Christians, in distinction from non-Christians; and 4) recognizing grief that accompanies the loss of a loved one and encouraging its expression.

Liturgical services alleviate the pain experienced in the loss of a loved one. In response to death, the Orthodox Tradition works to comfort a mourner by declaring the victory of eternal life through Christ's personal sacrifice. Moreover, it attends to the concerns of those left behind, addressing beliefs they have about the death of their loved one and providing graphic details about his or her well-being:

O God of spirits and of all flesh, who overcame death and abolished the devil and gave life to your world, the same hand, give rest to the soul of your departed servant _____ in a place of light, in a place of happiness, in a place of peace, where there is no pain, sorrow, or suffering. Gracious and merciful God, forgive every sin committed by him, whether by word, or deed, or thought. For there is no man who lives and does not sin. You alone are without sin. Your righteousness is eternal and your word is truth [15, p. 13].

Prayer from the Funeral Service

Likewise, hymns in the Funeral Service composed by St. John of Damascus offer perspective and consolation to the bereaved:

First Tone
What pleasure is there in life that has no sorrow?
Which glory remains on this earth without change?
All is more fleeting than shadow, more elusive than dreams.
A sudden change and all of these are followed by death. Yet in this light of your countenance and in the sweetness of your beauty, give rest to the one you have chosen, O Christ, Lover of humanity.

Fourth Tone
Indeed, the mystery of death is awesome. How the soul is suddenly separated from the harmony of the body. And how the natural bond of being together is cut off by the divine will. So we pray to you: O Life–giver and host of humanity, give rest to the one who departed this life in the company of the just.

Plagal Fourth Tone
I weep and I wail when I perceive death and see laid in the grave the beauty, fashioned for us in the likeness of God, to be without form, without glory, without beauty. What an amazing thing! What is this mystery that happened around us? How were we delivered to conception and how did we become united with death? Surely, by the will of God who gives to the departed rest [15, pp. 29-35].

Faith in the power of the Resurrection accounts for the joyful tone and hopeful passages in the funeral rite. This abiding optimism is joined with a communal recognition of grief and loss, which accounts for a more saddened, minor key. Interwoven, then, in the Orthodox funeral service are seemingly paradoxical moods, sounds, and actions that simultaneously express concern and empathy for loss in this world while celebrating faith and joy for eternal life in the next. Commenting on a sermon by St. John Chrysostom on an Epistle to the Thessalonians, St. Augustine explains this dual concept of *hopeful grief*, pointing out that although we are Christian, it is still natural to mourn, and yet we are "not to mourn as others who have no hope" [16, pp. 33-34].

As the greatest link between God and the faithful, prayer serves as a primary medium for the exchange of communication and love between the living and the dead. As such, prayer to or for the deceased affirms and deepens the bonds of the living with the departed. Additionally, the power of prayer establishes a personal, living connection between the dead and mourning, working both to mitigate the pain of loss and inform the journey of the immortal soul. All these features are illustrated in the following example from the funeral service:

> O Lord of Hosts, who are the consolation of the afflicted, and the comfort of those who mourn; and the succour of all those who are faint-hearted: Comfort through Your Loving-Kindness, those who are distressed with weeping for him (her) who has fallen asleep and heal every pain that does oppress their hearts. And give rest in Abraham's bosom unto Your servant, _____ , who has fallen asleep in the hope of resurrection into life eternal. For You are the Resurrection, and the Life, and the Repose of Your servant, _____ , Christ our God; and unto You do we ascribe glory, with Your Father who is from everlasting, and Your all-holy and good, and life-giving Spirit, now, and ever, and unto ages of ages. Amen [17, pp. 400-401].
>
> Prayer from the Funeral Service

Orthodox Burial

The liturgical message regarding death and rebirth finds fullest expression in the Good Friday service of Jesus Christ. In this dramatic liturgical event, a multitude of the faithful pray through the night, commemorating not only the Crucifixion of Jesus Christ but also the loss of the community's deceased. In this ritual moment, agony, emptiness, and loss are replaced by burgeoning triumph and celebration as the faithful anticipate Christ's Resurrection and the resurrection to come of all who have passed.

Burial customs for Orthodox Christians derive from Gospel accounts in which the apostles prepare Christ's lifeless body. With a remarkable concordance in details, the gospels describe several key elements in the burial regarding both the shroud and the tomb itself—elements that have become central images in the Orthodox funeral service.

Matthew's Gospel reports,

> And Joseph took the body and wrapped it in a clean linen shroud, and laid it in his own new tomb, which he had hewn in the rock; and he rolled a great stone to the door of the tomb [Matthew 27: 59-60].

Mark's Gospel states,

> Joseph of Arimathea brought a linen shroud and taking him down, wrapped him in the linen shroud, and laid him in the tomb which had been hewn out of the rock; and he rolled a stone against the door of the tomb [Matthew 15: 43-46].

Luke's Gospel says,

> Joseph from the Jewish town of Arimathea took [Jesus' body] down and
> wrapped it in a linen shroud, and laid him in a rock-hewn tomb, where no
> one had ever been laid [Luke 23: 50-53].

John's Gospel records,

> They took the body of Jesus, and bound it in linen cloths with the spices . . .
> there was a garden, and in the garden a new tomb where no one had ever been
> laid . . . they laid Jesus there [John 19:40-42].

Drawing from the descriptions in these accounts, strikingly visual passages from
the Good Friday Vespers and the Lamentations of the Good Friday service convey
in emotionally charged and resonant language the physical circumstances of
Jesus's death as experienced by those attending to Him, who re-enact the burial.

> O You who puts on light like a robe, when Joseph with Nikodemos brought
> You down from the Tree and beheld You dead, naked, and unburied, he
> mourned outwardly and grievously, crying to You with signs, and saying:
> Woe is me, sweet Jesus, whom but a while ago, when the sun beheld
> suspended upon the Cross, it was shrouded in darkness, the earth quaked with
> fear, and the veil of the Temple was rent asunder. Albeit, I see that You
> willingly endure death for my sake. How then shall I prepare You, my God?
> How shall I wrap You with linen? Or what dirges shall I chant for Your
> funeral? Wherefore, O compassionate Lord, I magnify Your Passion, and
> praise Your burial with Your Resurrection, crying, Lord, glory to You [1,
> p. 360].
>
> Good Friday Vespers

> When Joseph of Arimathea took You, the Life of all, down from the Tree,
> dead; he buried you, Bathing You with sweet and costly myrrh, gently he
> covered You with fine linen. And with sorrow and tender love in his heart
> and on his lips, he embraced Your most pure Body and yearned that it may
> be enshrouded; Wherefore, hiding his fear, he cried to You, rejoicing: Glory
> to Your condescension, O Merciful Master [1, p. 359].
>
> Good Friday Lamentation Service

Based on these traditions, acknowledging the body's sacred role as the
Temple of the Holy Spirit, the attending clergy seek to render the corpse incorruptible, wrapping it in shrouds to prepare the spirit for resurrection. In keeping
with ancient practices, priests anoint the body with myrrh and oil; shaping a cross
over the body, symbolizing the sacred and good struggles of the departed; and pray
to heal the sins of the deceased. At this point, the priest recites, from Psalm 51:7:
"Purge me with hyssop . . . and I shall be clean; wash me; wash me and I shall be
whiter than snow." Dressed and anointed, the body is positioned in the grave,
facing east, toward the Eastern European region of Christ's ministry, believed to
be the seat of the final resurrection.

The burial service is designed as much for the living as for the dead. Mourners place a handful of dirt within the coffin in a ritual recapitulation of God's words ". . . you are dust, and to dust you shall return" [Genesis 3:19]. Vassiliadis interprets this ritual as an excellent visual lesson regarding our own mortality and the vanity of earthly things [14].

Even so, referring to those believers for whom proper burial is rendered impossible, St. Augustine assures his reader of God's vigilance in tending to the dead:

> But even though the body has been all quite ground up to powder by some severe accident, or by ruthlessness of enemies, and though it has been so diligently scattered to the winds, or into the water, that there is no trace of it left, yet it shall not be beyond the omnipotence of the Creator—no, not a hair of its head shall perish [18, p. 499].

While God provides for those who have lost their body to war or disaster, *intentionally* disrupting one's corpse, as in the case of premeditated cremation, is not permitted in the Orthodox Church. However, as is the case in Japan, state law sometimes requires cremation of the dead. Therefore, while destruction of the body is not endorsed by the Orthodox community, in cases which are beyond one's control, such as the mandates of state law, one's resurrection is never threatened, as it lies within the domain of a protective God.

Iconographic Link between Death and Resurrection

Not distinguishing an importance between the death of God and the loss of the faithful's loved one, the Orthodox funeral service and the icons that it employs visually testify to the claim of Orthodox nuns, "Nothing was too good: the finest linen, the most expensive ointment, a brand new tomb" [19, p. 25] (see Figures 1 and 2). Dramatic liturgical conventions and symbolically-charged iconography work to express the gut-wrenching and profound agony of loss, as well as the miracle and joy of life anticipated in the promised Resurrection. In both visual and audible art forms, the tragedy at hand is staged against the backdrop of the Kingdom of God, an ephemeral space in which the past, present, and future—the temporal and the eternal—mingle interchangeably with one another. Experiencing fully the dynamic tension between the tragedy of death, on the one hand, and the miracle and joy of life, on the other, participants give full vent to the range of emotional expression.

The icon of the *Pieta* (called the Apokathilosis, in Greek) (Figure 3), a 15th century Italo-Cretan icon, depicts the Mother of God, Mary, and Christ's beloved disciple, John, mourning over Jesus' body following the Crucifixion. Bordered by angels, whose open hands convey shock and despair, the icon illustrates both heaven and earth grieving over the inconceivable act of destroying the Son of God [20, p. 327]. In the late 15th century Russian icon of the *Entombment* (Figure 1), the iconographer captures the grief of a woman cloaked in red, raising her arms in a

Figure 1. The Entombment.

gesture of ceremonial incantation. The scene depicts both a natural, human lament for the departed and participation in a solemn ritual. Against warm and dull tones of brown and white, the woman's bright red cloak draws the eye of the observer, focusing attention on the icon's central spiritual event [20, p. 285]. In an image that brings together the motifs of the *Pieta* and *Entombment,* the late 17th Century Byzantine icon *Epitaphios* (Figure 2), or "tomb," shows the preparation of Christ's body by Joseph of Arimathea, evoking the words of the Gospels in its depiction of both the cross itself and the linen shroud in which the corpse was wrapped [20, p. 327].

Liturgical theologian Rev. Alkivides Calivas describes the death of Christ as the "true birthday" [21, p. 64] of the Orthodox Church. His comments bring together the ecclesial images of iconography and liturgical practice concerning the message of the Church about death. Reflecting on the thoughts of theologian Boris Bobrinskoy [22], Calivas says that death takes on "positive value" [21,

Figure 2. The Epitaphios.

Figure 3. The Pieta (The Apokathilosis, in Greek).

p. 242], for even if physical death continues, it becomes the threshold of the passage from "death to life, rather than from life to death" [21, p. 242]. Calivas continues,

> ... through the Church we appropriate the transforming power of the death and Resurrection of Christ which places upon us the obligation to actualize the renunciations demanded of us by the Gospel in our everyday activities. It calls us to abjure the false values of the fallen world and inspires us to seek after all that is noble, good, natural, and sinless. It encourages us to struggle against all forms of oppression and unjust condition which devalue and diminish human life; do more for the life of others in the world; and work for the fulfillment of the Church's vocation in the world [21, p. 93].

Therefore, we see the connection between the Death and Resurrection of Christ and the liturgical practices in Orthodoxy.

PASTORAL PERSPECTIVE

The Greek Orthodox understanding of death exists within a broad cultural matrix of attitudes and approaches toward death. Foremost among theorists of thanatology in the past 35 years has been Dr. Elisabeth Kübler-Ross whose groundbreaking work *On Death and Dying* [23] outlines five progressive stages commonly experienced in the course of a terminal illness: 1) denial or isolation; 2) anger; 3) bargaining; 4) depression; and 5) acceptance. Dr. Ross's thesis initiated a revolution in medical and psychological literature by tackling a subject that had been carefully avoided in both professional debates and mainstream culture. Furthermore, her work triggered and facilitated a long overdue dialogue between health care providers and the terminally ill patients for whom they worked. Our collective understanding of death and dying has developed considerably in the decades following these breakthroughs. How has the Orthodox Tradition reconciled modern pastoral attitudes with an ever-growing field of psychological study? How has Orthodoxy assimilated its age-old theology with modern understanding of human needs?

Attunement to the Individual

The Orthodox Church seeks to comfort and console those touched by the experience of death and dying. Preserved through liturgical and theological channels, the Church's pastoral tradition calls for clerical attunement to an individual's feelings of loss and abandonment, revitalizing a connection with God at times of crisis and fear. A pastor cannot facilitate such a connection, however, through mere study of Scripture or theory or adherence to ritual. Innate compassion and genuine care lie at the core of successful clerical attunement. Effective clergy will observe, listen, and respond to the needs of the grieving and the sick with unrehearsed sensitivity and humane understanding [24].

We have considered how the Orthodox sacramental tradition creates a personal engagement between the suffering individual and the greater community. Clergy embody this connection by presiding over rituals of mourning. Bridging the gap between the isolated self and a collective spiritual identity, Orthodox practices of Holy Unction and laying on of hands literally represent the contact between Church and believer, uniting one with a greater, nurturing collectivity. A direct borrowing from Christ's own ministry, the Orthodox practice of touch resonates meaningfully for those who are dying [25].

While Orthodox clergy rely upon the liturgical practices of Holy Communion and Holy Unction in fulfilling their mission, personal attunement and an adherence to Christ's own approach to ministry are also essential to the effectiveness of pastoral care. In this respect Orthodox ministry to the dying is a twofold art: to listen to the dying and bereaved as unique persons; while through administration the sacramental role to facilitate the love that will solidify the parishioner's relationship to God, self, and others.

As a seminarian, I recall witnessing a pastoral visit in which a dying woman, suffering visibly from the aggressive course of her bone cancer, was counseled by a bishop. While the patient lay shaking from pain and fear, the esteemed clergyman launched into a liturgical speech, drawing exclusively from his theological knowledge rather than responding humanely to the woman's despair. Having quoted St. Paul's exhortation that she "fight the good fight of the faith" [I Timothy 6:12], the well-read bishop had little else to offer in the way of comfort. Without confronting the depths of her fear, he exited as quickly as he had come. Sadly, due to either an absence of genuine empathy, a lack of awareness of his task, or a pitiable inability to engage congregants compassionately, the bishop squandered a perfect opportunity to mitigate the woman's fears, to restore her wavering faith.

I also remember the story of a new priest who, like the bishop, missed a critical opportunity to minister because of his lack of preparation. Having learned of a birth in the community, the priest traveled to the hospital, prepared to congratulate and support the first-time parents. Delighted to share in their joy, the priest beamed with enthusiasm upon entering their hospital room, bursting out preemptively, "Congratulations! Is it a boy or a girl?" With a look of anguish, the young man replied, "Our son was stillborn." Devastated by the news and mortified by his mistake, the young priest froze in his tracks without a word of consolation. Immediately excusing himself from the room, the priest fled from the awkward situation, offering nothing in the way of comfort.

Whether these two cases represent individual failings or a lack of learned pastoral behavior, they dramatically illustrate how lapses in compassion and care can undermine one's ministerial responsibilities. As in any care-taking relationship, the infiltration of the care-giver's *own* emotional shortcomings, known as countertransference, often plagues the well-meaning cleric. If clergy narrowly conceive their roles as only liturgists, then emotional support for the suffering soul, as demonstrated and exemplified by Christ Himself, is often lost. While the theological and liturgical traditions of Orthodox Christianity aim to alleviate everyday sufferings and preserve the true spirit, the art of pastoral care remains fundamental to meeting the needs of the community members. In the absence of such care, the individual needs of a distressed layperson may be overshadowed by the observance of rituals that value the collective spirit over the particular experience. The powerful pastoral implications of Holy Tradition necessitate caring *application* of the learned wisdom of doctrine. When we look to Scripture we see Christ attuning Himself to the unique demands of each encounter. Attunement to the individual's experience of death requires a thoughtful and personal approach to the particular "stage" of that person's grieving. In pursuit of this goal, Orthodox Christian theologians have worked diligently to illustrate the implications of applied liturgy and, specifically, how it translates into effective care of the individual communicant [24, 26-29].

In the aforementioned case examples, the therapeutic failures of the hierarch and the priest may derive in part from their *own* fears of death and dying, expressed through mechanisms of avoidance and escape or withdrawal. One can certainly understand the human impulse behind the clerics' failings, considered in this light. Nonetheless, given the impact of these acts upon the psyche of the distressed individual, we must censure such negligent behavior. The hierarch turned away from the anguish of the dying woman; the priest fled at the news of the stillborn. As Orthodox Christian pastoral theologian Reverend Joseph Allen observes, the Church ritual calls not only for prayer and oil for healing, but also the laying on of hands—that is, when facing the fears of death, its isolation and loneliness, one feels a need to be closer, to be touched. Vividly exemplified by Christ Himself, physical *presence* at times of suffering works as a balm, providing comfort to the whole person—body, mind, and soul.

Death may serve as a barometer of both our faith and our ability to act upon a message of compassion—a call to share in someone else's vulnerability, to contemplate death and together, to rise above it. It is entirely natural that many shy away from this challenge, avoiding death, illness, and the kind of existential crisis brought about by moments of extreme emotional and psychological despair. St. Gregory of Nazianzos describes such despair after the death of St. Basil:

> You ask how I am.... Well, I am very bad. Basil I have no longer; Caesarios I have no longer; the intellectual and physical brothers are both dead. "My father and mother have left me," I can say with David. Physically I am ill, age is descending on my head. Cares are choking me; affairs oppress me; there is no reliance on friends and the Church is without shepherds. The good is vanishing; evil shows itself in all its nakedness. We are travelling in the dark; there is no lighthouse and Christ is asleep. What can one do? I know only one salvation from these troubles, and this is death. But even the world to come seems terrible to judge by this present world [30, pp. 101-102].

Emerging from the emotional depths captured by this passage, St. Gregory stabilized himself by re-establishing his relationship to God and renewing his commitment to the spiritual path [31]. Following the example of this great theologian, a man who recognized his own fallibility, members of the clergy must reconcile their powerful roles as teachers of doctrine with a humble admission of humanity, developing the art of pastoral care with the guidance of both spiritual and psychological resources.

Psychological studies have examined closely the positive impact of attunement, exploring the ways in which the perceptions and guidance of a caretaker can affect the experience of both the afflicted and their loved ones [32, 33]. The knowledge gained from such scientific assessments is vital to the improvement of Orthodox pastoral care. Bolstered by concrete data, the attunement of clergymen can clearly enhance the well-being of lay-persons in distress [34-38].

At the same time, studies exclusively scientific in nature often overlook the extent to which faith may influence the prognosis of a terminally ill patient or the outlook of an afflicted loved one. For example, while Kübler-Ross identifies five stages to death and dying, she does not fully examine the role of faith in each of them, overlooking a range of intense spiritual experiences that frequently accompany periods of grief. When she does acknowledge the impact of religious healing, Kübler-Ross arrives at a telling conclusion:

> Truly religious people with a deep, abiding relationship with God have found it easier to face death with equanimity. We do not often see them because they aren't troubled, so they don't need our help [39, p. 163].

From this perspective, psychology serves a positive and preventative role in mental health.

Acceptance, as the final stage in her model, represents a neutral stage of resignation rather than a positive, ideal approach to mortality. Kübler-Ross clearly articulates this distinction, warning that:

> Acceptance should not be mistaken for a happy stage. It is almost void of feelings. It is as if the pain had gone, the struggle is over, and there comes a time for the "final rest before the long journey" as one patient phrased it . . . [23, p. 100].

But strict adherence to this model fails to explain the enlightened experiences of many exemplary Christian figures. For instance, when St. Ignatios of Antioch desired to die for Christ, he demonstrated neither fearful denial nor neutral acceptance of death, espousing instead a transcendent view of mortality that escapes clinical categorization. As the second bishop of Antioch, St. Ignatios was sentenced to death during the reign of Emperor Trajan [AD 98-117] and condemned to be devoured by wild beasts. In the face of this horrific demise, St. Ignatios shocked his contemporaries, begging that his life not be spared. Driven by an ardent desire to die for Christ, St. Ignatios embraced his approaching death—for him it heralded the beginning of true life:

> . . . At last I am on the way to being a disciple. May nothing seen or unseen fascinate me, so that I may happily make my way to Jesus Christ! Fire, cross, struggles with wild beasts, wrenching of bones, mangling of limbs, crushing of the whole body, cruel tortures inflicted by the devil—let them come upon me, provided only I make my way to Jesus Christ. Of no use to me be the farthest reaches of the universe or the Kingdoms of this world. I would rather die and come to Jesus Christ than be the King over the entire earth. Him I seek who died for us; Him I love who rose again because of us. The birth pangs are upon me. Forgive me, brother; do not obstruct my coming to life—do not wish me to die; do not make a gift to the world of one who wants to be God's. Beware of seducing me with matter; suffer me to receive pure light. Once arrived there I shall be a man [Romans 5:3-6]—Why, moreover, did I surrender myself to death, to fire, to the sword, to wild beasts? Well, to be near the sword is to be near God; to be in the claws of wild beasts is to be in the hands of God. Only let it be done in the name of Jesus Christ! To suffer with Him I endure all things, if He, who became perfect man, gives me the strength [3, p. 71].

St. Ignatios' experience of death is not adequately understood by the stages of denial or acceptance. Therefore, pastoral care requires attunement, careful attention; that is, a "designer" understanding of the many elements which inform the dying or bereaved's response to death. Only through comprehensive understanding of the various elements that inform one's experience can we effectively respond. Ministry requires that we distinguish, understand, and attune to the individual experience of death and dying.

Spiritual Value

Understanding death and reflecting upon its Mystery allow us to give the appropriate spiritual value to life itself. Thus, the Orthodox Christian Church places great emphasis upon the study of meditation on death. Through such reflection one approaches the deeper meanings of faith, hope, and love. In contemplating death, one registers the shortness and fragility of life itself and is led to live according to the new life in Christ. St. Philothos of Sinai captures this sentiment when he asserts, "Ceaseless mindfulness of death purifies intellect and body" [4, p. 17].

The monastic tradition developed a rigorous practice of strengthening the soul, from which most forms of spiritual meditation are currently drawn. "Detachment from material things," as St. Peter of Damaskos wrote,

> gives rise to the contemplation of spiritual realities—contemplation not of created beings in this present life, but of the awesome things that take place before and after death. For the detached person is taught about these things by

> grace, so through inward grief he may mortify the passions and, when the time
> is ripe, attain peace and gentleness in his thoughts [4, p. 231].

As depicted in this passage, spiritual growth arises from our capacity to move beyond all material things. The practice of spiritual asceticism prescribed by St. Peter of Damasksos requires a controlled detachment

> . . . not only over external things, but also over the body, through our
> non-attachment to it, and over death, through the courage of our faith; then in
> the life to come we shall reign in our bodies externally with Christ, through the
> grace of the general resurrection [4, p. 125].

Within the framework of Orthodoxy exists a broad array of spiritual recommendations, ranging from conservative mandates (by which we denounce all that is material) to more liberal ideologies (by which we are instructed to embrace the attachments of this world, recognizing through them the teachings and sacrifices of Christ). From among these the believer must choose his or her personal path.

Hope

Hope is needed at no time of greater crisis than that moment in which we confront death. Residing on the frontier of death, hope is not only a living virtue of faith but also an eager anticipation of the promised Kingdom which Christ inaugurated, a time and place that is both "now and not yet" realized. While modern research demonstrates the power of hope, optimism, and faith in the regular maintenance of one's health and well-being [40, 42], these abstract concepts take on a new and urgent set of meanings when embraced by the dying believer. Faced with mortality, Orthodox Christians look forward to the communion with God to which their hope testifies, trusting in the Truth of life after death. For example, St. Ignatios equates Holy Communion with the "medicine of immortality, and the sovereign remedy by which we escape death and live in Jesus Christ for evermore" [16, p. 7]. In both liturgy and personal life, then, hope is perhaps the deepest expression of one's faith, exemplifying confidence in both one's life today and the promise of immortality. There are times, however, when a Christian does not feel hope at the time of death, overcome by feelings of doubt, despair, or fear. Nonetheless, a sense of abiding faith resides within the institutions of the Church itself, embodied in the stories of saints and martyrs, all of which testify to the redemptive value of trust in Christ.

A number of Orthodox pastoral guides address the importance of hope for those in the throes of loss [29, 43-46]. Reverend Anthony Coniaris delivers the message of hope as one of faith in the "transfiguration of Christ," a concept closely aligned with Orthodox understandings of death:

> He did not come to teach us to accept suffering and death because they
> are universal. He did not come to tell us that death is God's will for us.
> He came to tell us that death was something evil; something not part of

God's plan; something that needed to be destroyed. And he destroyed it for us. He gave us the victory. This is why for the Christian the final stage of life cannot be the passive acceptance of death, but its transfiguration in Christ! [43, p. 27].

By highlighting Christ's role as a "destroyer" of death and a "bringer of victory," Rev. Coniaris enjoins the dying to confront death actively rather than submitting passively to its power. This instructive paradigm for the Orthodox Christians finds its precedent in a description, based in Scripture, of believers as "nightwatch people" [16, p. 7], waiting expectantly for the return of the risen Lord [Matthew 28:1; Mark 16:2; Luke 23:50-56; Luke 24:1; John 20:1]. This description encompasses the experience of the thousands of martyrs who willingly served as human torches, enduring the cruelest of physical punishments and triumphing over death. Victorious and stoical in the face of their oppressors, these believers maintained their hope and faith in Christ.

REFLECTIONS

Conceptualizing death as the ultimate gateway into fuller communion with God, Orthodox believers are continuously preparing for this spiritual journey. Drawing from the teachings and practices of the Mystical Tradition, believers build their knowledge and faith, heightening their capacity to care and their love for God, self, and others. While many details about death necessarily remain a mystery, Orthodoxy professes that by living the precepts and the examples of the Easter Faith, one gains confidence in the Resurrection, which ultimately renders an individual's death a fearless time of transition.

In a penetrating article on the social implications of this Orthodox message, Reverend Alexander Schmemann criticizes theological perspectives that try to center mortality by endorsing "secularized religion" (where God is diminished in faith or replaced by humanitarian efforts) and its psychological approaches to the therapeutic healing of illness or death [47, p. 100]. He strongly distinguishes the Christian view from outlying ideologies, arguing that death is "abnormal" [47, p. 100] and that essentially this world, having accepted and normalized death, is "lost and beyond help" [47, p. 100]. Other Orthodox Christian writers do not perceive such consideration for health and well-being as examples of a tainted, syncretistic faith, but state a concern for one's physical welfare [49-51]. At the same time, they *do* argue that the effectiveness of Christ's message amounts to *much more* than a boost to the immune system. While today clinical evidence does confirm the medical impact of strongly-held faith [52], the spiritual tradition of instilling faith, goodness, and holiness goes far beyond the mere alleviation of symptoms.

Faith in Christ is more than a supplementary, alternative medicine: it dramatically affects the way we live our whole life, the way we perceive this existence as well as the next. The truth of Christ's life transforms death for us, demystifying a horrifying biological process. For Orthodox Christians, death is not a final stage but rather a transition in the Easter Faith, leading us toward resurrection. Schmemann is correct when he refers to Biblical sources in advising the faithful, directing the reader to the example of the disciples:

> The *great joy* that the disciples felt when they saw the risen Lord, that "burning of heart" that they experienced on the way to Emmaus, was not because the mysteries of an "other world" were revealed to them, but because they saw the Lord. And He sent them to . . . proclaim not the resurrection of the dead—not a doctrine of death—but repentance and remission of sins, the new life, and Kingdom. They announced what they knew, that in Christ this *new life* had already begun, that He is the Life Eternal, the Fulfillment, the Resurrection, and the Joy of the World [47, p. 97].

For the Greek Orthodox believer, death, as the ultimate embodiment of the Easter faith, actually clarifies life, orienting our relationship toward God, ourselves, and others. The Easter faith challenges us to recognize how death surrounds us in its many forms. Moreover, the Easter faith invites us to participate in the miracle of the Resurrection that confounds death. By living in Christ, the possession of internal joy manifests itself as eternal life.

Death where is your sting

REFERENCES

1. G. L. Papadeas (ed.), *Greek Orthodox Holy and Easter Services*, G. Papadeas, Daytona Beach, Florida, 1979.
2. V. Lossky, *The Mystical Theology of the Eastern Church*, James Clarke & Co. Ltd., Cambridge, England, 1968.
3. J. Quasten, *Patrology: The Beginnings of Patristic Literature*, Spectrum Press, Utrecht, Antwags, 1996.
4. Nikodimos of the Holy Mountain and Makarios of Corinth (ed.), *The Philokalia: The Complete Text*, Volume Two, G. E. H. Palmer, P. Sherrard, and K. Ware (trans. and eds.), Faber & Faber, London, England, 1981.
5. J. Karmiris, *Synopses Tes dogmetikes didaskalios tes Orthodoxou Catholikos Ekklesesis* [The Dogmatic Teachings of the Orthodox Catholic Church]. The Theological School, Athens University, Athens, Greece, 1957.
6. St. Athanosios, *Religious of CSMV, On the Incantarnation of the Word*, Mowbray & Co., London A.R., 1982.
7. P. Nellas, *Deification in Christ: The Nature of the Human Person*, St. Vladimir's Seminary Press, Crestwood, New York, 1987.
8. G. Abydos, *At the End of Time: The Eschatological Expectations of the Church*, Holy Cross Press, Brookline, Massachusetts, 1997.
9. M. Aghiorgoussis, *In the Image of God: Studies in Scripture, Theology, and Community*, Holy Cross Press, Brookline, Massachusetts, 1999.

10. C. Androutsos, *Dogmatics,* Athens, Greece, 1907.
11. L. M. Danforth, *The Death Rituals of Rural Greece,* Princeton University Press, New Jersey, 1982.
12. St. J. Chrysostom, Homilies on First Corinthians, in *Nicene and Post-Nicene Fathers, First Series,* Volume XII, P. Schaff (ed.), Eerdmans, Grand Rapids, Michigan, 1969.
13. R. A. Moody, *Life after Life,* Bantam Books, New York, 1976.
14. N. P. Vassiliadis, *The Mystery of Death,* P. Chamberas (trans.), The Orthodox Brotherhood of Theologians, Athens, Greece, 1993.
15. H. P. Hatzopoylos (ed.), *Funeral Services According to the Rite of the Greek Orthodox Church,* Harry P. Hatzopoylos, Boston, Massachusetts, 1985.
16. R. Rutherford and T. Barn, *The Death of a Christian: The Order of Christian Funerals,* The Liturgical Press, Collegeville, Minnesota, 1989.
17. I. F. Hapgood, *Service Book of the Holy Orthodox-Catholic Apostolic Church,* Antiochian Orthodox Christian Archdiocese, Englewood, New Jersey, 1975.
18. St. Augustine, "The City of God" 22:21, Nicene and Post-Nicene Fathers, First Series, Volume II, quoted from the Sisters of the Orthodox Monastery of the Transfiguration, in *Bodily Resurrection,* Ben Lomond (ed.), Conciliar Press, California, 1999.
19. Sisters of the Orthodox Monastery of the Transfiguration, *Bodily Resurrection,* Ben Lomond (ed.), Conciliar Press, California, 1997.
20. K. Weitzmann, G. Alibegosvili, A. Volskaja, M. Chantzidakis, G. Babie, M. Alpatov, and T. Voimescu, *The Icon,* Alfred A. Knopf, New York, 1982.
21. A. Calivas, *Great Week and Pascha in the Greek Orthodox Church,* Holy Cross Orthodox Press, Brookline, Massachusetts, 1992.
22. B. Bobrinskoy, Old Age and Death: Tragedy or Blessing? *St. Vladimir's Theological Quarterly,* pp. 232-244, 1979.
23. E. Kübler-Ross, *On Death and Dying: What the Dying have to Teach Doctors, Nurses, Clergy, and their Own Families,* The Macmillan Company, London, 1969.
24. J. T. Chirban, *Interviewing in Depth: The Interactive-Relational Approach,* Sage, Thousand Oaks, California, 1996.
25. K. Piligian, Therapeutic Touch: Using Your Hands for Help or Heal, in *Health and Faith: Psychological and Religious Dimensions,* J. T. Chirban (ed.), University Press of America, Lanham, Maryland, 1991.
26. J. J. Allen, The Orthodox Pastor and the Dying, *St. Vladimir's Quarterly,* pp. 23-35, 1979.
27. J. T. Chirban (ed.), *Coping with Death and Dying: An Interdisciplinary Approach,* University Press of America, Lanham, Maryland, 1985.
28. J. T. Chirban (ed.), *Sickness or Sin? Spiritual Discernment and Differential Diagnosis,* Holy Cross Press, Brookline, Massachusetts, 2001.
29. P. Pharos, *To Penthos,* Athens, Greece, 1988.
30. H. Campenhausen, *The Fathers of the Greek Church,* Pantheon, New York, 1955.
31. J. T. Chirban, Developmental Stages in Orthodox Christianity, in *Transformations of Consciousness: Conventional and Contemplative Perspectives on Development,* K. Wilbur, J. Engler, and D. P. Brown (eds.), New Science Library, Shambala, Boston, 1986.
32. J. Bowlby, *Attachment and Loss: Vol. 1. Attachment,* Basic Books, New York, 1969.
33. D. Stern, *The Interpersonal World of the Infant: A View from Psychoanalysis and Developmental Psychology,* Basic Books, New York, 1985.

34. I. R. Byock, *Dying Well: The Prospect for Growth at the End of Life*, Riverhead Books, New York, 1997.
35. M. Field and C. Cassel (eds.), *Approaching Death: Improving Care at the End of Life*, National Academy Press, Washington, D.C., 1997.
36. R. Kastenbaum and R. Aisenberg, *The Psychology of Death*, Springer, New York, 1976.
37. T. A. Rando, *Grief, Dying, and Death: Clinical Interviews for Caregivers*, Research Press, Champaign, Illinois, 1984.
38. T. A. Rando, *Clinical Dimensions of Anticipatory Mourning: Theory and Practice in Working with the Dying, Their Loved Ones, and Their Caretakers*, Research Press, Champaign, Illinois, 2000.
39. E. Kübler-Ross, *Questions and Answers on Death and Dying*, Collier Books, New York, 1974.
40. H. G. Koenig, K. I. Pargament, and J. Nielsen, Religious Coping and Health Status in Medically Ill, Hospitalized Older Adults, *Journal of Nervous and Mental Disease, 18*, pp. 513-521, 1998.
41. J. S. Levin and H. I. Vanderpool, Religious Factors in Physical Health and the Prevention of Illness, *Prevention in Human Services, 9*, pp. 41-64, 1991.
42. S. Sethi and M. E. P. Seligman, Optimism and Fundamentalism, *Psychological Science, 4*, pp. 256-259, 1993.
43. A. M. Coniaris, *Christ's Comfort for Those Who Sorrow: Messages of Hope for Those Who Have Lost Loved Ones*, Light and Life Publishing Company, Minneapolis, Minnesota, 1978.
44. A. M. Coniaris, *61 Talks for Orthodox Funerals*, Light and Life Publishing Company, Minneapolis, Minnesota, 1969.
45. A. M. Coniaris, *Surviving the Loss of a Loved One*, Light and Life Publishing Company, Minneapolis, Minnesota, 1982.
46. S. Papakostas, *For the Hours of Pain*, L. J. Newville (trans.), ZOE Brotherhood of Theologians, Athens, Greece, 1967.
47. A. Schmemann, *For the Life of This World: Sacraments and Orthodoxy*, St. Vladimir's Press, Crestwood, New York, 1973.
48. S. Harakas, *Health and Medicine in the Eastern Orthodox Tradition*, Crossroad, New York, 1990.
49. D. Constantelos, The Interface of Medicine and Religion, in *Health and Faith: Medical, Psychological and Religious Dimensions*, J. T. Chirban (ed.), University Press of America, Lanham, Maryland, 1991.
50. J. T. Chirban, The Power of Medicine, Psychology, and Religion, in *Healing*, J. T. Chirban (ed.), Holy Cross Press, Brookline, Maaaschusetts, 1991.
51. J. T. Chirban, Healing and Spirituality, in *Health and Faith: Medical, Psychological, and Religious Dimensions*, J. T. Chirban (ed.), University Press of America, Lanham, Maryland, 1991.
52. T. G. Plante and A. C. Sherman, *Faith and Healing Psychology: Exploring the Impact on Health of Religion and Spirituality*, Guilford, New York, 2001.

CHAPTER 7

Spirituality, Protestantism, and Death

Dennis Klass

This volume is about *spirituality* and death. This chapter is about a *religion*, Protestantism. As a beginning, we ought to spend a moment thinking about the relationship between *spirituality* and *religion*.

SPIRITUALITY AND RELIGION

The *spiritual* is a dimension of our humanness. Most dimensions of our humanness are not uniquely human. We share with all matter the quality of physical existence, for we have weight, chemical composition, and spatial relationship to all other hunks of matter. We share with all living beings the processes of reproduction and adaptation to our environment. We share with vertebrates a sense of bonding with others of our species as well as a need to guard ourselves from some other members of our own species and from some other species. We share with many animals consciousness of our environment, of our selves within that environment, of our own pain, and, sometimes, of the pain of others. Spirituality, however, probably is limited to our earlier ancestors, *homo habilis* and *homo erectus*, who had tools and fire, and to ourselves, *homo sapiens*.

Like *life, spirituality* is not a thing or a state of being, but is a process of interaction. Like *consciousness, spirituality* is an awareness of relationship. As consciousness is an awareness of ourselves in relation to objects of our senses, spirituality is an awareness of a relationship to that which is beyond our senses. We know our spirituality in the awe we feel, as Kant told us, when we stare into the

---

*The chapter was originally published in *Death and Spirituality*, K. A. Doka and J. D. Morgan (eds.), Baywood, Amityville, New York, 1993.

vastness of the starry sky above and in the righteousness we feel when we act against our own immediate advantage and follow, instead, the moral law within. We know our spirituality when we feel the boundaries of our individual ego soften and we know the truth that is in us is also out there: or in Christian terms, when we know that the reality in our hearts is also the reality of the creator of heaven and earth; or in Buddhist terms, when we know that the separateness of the reality I call my "I" is an illusion.

Spirituality is experienced at the meeting point, or as some would say, the merging point, between our self and that which we usually feel is not our self. D. W. Winnicott told of a realm of experience which is both inner experience and outer experience [1]. It is like music which is a series of notes mathematically related, but which, when we are open to it, feels like flight in our soul. Ken Wilber tells us that we know the spiritual when we break through the boundaries of our ordinary self and come into contact with that which used to feel only outside ourselves [2].

And *death* seems the end of that spirituality, for it would be the end of life, of consciousness, of contact with the eternal. To be sure, spiritual teachers have often talked of death in a metaphoric sense as necessary to the spiritual life: "Unless you die and are born again you are not fit for the Kingdom of Heaven." But death as a metaphor is quite different from death as a physical, bloody, painful reality. Yet the spiritual is our aid and comfort in the face of death, for it is our sense of connection with that which is beyond the limitations of this physical and conscious self. To understand the lived relationship of the spiritual to death we must turn to *religion*, for there is no spiritual to be lived in the abstract. The spiritual, like the soul, must wear a body if we are to see it; the body is *religion*.

Religion is a cultural institution. It exists in a particular form in a particular place and changes over time. In many ways, the religion to which we belong is an accident of birth. A Presbyterian elder in the suburban St. Louis would have been of a quite different religion if he had been born in Boston in 1670, and of a very different religion had he lived in South America during the time of the Inca civilization. Religions bind communities together in shared symbols, ritual, myth, and ethical norms.

At best, the symbols, myth, ritual, and ethics of a religion provide the means by which the spiritual may be channeled and nurtured. And at their beginnings, all religions seem to have been the effect of a burst of spirituality. But there is another side as well. Religion is also a way to kill the spirit and turn it into letter. Religious symbols, myths, rituals, and ethics often become ends in themselves, preserved and passed on for the habitual comfort or social advantage they afford the pious. Still, no matter now hypocritical it seems to the outsider, religion always seems genuine to those who order their lives by its map, so in this chapter we shall treat religion with the respect due to spirituality.

We turn now to one religion, *Protestantism*. At its best, it provides its members a map by which their spiritual encounter with death can be navigated. At its worst, it has offered dead-end channels or rocky shoals for those who have tried to follow its charts. We will try to give a brief overview of its map. The metaphor of religion as a navigational chart is appropriate for Protestantism, for the image of the individual making his or her way through a difficult passage is at the heart of the Protestant view of life. One well-known Protestant hymn reads:

Jesus, Savior, pilot me
Over life's tempestuous sea;
Unknown waves before me roll,
Hiding rock and treacherous shaol.
Chart and compass come from thee.
Jesus, Savior, pilot me.

In some ways, it is difficult to distinguish the spirituality of Protestantism from the general spirituality in North American civil religion, for U.S. and English Canadian culture was born out of Protestantism. European settlement came from the Protestant sections of Europe. When Catholics and Jews came in sufficient numbers to do so, they started their own schools for their children, for it seemed to them that the "public" schools were Protestant. For some of the Protestant settlers, North America was to be the proving ground of their ideas. They would found a "city on a hill" for all the world to see the perfect society of men which could be built on Protestant principles. Most scholarship on contemporary North America culture finds that the "protestant hegemony" is over. Often the election of Catholic John Kennedy as president is cited as a date to mark the end of the dominance of Protestantism. But still, for the first three and a half centuries, North American politics, art, economics, and home life grew out of the Protestant heritage. The intellectual questions grew from Protestant soil.

In this chapter, we will try to stick to Protestantism as it has provided forms for the spiritual dimension of humanness. But we will bear in mind that the themes we will see in Protestantism, such as the importance of the individual and the individual's immediate access to God, are often the unexamined assumptions of a wide range of spiritual alternatives which have moved out of the church but remain essentially Protestant in their worldview.

AN OVERVIEW OF PROTESTANTISM

In its very soul, Protestantism is a diverse and fragmented religious tradition, for in its beginning it was a protest against the standing order; and throughout its history, renewed protests ended in the creation of new schools, denominations, and movements. Historically we think of Protestantism as beginning when Martin Luther protested against the corruption of the Catholic indulgence system or when John Calvin set up his theocratic government in Geneva, or perhaps when the anabaptist communities vowed to live the simple communal life they found in the New Testament. We can also think of Protestantism beginning with a change in historical consciousness, *individualism*, and with a change in technology, the invention of the *printing press*. As a way of outlining the diversity of origin and historical development, we will look at a series of interrelating themes in Protestantism: its individualism, its view of authority, its understanding of God, its understanding of the God/person relationship, and its organization of the community of believers.

Individualism

For whatever reasons, beginning about 1300, Europeans began, for the first time since antiquity, to feel themselves to have an individual soul whose destiny was their individual responsibility. By 1200, Western Christianity had recovered from the fall of Roman Civilization, and from its split from the Eastern Church. Western Christianity had made accommodation to the triumph of Islam in most of Christianity's old territory. The papacy had asserted spiritual and temporal powers, worked out methods of dominating kings and emperors, and tamed the monastic piety into orders obedient to Rome. Northern Europe began to feel a new autonomy. Rome seemed a long way away. Latin did not seem to fit the world as did the native tongues. The kings and nobles did not like the heavy hand of the church restricting their powers. At the same time, trade was increasing and serfs were being freed. A new class of merchants emerged whose wealth depended on commerce, not on the land as did the wealth of the nobility. In some places, this new class gained control of their own political lives. In Geneva, after a series of other arrangements, the Town Council, an elected body, was free from any interference from the nobility and from the church.

Individuals began to have more of a sense of themselves apart from their collective identifications. They began to feel that there was a "me" who is important in my own right, and that "my life" counts in the eyes of God and in my eyes. Phillipe Ariés notes that the period saw a change in the way death was understood. Earlier, he argues, death had been tamed, for it was a part of the natural processes and could be made acceptable by the rituals provided by the church. With the sense that "I am an individual," death became a crisis which Ariés names, "My Death" [3].

People became concerned with the destiny of their own soul. Among the earliest indications of this development was a flood of visions akin to the present near death experiences [4]. Individuals who thought themselves as just back from the edge of death reported that their soul journeyed to another world where they were judged by the quality of the life they had led on earth. From those visions, an idea of the after-life developed rather fully. It included a Heaven where the souls of good people went and a Hell where the souls of sinners went. We can see another indication of this rise of concern with the individual's death in the woodcuts of the dance of death. Everyone, regardless of their station in this life, must dance their individual dance with the smiling skeleton.

The new autonomous individuals began to trust their own reason and conscience to test religious truths. With the rediscovery of the ancient philosophers, the new knowledge of the world gained by expanded trade, and the establishment of independent universities, learning moved out of the narrow, deductive limitations imposed by scholasticism. With intellectual autonomy, science as we know it now began to develop, first as practical experiment with new tools for competitive advantage in the rapidly developing commercial world, and later as the human mind seeking to comprehend nature. Astrology gave way to astronomy and later alchemy to chemistry. We already feel ourselves in modernity when in 1408 the early reformer John Huss, in an address at the University of Prague, said:

> From the beginning of my studies, I have made it a rule whenever I found a better opinion on any matter, gladly and without a struggle to give up the old one, being well aware that what we know is vastly less than what we do not know [5, p. 39].

Religious Authority

The introduction of the printing press in the late medieval world made as much difference in the way humans processed information as the introductions of the computer and satellite television are making in ours. Hand copied manuscripts were usually read aloud. Their use could be controlled. With the rise of mass reading, the eye replaced the ear as the primary sense that gathered abstract information. The linear thinking described by McLuhan replaced the more uncritical holistic thinking of the oral world. A text could be discussed, read again, and compared to other texts in the privacy of the home. The Bible, translated into the languages of the people, could be an authority against which to judge all other authority. It could be the authority for the new autonomous individual and it could be the authority on which to base the political struggles against the Pope. The Word was not the Body of Christ which was the church. The Word was on the page. The people could read it and search for their own truth; and they would then be responsible for that truth as they stood alone and autonomous before the Judgment Seat.

While the Bible is in theory available to each believer to interpret according to his/her own faith and reason, the history of Protestantism can largely be read as a history of conflict, often bitter, about the correct interpretation of the Bible. The major conflict today is over the nature of the revelation in the Bible. Conservatives hold that the Bible was given word-for-word by God and is therefore without error and should be interpreted literally. Liberals tend to hold that the Bible is a product of a historical process, and that it should be interpreted in light of its time and in light of human scientific reason.

God

Just as the Protestant could not feel the spiritual outside of his/her sense of unique individuality, neither could the Protestant experience the spiritual outside of a sense that there is one God who is the Father in Heaven. God is understood to be a single being who existed at the beginning of time, created the world, spoke to his people through the law and prophets of the Old Testament, and, especially, who came to earth as Jesus, who was God in human form. God remains for Protestantism a God who is transcendent, creator, judge, and redeemer. Although Protestantism came into being almost at the same time as astronomy proclaimed a heliocentric solar system rather than an earth surrounded by crystal spheres, the new science did not affect the basic cosmology which Protestantism brought from its Catholic roots. The God of the Protestants remained the Heavenly Father and the reformers firmly remained His children. This God had a history. He created the world. He made Adam and Eve and drove them out of the Garden when they tried to usurp His place by knowing Good and Evil. He had chosen the people of Israel to be His own and given them the Law through Moses when He had led them to their promised land. He had reproved His people by the prophets when they did evil. And finally, though modern revisionists often wish otherwise, the reformers believed that God had withdrawn his choice from the Israelites (now called Jews) and had sent his son in the form of a man, Jesus. Jesus was sinless, but died to take away the sins of all humans. After Jesus died, he rose from the dead and is now in heaven. All who believed in him were now the chosen people and at death, they would also rise and join him.

The experience of God has been described in many ways in the history of Protestantism, but for the most part it remains within the experience of a child with a parent. Jesus used the word "Abba" when addressing God. It literally means "daddy." Like a parent, God is felt to be all powerful and all knowing. Protestant founder Martin Luther wrote a hymn, "A mighty fortress is our God, a bulwark never failing." God is a being who the believer can trust as a child trusts a parent, and in return God cares for the believer. Jesus once asked what parent whose child asked for bread would give a stone. So God the father should be experienced as caring for the believer. Fredrick Schliermacher distilled the experience of the Protestant with God as "the feeling of absolute dependence." Another Protestant, Rudolph Otto, said the experience of God is the *Mysterium Tremendum* made up of awe, fascination, fear, and a sense of belonging.

Because the presence of God is offered by Protestantism as so immediate, the absence of God can be felt just as strongly. The individual can feel a lack of autonomy if God is not there for support. The plaintive gospel hymn "I need thee every hour" and the joyful claim of "Leaning, leaning, leaning on the everlasting arms" point to the potential terror that could be felt were the everlasting arms to fail or one's hour of need be unmet.

Priesthood of All Believers

In a radical sense, the understanding of access to God changed for the autonomous individuals of Protestantism. Each Protestant has a direct and personal relationship with God unmediated by priest or sacrament. The reformers believed that salvation was to be had only by faith and the only authority was scripture. They removed the church as the mediating institution between humans and God. The idea of sainthood changed in Protestantism. In some places, statues of saints were smashed. No longer could the believer find a saint who could grant special favors or insure that petitions would get through to God. In some later Protestantism, the "saints" became a word that referred to believers (as when they "go marching in").

The ritual aspect of worship was simplified by the early reformers as native languages were substituted for Latin, so the action no longer seemed far off and removed from the life of the worshipper. The medieval church had developed a doctrine that the bread and wine of the mass were turned into actual body and blood of Christ on the altar. In language which seems strange to us today, Luther argued for "consubstantiation" rather than the Catholic "transubstantiation." But for most Protestants such fine distinctions were not enough and the bread and wine which Jesus had shared with his disciples on the night before he was executed became a meal which the community of believers shared with each other in memory of Jesus. For many Protestants, the altar became a table. We can see the simplification of worship in the clean and unadorned lines of the New England "meeting house." The central focus is a pulpit. From there the Word was preached to members of the community who sit in pews. In front of the pulpit is a small table which may be pulled out so the minister and deacons can sit behind it as the sacrament is shared. The human-scale table replaced the awe-inspiring altar.

Nothing stands between the believer and God. Indeed, the direct access to God became the center of much Protestantism. Luther's exposition of the commandment "You shall have no other gods," begins with:

> A god is that to which we look for all good and in which we find refuge in every time of need. To have a god is nothing else than to trust and believe in him with our whole heart. As I have often said, the trust and faith of the heart alone make both God and an idol. If your faith and trust are right, then your God is the true God. On the other hand, if your trust is false and wrong, then you have not the true God. For these two belong together, faith and God. That to which your heart clings and entrusts itself is, I say, really your God [6, p. 9].

Later evangelical Americans would not admit anyone as saved until they could individually testify that they had a "personal relationship" with God. There is no sense in the Protestant soul that any other person or office has special access to God. God can be experienced in the life and in the heart of the individual. Prayers are not directed toward saints who have closer access to God. Confession may be made directly to God and forgiveness may be received directly from God. A priest is not needed to mediate the confession-forgiveness process. It is the individual and the individual's relationship with the divine which is important. As the spiritual says, "It's a me; it's a me; it's a me, Oh Lord, standing in the need of prayer."

But if God be a judgmental parent, then the individual stands in terror with no protection before the wrath. Jonathan Edwards' sermon "Sinners in the Hands of an Angry God" has a flavor of the more frightening side of the idea of priesthood of all believers:

> The God that holds you over the pit of hell, much as one holds a spider, or some loathsome insect over the fire, abhors you, and is dreadfully provoked; his wrath towards you burns like fire, he looks upon you as worthy of nothing else, but to be cast into the fire; he is of purer eyes than to bear to have you in his sight; you are ten thousand times more abominable in his eyes, than the most hateful venomous serpent is in ours. You have offended him infinitely more than ever a stubborn rebel did his prince; and yet it is nothing but his hand that holds you from falling into the fire every moment [7, p. 159].

Since all were equal before God, all were responsible for God's work. The clergy became preachers and teachers of the Word. But preaching and teaching are not accepted automatically. Criticizing the minister's sermon is often a favorite activity among Protestants. The goal of preaching and teaching is to enable an individual believer to live out his or her life in the faith, for the important acting in Protestantism is not the sacrament in church, but the individual life in the world. Thus, the Protestant soul is often called to higher than average living. As the hymn says:

> Rise up, oh men of God.
> Have done with lesser things.
> Give heart and soul and mind and strength
> To serve the King of Kings.

The priesthood of believers means that each individual has direct access to God, so it would seem that the gap between man and God is closed, and so it seemed to the early reformers. But it is difficult to relate directly to God, for He is maker of heaven and earth, who was before all things and will be after all things. This God not only protects, but also judges. Soren Kierkegaard, the Protestant existentialist, described worship as a theater [8]. The preacher is the prompter in the wings; the individual worshipper in on stage; and God is the audience. Such lonely self consciousness has often been the hallmark of the Protestant inner life, especially among the intellectuals (see for example, Dag Hammarskjold [9]).

Most Protestants in the pew, however, would be uncomfortable with Kierkegaard's stage or on Edward's spider thread. They find it easier to focus on Jesus, God in human form with whom one may have personal attachment.

I've found a friend, O such a friend!
He loved me ere I knew him.
He drew me with the chords of love
And thus he bound me to him.

Thus Protestantism maintains a tension between a sense of aloneness and unworthiness in the face of God the father and a sense of immediate presence of the God who came as Jesus. In the high moments of Protestant experience, the tension is resolved in *justification* or *atonement* as the individual feels him or herself to be known, to be called, and to respond. A well-known account of one of those very Protestant moments was written by John Newton:

Amazing Grace, how sweet the sound
That saved a wretch like me!
I once was lost, but now I'm found;
Was blind, but now I see.

The individual alone encounters the infinity of the universe and the depth of his/her own soul. Such a disparity produces the feelings of fear, guilt, and smallness. When those feelings are overcome, the individual knows him/herself to be safe, forgiven, and important in God's eyes.

The Community of Believers

If the individual is radically alone in the presence of God, the individual need not be alone in human society. In Protestantism, the church became a voluntary association of believers. Humans needed an institution in which they could study the Word, and gather to worship. This varies a good deal from place to place, but in many groups which are important to the development of North American Protestantism, church membership was a voluntary act, made in a public confession of belief and public testimony of an inner experience.

Thus the membership the Protestant feels is a particular membership. While a few clergy or very active laypeople might feel themselves affiliated with other believers around the world, the Protestant community of reference is, for the most part, a local *congregation* or a particular *denomination*. The church is a series of interpersonal relationships. The traditions of moral correctness and upright behavior are vested in senior matriarchs of the congregation whose approval or disapproval is communicated through a network of family and organizational relationships. If the Protestant stands alone before God in his inner faith, the Protestant stands before the congregation in the moral and behavioral life. For this reason, Protestant congregations tend to be split along racial, ethnic, and social class lines. While the ideal held by the official theology is of the inclusiveness of humanity and while the Sunday School children are taught to sing, "Red and yellow, black and white, all are precious in His sight," Black folk tend to congregate with Black folk and White folk with Whites, while rich and poor each have their own church. The feeling, then, is being with one's own. The congregation is often referred to as a family. The community gathering for a hot-dish supper may be as important as the community gathering to study the Word. The communal singing in worship blends into communal singing of "spirituals" for the joy of "fellowship." Larger congregations are divided into smaller groups of young people, young married, singles, middle-aged couples, men's fellowships, and women's guilds.

DEATH, SALVATION, AND SUFFERING

Death is a challenge to Protestant spirituality, first because it opens the possibility that the individual might not survive death. That challenge is answered in Protestantism in the theme of salvation. Second, death is a challenge because it often raises the problem of evil and the problem of meaningfulness of suffering. We will deal first with the salvation, then with the issue of suffering.

Salvation

In the individualistic spirituality of Protestantism, death raises the possibility that the individual ends with the demise of the physical. For Protestants, the answer to death is salvation. Indeed, the goal of Protestant religion is salvation. At its simplest, the idea is that the human is born into a condition of damnable sinfulness because Adam and Eve disobeyed God and lost their original goodness. Protestants of most theological stripes have preached that God made salvation possible because He became human in Jesus, who was sinless. Jesus' dying and rising from the dead means that those who participate in Jesus' death and resurrection no longer participate in the sinful human nature and thus are fit for the Kingdom of God.

Christianity was founded in a world which had competing ideas of the new world. In the exile (598-521, BCE) the hope of the Jewish people shifted from a this-worldly nationalism to a vision of a perfect world beyond history. We see this primarily in the latter sections of Ezekiel in the Old Testament. But some also looked to a perfect world in a New Jerusalem on an Earth transformed by the intervention of God. There was also the idea that each individual has two bodies, one physical and one spiritual. Within this tradition, St. Paul explained, "So it is with the resurrection of the dead. . . . It is sown a physical body, it is raised a spiritual body. If there is a physical body, there is also a spiritual body" [I Corinthians 15:42-44]. Both Jesus and Paul speak at different times as if the resurrection of the dead will come on earth after a final act of God and also as if there is a Heaven and Hell which occurs immediately after the death of the individual. Most of the possibilities which might arise from this mixture of competing ideas have been emphasized at one time or another in various Protestant groups.

Over the history of Protestantism, the actual possibility and nature of salvation has varied considerably. Indeed, one of the conflicts of the English reformation was whether the burial service in the prayer book should omit the words "sure and certain" in the line "we therefore commit his body to the ground in the sure and certain hope of resurrection to eternal life" [10, p. 73]. The Calvinists, best known in America as the Puritans, thought that God rightly damned everyone, for no one deserved to be saved. But from his love, God elected a few and predestined them for a heavenly life after death. One could never be sure, however, that one was a member of this select few, so one had constantly to be monitoring one's thoughts and actions for vestiges of the lower man. On the other hand, among the Pentecostals, salvation is self-evident, for God's primary activity in the present world is as the Holy Spirit who will come to anyone who opens the self to the Spirit. One needs to "Give your heart to Jesus," and the Holy Spirit will enter the person. Pentecostals know when the Spirit has possessed a believer, for the Spirit speaks through them in the phenomenon of glossolalia, "speaking in tongues." Thus, so long as one still believes and so long as the spiritual gift of tongues lasts, one can be sure of a place in heaven.

Contemporary conservative or evangelical Protestants make salvation the center of their organizational life. The prime reason for the church is to spread the Word and provide opportunities for people's salvation. Most religious programs on television are put on by conservatives in the service of saving souls. For liberals, on the other hand, salvation seems more elusive. Since liberals accept a greater role for human reason, the experience of salvation is less likely to be highly emotional. Rather, a liberal is more likely to gain conviction over a longer period of time. Further, liberals are less likely to believe that God would damn anyone to Hell, so the question of what is one "saved from" and "saved to" is somewhat more difficult to articulate. In the face of death, both the liberal and conservative come against the test of their faith. For the liberal, the test may be whether anything is known surely enough to overcome the pain, doubt, and fear of death. For the conservative, the test is whether the certainty, which was supported by the church community and which often brought higher social status in the church community, can now hold in the very solitary experience of dying.

Salvation has both the *eschatological* and an *ethical* dimension. The eschatological idea is that there is another world or age after this one. Jesus' teaching that the Kingdom is at hand, that it is like a mustard seed or the yeast in the dough, has led liberal scholars to the idea of "realized" eschatology—that the Kingdom of God is actually a present reality. But for most Protestants in the pew, salvation has a future orientation. Throughout Protestant history, there have been groups which have read the Bible as a guide to present history and have predicted that the Kingdom of God will be an event on earth, that it is coming soon, and that the dead will be raised and judged as the sinners are damned forever. But too many predictions about the end of time dull the nerves. Individually, people bet on the future by marrying and having children. They grow old, get sick, and know that they will probably die before history ends. Several Protestant denominations had begun with the claim that the end of history was coming soon, but as the first generation passed on, the churches became more comfortable in the present.

The basic teaching in the New Testament is an eschatological understanding of history, with a new age—a new relationship of humans to God; but for most Protestants in the pew, the teachings about the Kingdom of God and a "new world is happening" come down to the question, "What happens to me after I die?" It is about what will happen to the individual after death.

The ethical dimension of salvation determines the answer, because the autonomous individual of Protestantism is responsible for the moral quality of life lived on earth. If one is saved, it is salvation to a more moral and ethical life than that of the sinner. That moral life in this world is an indication that the individual is qualified for Heaven in the afterlife. The sins which have been of most concern to Protestants are those which are immediately applicable to the autonomous individual's decision. In general, Protestants have been more concerned with sins which are private and personal than with sins which are public and corporate. Thus, Protestants are more likely to fear God's judgment for extra-marital sex or thoughts about extra-marital sex, than they fear God's judgment because they work for a corporation which pollutes the environment.

The question of how strict a judge God will be has been a matter of disagreement among Protestants throughout their history. All Protestants would probably agree that there is a Heaven. Protestant funeral sermons offer a better world after this one. At times Protestant literature has been rather detailed in its description of the world after death. For example, in the consolation literature of the middle 19th century United States, the writers seemed to know the streets and houses of heaven as well as they knew their own neighborhood. Usually, however, Protestants have been content to offer Heaven, but leave the details to the individual imagination and later experience.

Hell, the other possibility for a life after death, brings considerably more disagreement among Protestants. For some, there cannot be a just God without Hell, for there is no purpose in leading a moral life if there is no punishment for the immoral. For others, however, the idea of a loving God seems to exclude the idea that God would leave anyone out of heaven. At present, those for whom Hell is a live possibility seem outnumbered by those for whom Heaven is the only possible destination they can imagine for themselves and for those they love. Still, in counseling we see people for whom the fear of death is linked to fear of punishment for real or imagined shortcomings.

It would seem that the more sure a person is that there is life after death and that the soul is bound for heaven, the more the shock of death would be softened. If the soul will be in heaven, death is not final; it is just a temporary separation. And for some people, heaven seems a sure thing. But for most Protestants, heaven is known in hope, not in guarantee, so the anxiety at one's own death can only be partly assuaged by belief.

If we ask what kind of experiences do Protestants bring to their hope of an afterlife, we find phenomena which sometimes seem surer than the data-free speculation about God's judgment and the existence of Hell. There is a difference between the life-after-death people experience when others die and the life-after-death we hope for in our own death. Almost everyone in my study of parents whose children have died experiences their child in heaven [11]. We found no parents with a sense of their child in Hell. I know of no research in which contemporary people experience significant others who have died as in Hell. For those in the study with active prayer lives, when they experience the presence of God, they also experience the presence of the child who had died. When others feel the wonder of the natural world, they also feel the presence of their child. In the study, we also found several parents who said that intellectually they did not believe in an afterlife, but still they felt in touch with a dead child who seemed to be in heaven. For many people, the inner representations of everyone they had grieved were joined. It is not unusual for people to think of someone dying and going to heaven to join another significant person who has died. Thus, the belief in an afterlife holds together experiences of memory, a sense of presence, a sense of the enduring quality of a person who has died, and a sense of the human community which we have shared. These experiences are strongly supported in Protestantism, though the theology is apt to be softer than the sentiment. The experiences which support the belief in the afterlife have little place in the prevailing theology of most Protestants, but still, they remain a strong part of the resolution of grief and are supported within the practical life of a Protestant congregation.

For the people facing their own death, afterlife may be somewhat harder to verify. The specific theological issue that began the Protestant reformation was the sale of indulgences, a kind of sacramental coupon redeemable at death. The Catholic church had provided prayers and masses for the dead which would insure heaven. The sacrament of last rites could absolve dying persons of their sins and give a guarantee of heaven. The sacrament of confession and penance could give immediate assurance of the soul's worthiness for a good afterlife. But the Protestant faces death with none of those aids. The individual faces the cosmos alone.

For those whom William James called the "sick soul"—who feel that the world and themselves are not right and that evil may have the final innings—death may hold the terror that there is nothing after life [12]. Or they may feel the judgment they face in the same way Kierkegaard described the individual on the stage with God as an audience. This individual Protestant alone with death and with God may well have experiences upon which to draw which provide what Wordsworth called "intimations of immortality." A saving experience where God seemed personal and close may very well be enough to last a lifetime so that on the deathbed, the believer may still know the certainty of the "hour I first believed."

For others, however, an untimely death and great suffering may very well make sure certainty seem dim indeed.

For those whom James called the "healthy minded," life seems basically good and their life in conformity to prevailing ethical standards seems blessed by God. The healthy minded have lived with a sense of blessedness all their lives, so the blessing of heaven, if death be acceptable, seems a natural extension of their habitual way of living.

All religious belief is held as part of the individual's affiliation with the community; that is, we verify our mental world by holding much the same world as the community in which we are members. If the individual is in synch with the community—that there is a heaven and that the individual's life merits entry—and if the individual feels the community bonds as he or she dies, then the bond with God can be maintained easier. But if the individual is out of synch with the community, the bond with God may be less sure. Except for the faith in the center of the soul and the bonds with the community of faith, Protestantism provides few certainties with which to face the terror of one's own death.

The Problem of Evil and the Meaningfulness of Suffering

Salvation answers the challenge death presents that the individual may end with the end of the physical body. The second challenge death presents is the problem of evil and the potential meaninglessness of suffering. The problem of evil may be defined simply as: Does the spiritual force work for good, especially my good? The problem of the meaningfulness of suffering is an important subset of the problem of evil. It may be simply defined as: Does the physical, social, and psychological pain I experience have any positive value?

Because the question of evil and the meaningfulness of suffering are so central a challenge to the spiritual, religions make the issues central to their teachings. The first noble truth in Buddhism is that "All life is suffering." Suffering is in the core of Protestant teaching. Jesus died a painful death on a cross. The broken body and shed blood are central themes in Protestant preaching. Yet it is not easy for any believer to bring the teaching of religion to bear as the pain of bone cancer does not respond to the medication. Overcoming evil is at the core of the Protestant teaching. Jesus rose from the dead, so death, sin, and the devil have been overcome. Yet the resurrection of the Son of God may be scant solace to parents who stand at the bedside of their teen-age son lying brain-dead from a self-inflicted gunshot wound. We will look at the means Protestantism has to meet this challenge.

Evil

Protestantism has rather mixed answers to the problem of evil. For most of the first two centuries of Protestantism, there was little question in anyone's mind that the Devil did exist, that evil spirits could be loose in the world, and that the Protestant needed to be wary. Luther thought he was personally beset by devils. He wrote the hymn words:

For still our ancient foe
Doth seek to work us woe.
His craft and power are great
And armed with cruel hate.
On earth is not his equal.

There are still a good many Protestants for whom evil is an active and personal force in their world. They believe that there is a large cult of devil worshippers who speak in the lyrics of heavy metal rock songs. Symbols like the '60s peace symbol and the ancient Egyptian life symbol are displayed and solemnly pronounced the marks of Satanic cults. Obviously, there is a cultural need for such Protestant theology, for these ideas get rather full airing in the mass media.

Another Protestant answer to the presence of death and suffering is that these came into the world as a result and as a punishment for humanity's disobedience and sin. "The wages of sin is death," said St. Paul. One of the possibilities of faith is that the faithful no longer need fear God's extracting those wages. Protestantism's God is a powerful protective father who is said to count the hairs of the believer's head and know when the sparrow falls. There is a kind of contract in the belief of many people that if they are good, then God will protect them personally from harm. The reverse of that contract is that harm comes to those who have not been good. There are few people who, when they are diagnosed with a serious illness do not spend at least moments considering whether they are being punished for some real or imagined shortcoming.

For most moderate and liberal Protestants, however much their necks tingle at reports of satanic rites and however much they might wonder about their sins being punished, the problem of evil is more likely to be cast as a problem of the limitation of the power of God; that is, moderate and liberal Protestantism has tended to move to an old tradition which sees evil as the absence of good, just as cold is the absence of heat. In matters of suffering and death, good tends to be defined as "good for me." When we are in pain, we tend not to care that as a severe infection is harming one human, it is also the flowering of bacterial civilization. Though written by a Jewish Rabbi, Harold Kushner's book *When Bad Things Happen to Good People* has been widely read by Protestants trying to understand why bad things are happening to them [13]. He argues that there is a God, but that God's omnipotence is limited. That is, God does not interfere with natural laws; so that if two cars are headed toward each other at 60 miles per hour, the natural laws by which the universe is sustained cannot be abridged for the sake of the people in those cars. Obviously, those who find comfort in the limitation of God's omnipotence are also likely to believe in a more active and responsible role for humans. If God is not all powerful, many other questions of faith and salvation must be reworked if the theology of the belief system is to be kept consistent. Most people, however, seem not to need a great deal of consistency in their working theology.

Suffering

Suffering is physical as we experience our body's pain or incapacity. It is social as we experience the loneliness of being isolated from family and community. It is psychological as we feel the accusations of shortcomings from our conscience and memory. Obviously, there are many kinds of suffering from the economic devastation of homelessness to the social outcast status of the homosexual to the uncontrolled inner conflict of schizophrenia. But this volume is about death and dying, so we will limit ourselves. Each year I survey may class about what frightens them about death. The answer for most is that death itself is less frightening than dying. When I ask what is worse than death, the majority speak of long, unrelenting suffering or of losing bodily function without a full loss of consciousness. Most people in the modern world would like a quick death, or at least a painless one.

Quick and painless deaths are a rarity. For example, the trajectory of a terminal cancer is several months to several years with a cycle of hope and dashed hope, with a gradual loss of bodily functions, and with treatment which may bring as much pain as the disease. Suffering is difficult for the person dying and is difficult for family and friends.

Some of the answer to the problem of suffering is found in the answer to the general problem of evil: Why does it happen? But the more immediate problem of suffering is: How shall I live through it? How shall I play the role? How do I do this? We do not live life as if no one had ever lived before. We use models on which to pattern parts of our lives: a good father is a model for our own parenting; a sports hero is our model for gracious winning and losing. Protestantism has basically two models for suffering. Those models are personified by *Job* and *Jesus*.

Job is the central character of a story in the Old Testament which deals with whether faith in God is dependent on God providing the believer with the good life. Satan, in this story, is God's debating opponent rather than the personification of evil. Satan says the only reason Job is faithful is that Job and his family are healthy and he is rich. Satan challenges God, "Put forth thy hand now and touch all that he has, he will curse thee to thy face" [Job 2:11]. God takes the challenge and with the proviso that Job not die, allows the destruction of Job's crops, livestock, and finally his children. Then Job gets sores all over his body and he sits in the ashes scraping the sores with a broken piece of pottery. Then begins a long series of dialogues first between Job and his wife, then between Job and three friends, then between Job and one younger friend, and finally between God and Job. All the dialogues center on the question: Should Job accuse God for what has happened to him? Or should Job accept responsibility for his suffering? Job refuses to admit that he did anything to deserve his condition:

> My foot has held fast to his steps;
> I have kept his way and have not turned aside.
> I have not departed from the commandment of his lips [Job 23:11-12].

But it is not enough for Job to find himself righteous, the later arguments of the story insist that the sufferer must also find God is without fault even though He created a world that included Job's suffering. Near the end of the story, God, himself, speaks out of a whirlwind, "Where were you when I laid the foundations of the earth?" [Job 38:1]. God then goes on at some length showing that He has power and knowledge, neither of which Job has. Job's right to question God is denied, for it is only for God to question Job. God says to Job:

> I will question you, and you will declare to me.
> Will you even put me in the wrong?
> Will you condemn me that you may be justified [Job 40: 7-8]?

At the end, Job gives up any claim to his own goodness and he gives up any claim to understanding why this is happening. As he understands that only God knows the truth and only God has the power to understand, Job sees the truth about Man's relationship to God:

> I know that thou canst do all things,
> and that no purpose of thine can be thwarted
> Therefore I have uttered what I did not understand,
> things too wonderful for me, which I did not know
> I had heard of thee by the hearing of the ear,
> but now my eye sees thee;
> Therefore I despire myself
> and repent in dust and ashes [Job 42:2-6].

With that confession, the argument is won, for God has proved to Satan that Job's faith does not depend on Job's being rich and healthy. To give the story a happy ending, Job's family and possessions are restored.

In Job's model, the Protestant endures suffering without the loss of faith because the Protestant has no claim of righteousness or goodness on his or her own account, and because any answers about why and to whom suffering comes are human answers which do not count. Though Job seems not to know it in the story, his sufferings happened merely to settle an argument between Satan and God. Yet even this is discounted, because it is not for Job to understand; it is for Job to be faithful. When Job stops asking questions, stops thinking that humans can know the answers, then Job moves to a new level of faith, for before he had "heard of thee by the hearing of the ear, but now my eye sees thee."

The high theology and philosophy of Job is encapsulated for Protestants in the pew by the phrase "the patience of Job," for it is not the arguments which need to be understood in the face of suffering. The patient is to endure as Job did. Job is an oft-used model for Protestants. The mere fact of endurance without complaint against God and without self righteousness is proof of faith and therefore proof of the suffering Protestant's fitness for Heaven.

Jesus provides a quite different model of suffering, for Jesus was the sacrificial lamb who in death took the sins of all of humanity upon himself. It is his death which redeems humankind. The first idea of this model of suffering is in Isaiah in the Old Testament:

> He was despised and rejected by men;
> a man of sorrows, and acquainted with grief . . .
> Surely he has borne our griefs and carried our sorrows;
> yet we esteemed him stricken, smitten by God, and afflicted.
> But he was wounded for our transgressions,
> he was bruised for our iniquities;
> upon him was the chastisement that made us whole [Isaiah 53:3-6].

Suffering is here not to be endured as if it were a test of faith. Rather, suffering is self-chosen because by Jesus Christ's suffering the effects of sin and evil are removed.

Although Christ's suffering is a central part of the Protestant theology, too much talk of humans sharing the suffering of Jesus sounds too Catholic for Protestant sensibility. Protestants read the Word and wrestle with God within their own soul like Job did. There is no place in Protestantism for the stigmata such as St. Francis had when the wounds of Jesus' crucifixion appeared on the saint's body. There is no place in Protestantism for pilgrims to whip themselves bloody in order to share Jesus' pain. Protestants of all sorts tend to think of Jesus' suffering as something Jesus did "for my sake." Therefore the issue for Protestants is whether the individual can accept the gift of God's grace in Jesus' death, not how the individual can participate in Jesus's suffering. Indeed, this difference between Protestant and Catholic Christians is exemplified in the representations of the cross. Catholics tend to display the cross with the limp, dying body of Jesus on it, while Protestants tend to display the bare cross, that is, the cross after the crucifixion, which represents the resurrection rather than the suffering.

Because Protestantism has so often been a protest against what it considered a degenerate standing order, Protestants have often spoken of suffering on behalf of Jesus when they were persecuted or opposed by those they believed to be in league with the devil. This kind of suffering is real, but somewhat beyond the scope of the theme of this book: death and spirituality.

There have been significant movements of non-violence in Protestantism in which the powerless suffering of Jesus has been understood as a way to redeem those who rule in society as well as to change the power relationships. For example, George Fox, the founder of the Quakers, would not return hate for hate or blow for blow because the kindness of love could be stronger than the cruelty of the world. In the 20th century, American Protestant minister Martin Luther King, Jr., developed the idea of suffering for others in a political direction. Hundreds of Protestant clergy from around the country traveled the South to march, facing death while pledging neither to run away nor fight back. They would, they believed, redeem the souls of the racists who opposed them. But while King is honored as a person, his ideas about redemptive suffering have not been incorporated into the common fund of Protestant theology.

Still sometimes we do find that the suffering of Jesus is a model for Protestants as they face their own death. Often cited are the deaths of heroes or the deaths of those who have sacrificed their lives or have suffered for others. Suffering of the innocent children has often evoked a sense of the suffering of Jesus who was innocent, without sin. The theme of innocent suffering, as the suffering of Jesus, was strong in Victorian American Protestantism. The dying child in *Uncle Tom's Cabin* had insight beyond the learned men and could be the incarnation of the dying Christ [14].

Rather than the theme of the believer participating in Jesus' sufferings, contemporary Protestant pastors seem more likely to turn the focus around. Unlike Job whose suffering seemed to put him beyond the scope of God's care, and who only saw God when he confessed he could not understand, Protestants find comfort in the fact that God can empathize with humans. "God understands our pain because he experienced pain himself," is a theme which finds resonance in the present day when understanding is defined as the feeling of empathy rather than intellectual rational comprehension. Thus, because God suffered in Jesus' dying, suffering does not put the believer out of harmony with God, but is an occasion in which God can empathize and understand the experience of the believer. In my study of parents whose children have died, some identified their suffering with God's. They say "God is a bereaved parent." So long as God understands and cares, suffering does not separate them from God.

CONCLUSION

The core of Protestant Christianity is the relationship of the individual to his or her God. Death challenges this relationship in that it may end with the disappearance of the individual. Protestantism answers that challenge with the claim of salvation: that there is life after death and that faith will deliver the believer into the better world. Death also challenges the relationship between the individual and God insofar as death often brings with it the problems of the meaningfulness of suffering and the existence of evil. Protestant answers to the problem of evil range from the existence of a Devil who has been overcome by Jesus' death to defining God as limited in power. Two models are available to the Protestant to find meaning in suffering: Job, whose suffering teaches the limits of human understanding, and Jesus, whose suffering redeems humankind.

REFERENCES

1. D. W. Winnicott, *Playing and Reality*, Basic Books, New York, 1971.
2. K. Wilbur, *Up From Eden*, Shambhala Press, Boulder, Colorado, 1981.
3. P. Ariés, *Western Attitudes Toward Death*, P. M. Ranum (trans.), Johns Hopkins University Press, Baltimore, 1974.
4. C. Zaleski, *Otherworld Journeys: Accounts of Near-Death Experiences in Medieval and Modern Times,* Oxford University Press, New York, 1987.
5. H. B. Workman, *The Dawn of the Reformation*, Vol. 1, Epworth Press, London, 1933.
6. M. Luther, *The Large Catechism*, R. H. Fischer (trans.), Fortress Press, Philadelphia, 1959.
7. J. Edwards, *Basic Writings*, O. E. Winslow (ed.), New American Library, New York, 1966.
8. S. Kierkegaard, *Purity of Heart is to Will One Thing*, D. V. Steere (trans.), Harper & Row, New York, 1938.
9. D. Hammarskjold, *Markings*, Leif Sjoberg and W. H. Auden (trans.), Alfred A. Knopf, New York, 1964.
10. D. E. Stannard, *The Puritan Way of Death*, Oxford University Press, New York, 1988.
11. D. Klass, *Parental Grief: Solace and Restoration*, Springer, New York, 1988.
12. W. James, *Varieties of Religious Experience*, New American Library, New York, 1958.
13. H. Kushner, *When Bad Things Happen to Good People*, Schocken, New York, 1981.
14. A. Douglas, *Feminization of American Culture*, Alfred E. Knopf, New York, 1977.

FURTHER READING

In this chapter I have passed over a great deal of the history and denominational differences within Protestantism. The following books are good general introductions to Protestant history, thought, and practice. Some are quite old, but they were widely distributed and should be found in many libraries.

Brown, R. M., *The Spirit of Protestantism*, Oxford University Press, New York, 1964.
Cobb, J. B., *Varieties of Protestantism*, Westminster Press, Philadelphia, 1980.
Dunstan, J. L. (ed.), *Protestantism*, George Braziller, New York, 1962.
Marty, M. E., *Protestantism*, Holt, Rinehart and Winston, New York, 1972.
Rausch, D. A. and Voss, C. H., *Protestant—Its Modern Meaning*, Fortress Press, Philadelphia, 1987.

CHAPTER 8

Dying and Grieving Ministry in Mennonite Churches

P. Albert Koop

The article on "Funeral Customs" in the *Mennonite Encyclopedia* [1] claims that, at the time of publication (1956), no systematic study of Mennonite funeral customs and practices had been made. A search of the literature and the article on "Funerals" in the supplement [2] published in 1990 confirms that this is still the case. Both encyclopedia articles offer anecdotal evidence only, with some speculation as to origins. In this chapter I will summarize this evidence and speculation. As well, I will present some of my own observations and the results of my own investigations. I cannot, however, claim this to be a comprehensive, definitive treatment of the topic.

A problem in dealing with this topic is the tremendous variation in practices to be found within the Mennonite community. In part, this stems from their congregational governance structure. There is no central seat of authority on issues of doctrine and practice. Indeed, in some of the most traditional groups, often referred to as the Old Order Amish or Old Order Mennonites, their beliefs and practices, called "Die Ordnung," are deliberately not written down or codified in any formal sense [3]. It represents the community's understanding of what the traditional, proper ways are. Change occurs only after debate by the community and a consensus that it is acceptable. Over the centuries, change has occurred, but only at a slow pace and with many local variations. Funeral practices fall within this framework. These traditional groups are in a minority within the larger Mennonite world.[1] The majority of Mennonites have accepted modernity. They

---

[1] Leo Driedger, a sociologist at the University of Manitoba, documents the astonishing rate at which the rural, peasant village model which is consistent with "Die Ordnung" is being abandoned by North American Mennonites [4].

have been influenced by other Protestant groups, especially by evangelical groups, but have retained the congregational governance structure.[2] Again, this makes for variation in practices. One implication of all this is that my discussion here has to be set in a proper historical context.

Mennonite and Amish religious roots are to be found among the Anabaptists, those radical reformers who were not satisfied by the paths taken by the major reformers during the Protestant Reformation of the early 16th century.[3] Their opposition to both the Catholic Church and the Lutheran and Reformed variants of the Reformation led to a period of severe persecution and, in many cases, martyrdom [6]. Persecution drove many of them from their homes, setting in motion a pattern of migration and dispersion which, to some extent, persists to this day. Two major streams of migration can be identified. Dutch and North German Anabaptists fled to Poland and from there further migration took them to the Ukraine, then on to Kansas, Nebraska, and Manitoba, and finally to various Latin American countries. Swiss and South German Anabaptists found refuge in the British colony of Pennsylvania and from there they have spread out in North America, primarily Virginia, Ohio, Indiana, Michigan, and Ontario. It is the customs of these two groups that will form the basis of my observations here.[4]

Recently, my wife and I have attended a number of Mennonite funerals, primarily of parents of friends of ours. The services have been in churches which identify them as "modern Mennonites," i.e., they were not "Old Order Mennonites" or "Old Order Amish." There are many similarities between these funerals and those of other Christian denominations, but there are also some differences. Perhaps a brief description of our experience at one such funeral is appropriate.

We arrived at the Oak Street United Mennonite Church in Leamington about half an hour before the appointed time. The open casket was set up in the foyer of the church with members of the immediate family on either side. We filed by the casket, paid our respects to the deceased, had a few words of condolence with the family, and then proceeded into the sanctuary where the ushers showed us to our seats. At the appropriate time the casket was closed and was wheeled up to the area in front of the pulpit. A short service of about 45 minutes followed. There were two brief sermons, one in English and the other in German.[5] A choir sang and there was

---

[2] Consensus has, for the most part, been abandoned.

[3] Williams calls them the radical reformers. See [5].

[4] 45.3 percent of the world's 1,060,000 Mennonites in 1998 lived in Asia and Africa, the result of missionary activity that began in the late 19th century. These are not included here. Also not included are the Hutterites. They trace their roots back to Austrian Anabaptists who adopted communalism and have maintained it to this day. Today some 45,000 Hutterites live in communes scattered across the Dakotas, Montana, and the Canadian Prairie Provinces. Demographic data is taken from Table 1.2 [4]. For more on the Hutterites, see [7].

[5] The German service reflects the fact that most of us at the funeral had come to Canada as refugees from German settlements in Poland and the Ukraine or we were their first generation descendants.

some congregational singing. After the service a procession of cars followed the hearse to the local community cemetery for the burial.[6] Everyone was invited back to the church for "faspa,"[7] which had been prepared by women from the local church. It was a substantial meal—buns and bread, cold meats, cheeses, platters of fresh vegetables with various dips, cookies, tarts, cakes, and, of course, lots of coffee.

The scenario I have just presented could well have described a funeral in any of a number of different religious settings. Was it explicitly Mennonite? If so, what exactly was it that made it Mennonite? There were some aspects of the service that may well have received more emphasis here than would have been the case in most other churches. As I was preparing for writing this chapter, I asked our pastor[8] what the ideal Christian funeral service should accomplish. His answer was that at this service the congregation should meet God, the grieving—especially members of the immediate family—should be comforted, and the life of the deceased should be honored. He made it clear that these were listed in order of importance. The two brief sermons followed this model and maintained the suggested priority. Perhaps this emphasis would have been different in different churches. If so, this was only a matter of degree. Others, especially other Protestant groups, might well have emphasized the life of the deceased to a greater degree.

To me, however, it was at the "faspa" that I truly became aware that I was attending a Mennonite funeral. We helped ourselves to the food and the conversations began. Although a large number of people were in attendance from all across Southern Ontario and we did not all know each other personally, we felt comfortable in each other's presence. In our daily lives we were professional people, farmers, laborers, retirees, old people, young people, and so on but we were from the same community and the buzz of conversation showed it. A microphone was set up and one by one, starting with members of the family, people told stories of their memories of the deceased. Small songbooks, with favorite hymns appropriate for the occasion, were distributed and from time to time one of the mourners would suggest a song and we all sang. There were tears and there was laughter. The community was celebrating the life of one of its own. The strength of this community orientation made it a unique Mennonite experience. A brief look at historical practices and at current practices of the "Old Orders" help to put our experience into context.

As indicated earlier, no comprehensive study of Mennonite funeral practices exists. The *Mennonite Encyclopedia* presents anecdotal evidence only.[9] Early persecution left an indelible mark on the Anabaptist movement. The services and facilities of the established churches were closed to them. It became customary to

---

[6] Although cremation is not forbidden, it is extremely rare in Mennonite circles.

[7] Faspa is a low German expression for a substantial serving of afternoon refreshments.

[8] Rev. Harold Peters-Fransen, pastor of Valleyview Mennonite Church in London, Ontario.

[9] See articles on "Burials," "Cemeteries," and "Funeral Customs."

conduct the funeral in the home of the deceased without the benefit of clergy. A relative, or perhaps a close friend, would compose a long poem that was read at the funeral. Sometimes the poem was adapted to the music of a popular folk tune of the day and sung. As persecution subsided, and eventually disappeared, the Mennonite churches adopted funeral practices closer to societal norms but traces of the old practices remained. Long funeral hymns were still being written.[10] Special collections of hymns appropriate for funerals were published. They are still with us today. It was just such a special collection that we were using in the church at Leamington, although singing long hymns of 28 stanzas is no longer in fashion. The long obituary, no longer in the form of a poem, is still with us. This is evident in many Mennonite publications[11] and in newspaper columns of the general press in a city such as Winnipeg that has a large Mennonite population.

A segment of the Mennonite population has consciously rejected modernity. They are sometimes referred to as the "Old Orders." For the Mennonites from the South, Germany and Switzerland the are the Old Order Amish and the Old Order Mennonites. They live among the general population[12] in various regions of North America. They are distinguished by their rejection of modern technology, most visibly in their use of horses and buggies for transportation. For the Mennonites from the Netherlands and North Germany they are the Old Colony Mennonites. They are more accepting of new technology but they try to remain geographically isolated. Today most of them live in Mexico, Paraguay, Belize, and Bolivia, but some have returned to Canada. What these two groups have in common is their determination to remain true to the old ways, as they perceive them. At the heart of each is an egalitarian concept of the community. Their funeral practices adhere strictly to this concept and may be said to represent the true Mennonite way.

In the Old Colony Mennonite Church, funerals are very much a community affair. Let's see how it works in a particular location, the Aylmer Old Colony Mennonite Church.[13] The church has its own cemetery and a funeral fund that covers all associated expenses. Each family contributes $100.00 to this fund.[14]

---

[10]The Danzig (today Gdansk) Mennonite Church published a hymn of 28 stanzas on the death of Elder Dirk Jantzen in 1750. Singing it took as much time as preaching a sermon.

[11]*Der Bote* is one of these. It is read by many of the German speaking Mennonite refugees who left the Ukraine in the 1920s or Poland in 1945. Each biweekly issue has many of these long obituaries. They take up as much as 1/4 of each biweekly issue.

[12]To use their terminology, they live among "the English."

[13]The information in this section is based on an interview with Rev. Herman Bergen, one of the pastors of the Aylmer Old Colony Mennonite Church in Aylmer, Ontario. The Old Colony Church does not have a paid ministry. A large church such as this one will call a number of its male members to serve as pastors. All have to earn their livelihood at other occupations, usually farming. Mr. Bergen made it clear that he was describing their practices in the Aylmer church and that there might be some local variations in other locales, especially in the Latin American countries, but that these were minor. I want to take this opportunity to thank him for sharing this information in such a forthright manner.

[14]This illustrates both a strong commitment to family values and an egalitarian ethic within the community.

They have a contract with a funeral home in Aylmer for their services, but this seems to be in order to meet legal requirements.[15] Family and friends within the congregation do many of the services, such as building the coffin, a simple pine box, and digging the grave, normally provided by funeral home or cemetery staff.

When a member of the Aylmer Old Colony Mennonite Church dies, the body is taken to the funeral home for the necessary preparations. It will remain there till the day of the funeral. Friends may send flowers to the home of the deceased's family or to the funeral home, but these are not taken to the church for the funeral service or to the cemetery. The casket is open before the church service and before the burial at the cemetery. The church service will be simple, perhaps with two sermons and some congregational singing. No musical instruments will be used and there will be no choir. After the church service the body is transported to the cemetery. The mourners follow the hearse[16] as is customary in the other settings. After a brief grave-side service, the casket is closed and lowered into the grave by the pallbearers. Friends and family fill the earth back into the grave. It is after this has been completed that the mourners return to the church for "faspa."

A few words about the cemetery may be of interest. It is a plot immediately adjacent to a small rural public cemetery. There are no family plots here. Bodies are buried in chronological order, by the date of the funeral. No headstones are permitted. A small plaque showing name and dates of birth and death only marks each grave. These practices recognize the centrality of the community in the life of church members, the strong egalitarian ethic implied by Mennonite religious beliefs, and the traditional Mennonite emphasis on simplicity. In part, they are shared with many other Mennonite groups. The Old Order Amish do it the same way, i.e., no headstones and chronological order of burial. Family plots and headstones are permitted in most Mennonite cemeteries, however, ostentatious monuments are uncommon. Rarely is a headstone much higher than its neighbor.

A final example to illustrate the nature of the hospitality involved in the celebration of the life of the deceased is to be found in the report on the funeral of John P. Mast, Bishop of the Old Order Amish in Berks County, Pennsylvania in 1888 [8]. Although this took place more than a century ago, similar events still occur in Amish country today. Almost 2,000 people arrived in more than 350 buggies for the funeral at the Mast farm. After the service the funeral cortege of most of these buggies must have been an impressive sight. As soon as the cortege

---

[15]Rev. Bergen said embalming or an autopsy might be required. They do not object to either of these procedures. To my knowledge, there is no such objection in any of the Mennonite communites.

[16]Rev. Bergen indicated that the deceased's family would have to pay an extra $150.00 for the hearse to transport the body to the cemetery. Why this should be an extra cost when everything else is paid for by the funeral fund was not explained. Perhaps this may be one of those local variations. The Aylmer church's cemetery is located some 7 kilometers away from the church. It may be common for the cemetery to be adjacent to the church building, or it may be customary to use vehicles such as farm wagons, trucks, or vans for the purpose. In any case, the use of the hearse at an extra charge was the norm in Aylmer.

had left, tables were set up for the meal in all suitable areas, downstairs rooms in the home, adjoining porches, barnyard sheds, and barn floors. Three hundred pounds of choice beef, 35 large loaves of bread, 900 buns, hundreds of pies and cakes, two boxes of cream cheese, gallons upon gallons of coffee, and heaps of fruit and vegetables were consumed. "Bishop Mast had had a fine funeral and everyone agreed that he had been a model. 'Peace to his ashes!'"

In summary, Mennonites tend to follow funeral practices that adhere quite closely to the norms of the larger society around them. Distinct features are related to a strong community orientation, an egalitarian ethic that comes from their religious beliefs, and an emphasis on simplicity. The more tradition-oriented groups emphasize the old ways. Their practices tend to reflect societal norms of a bygone era.

REFERENCES

1. *The Mennonite Encyclopedia,* 4 vols., Mennonite Publishing House, Scottdale, Pennsylvania, 1956.
2. *The Mennonite Encyclopedia,* Vol. 5, Herald Press, Scottdale, Pennsylvania, 1990.
3. J. F. Beiler, On the Meaning of Ordnung, in *Amish Roots: A Treasury of History, Wisdom, and Lore,* J. A. Hostetler (ed.), The Johns Hopkins University Press, Baltimore, pp. 84-85, 1989.
4. L. Driedger, *Mennonites in the Global Village,* University of Toronto Press, Toronto, 2000.
5. G. H. Williams, *The Radical Reformation* (3rd Edition), Sixteenth Century Journal Publishers, Inc., Kirksville, Missouri, 1992.
6. T. van Braught, *The Bloody Theater or Martyrs Mirror,* J. F. Sohm (trans.), Herald Press, Scottdale, Pennsylvania, 1951.
7. R. Janzen, *The Prairie People: Forgotten Anabaptists,* University Press of New England, Hanover, New Hampshire, 1999.
8. J. A. Hostetler (ed.), *Amish Roots: A Treasury of History, Wisdom, and Lore,* The Johns Hopkins University Press, Baltimore, pp. 128-129, 1989.

CHAPTER 9

Islam

John D. Morgan

ISLAM, THE RELIGION

Islam, the fastest growing religion in the world today, sees itself as part of the Abrahamic tradition, the tradition that includes Judaism and Christianity. Muslims trace their ancestry to Ishmael, the son of Abraham, the first patriarch of the Jews, had by Hagar, who was his wife's maid [1, p. 175]. Muslims considered Islam to be the final statement of the Abrahamic traditions, honoring the prophets of the Hebrew and the Christian Bibles.

> Jesus himself was part of the Abrahamic tradition. He is my Prophet and I cherish him, deeply. I write about him, I talk about him. Jesus is very much a part of me, as is Moses, as is David, as is Salomon [2].

Islam was revealed through the prophet Mohammed. He was born in Mecca, Saudi Arabia around the year 540 CE. His father Ábd-Allah died before his birth and his mother, Aminah, died when he was about six years old. The Prophet died in the year 633 [3, p. 135]. Islam was revealed to Mohamed, and thus is believed to be founded by no one but Allah [p. 136]. Allah, the Arabic word for God, refers to the Transcendent Reality worshipped by Christians, Muslims, and Jews [2]. The way that the religion is customarily understood in the West does not really apply to Islam. In Islam, religion is not separate, something sacred done on Sunday. Islam is a way of life [2]. The word Islam means peace. Peace how? Peace from submission, understanding of reality, coming to terms with the transcending reality. When one comes to terms with the transcending reality, one has peace [2]. A Muslim is anyone who has this attribute of "Islam"; anyone who submits to the will of God. "In the Koran no distinction is made between Christian, Muslims, and Jews. The only thing that matters is the right conduct" [2].

There are seven articles of faith in Islam: The first is a belief in the oneness of Allah; second, belief in the angels of Allah; third, belief in the revelations of Allah;

fourth, belief in the prophets of Allah; fifth, belief in the day of Judgement; sixth, Belief in Predestination; and finally, belief in resurrection after death [3, pp. 137-138.]

In addition to these articles of faith, there are behavioral aspects that identify Muslims the world over. These are called the "Pillars of Islam," the fundamentals of the Islamic way of life. There is first of all, the Declaration of faith—"To bear witness that there is none worthy of worship except Allah and that Muhammad is His Prophet and Messenger to all human beings until the Day of Judgement." Second the commitment to constant prayer—"To establish prayers five times daily as a duty toward Allah. They strengthen the relationship with Allah and inspire man to a higher morality. They purify the heart and prevent temptation towards wrong-doings and evil."

> When one asks, therefore, why the Muslim prays, a partial answer is doubt-less: in response to the natural yearning of the human heart to pour forth its love and gratitude toward its Creator. But accompanying this desire is a need to keep his life in its proper perspective; to see it in its objective setting; to acknowledge his creatureliness before his creator, and to submit himself to the will of God as rightfully sovereign over his life [4, pp. 322-323].

Third, fasting for those who are well enough and old enough—"To observe Fast during the Holy Month of Ramadan. During this time Muslims abstain from food, drink, sexual intercourse, and evil intentions and actions. Fasting aims to train the Muslim to live a complete life of total submission to Almighty God." The fourth pillar is charity—"To pay the annual charity. It is 2.5 percent of one's net savings for the year and serves to purify the wealth of the giver and to improve the well-being of the receiver (poorer sections of society)." The final pillar is the Pilgrimage—"To perform pilgrimage to the Holy City of Mecca once in a lifetime, if one can afford the means of the journey" [2, pp. 136-137].

For Islam, the individual person is fully real and good in principle. The human soul is eternal, for once created the soul lives forever. Value, virtue, goodness, and spiritual fulfilment come by expressing one's unique self by virtue of which one is different from anyone or anything else [4, p. 317]. Humankind was not created in vain. One is held accountable for one's faith, actions, and the blessings which God gives in this life [3, p. 142]. Therefore, the primary purpose of life is to walk in the path of God, to abide by God's ordinances, and to secure God's pleasure [5, p. 51].

CEREMONIES AT DEATH

The *Azan,* the five-time-per-day call that is announced from the mosque asking the leaders to come and join in a prayer, is the first thing a Muslim hears at the moment of birth. Ideally, it also is the last thing that s/he hears before death. This congregational prayer occurs five times per day: sunrise or just before sunrise; mid-day; late afternoon; sunset; and night. It is a call to recognize the supreme reality, to orientate one's life according to that transcendent reality [2]. In Islam, as in Christianity and Judaism, life is viewed as a preparation for the next life where one will be held accountable, the day of reckoning [2].

Death is viewed as a passage. When a person hears about a death, the Koranic passage that is most often heard is "surely we are for Allah and to Allah we return" [2]. The family turns the face of the dying person toward the Ka'ba in Mecca, and whispers the *Azan* in his or her ear. After death occurs, the body is placed on a stretcher with the head in the direction of Mecca. "It is as if dying is an act of prayer with the rituals of prayer being applied" [5, p. 52].

The Imam should be called for someone who is sick. If the Imam is not available, readings and prayers from the Koran may be done by a friend or family member. Muslims will usually accept Christian ministers and chaplains as they accept Christ as one of the prophets. The dying Muslim will wish to face Mecca as s/he dies (wsw), his or her head should be elevated so that it is higher than rest of body. The dying person may wish to have a confession of faith, a confession of sins, may injure self as a way of sorrow for sins before s/he dies. It is important that in a health care situation great attention be spent to provide modest surroundings. To the extent possible a male patient should be cared for by male attendants, female by female. However, contemporary Muslims in industrialized societies recognize that this is not always possible. What is important is that the attendant should be mindful of the modesty requirements of Muslims.

After death the individual's eyes should be gently closed, his or her mouth closed with a bandage under the chin and tied over the head, and arms and legs straightened. When a person dies, the body is washed, a female member is washed by a female member of the family, the male body is washed by a male member of the family. The body is also washed in the way that a Muslim washes before prayer. "You know you wash yourself to enter the *mosque* or in the privacy of you own home. You find that you are orienting yourself to the transcending of reality. You focus your mind, get ready and then pray" [2]. After the bath, the dead body is wrapped with two pieces of white cotton, wrapped around loosely, and is ready for internment. Ideally, only other Muslims should handle the body. If it is necessary to handle the body, non-Muslims should use gloves as a sign of respect. The eyes should be closed, the jaw bound, body placed in a straight position, arms and legs straight out, hair and nails cut, turn to side to face Mecca for burial.

Since it is assumed that the soul leaves the body immediately, the body should be buried within two intervals of prayer. If the death takes place at mid-morning after the morning prayers, then it is desirable that the body should be buried by late-afternoon prayer so there is enough time to prepare the body, to get the people around, and then have it buried [2]. Circumstances may affect this tradition. Muslims do not believe in the physical display of the body. The wrapping of the body, and shrouding the face, is a way of showing respect for the dead. The person is no longer in control of his or her privacy. It is up to the living to provide that privacy for the dead. The body is usually taken out of the coffin before it is buried in order to speed decomposition [6, p. 192].

In Islamic tradition, women do not go to the cemetery. Women do not participate in the act of burial. The grave is dug, two feet by six feet normally, about five to six feet below. Because the body is not buried in a coffin (it belongs to the earth and is returned to the earth), a mat is placed over the body so that earth does not fall directly on the body [2]. The body is buried with head north, the feet south, and the face is turned toward Mecca, the direction of prayer. The earth is thrown, the people depart. The story for that living person is over.

Non-essential autopsies are opposed; organ donation only for medical need (not for education purposes); blood transfusions acceptable.

While death in its most fundamental sense is a passage to accountability before Allah, it is also a tearing away from our loved ones in this life. A hole is created in that relationship that had existed. The person has gone away in a physical way. There is that moment of grief and shock, but Islam, like Judaism and Christianity, asserts that ultimately the human being is not dead, there has been no death, there has been a passage [2]. Attending a funeral, and in particular helping to carry the dead in the funeral procession, is considered an act of piety. The coffin is usually carried by relays of male relatives and friends [6, p. 191]. The surrounding people can grieve and shed tears, but are forbidden to wail, beat the breasts, slap the face, tear their hair or garments, or complain, or curse [3, p. 143].

BEREAVEMENT SUPPORT

The community, the family system, the friends, other institutions, are supposed to come in and support the family where the death has taken place. It is important to meet the normal demands of family life, the most essential, food. In traditional societies, for three days no activity takes place in the home, no fire is burned [2]. "This is as normal as in any other culture, you go and you share, you're sorry about this loss that has taken place, there is no particular formula that you have to say, it is simply sharing the loss and consoling each other" [2].

The recognition of transcendent reality comes through in prayers, in verses of the Koran, in the language. Death is something that each has to deal with, each has to orientate ourselves to the transcending reality. Prayer and ritual gives you strength, particularly in the moments of illnesses and death and dying. It restores a new relationship to these matters. There is no particular formula [2].

Reciting the Koran during the period of mourning is the main tradition. People recite the Koran, get together, read a prayer. During that three-day period a number of the family and friends often go to the grave and recite the Koran as a way of coming to terms with there own loss. The three-day period is a psychological way of coming to terms with one's own loss. There is no precise grand scheme, nothing of that sort.

CONCLUSION

Allah takes care. He knows all, he is the omniscient. The person has committed what ever he or she has committed and now his soul is in a stage of transition, where he will, if he or she is a believer: if he or she is not a believer than everything has come to an end.

REFERENCES

1. A. J. Magida (ed.), *How to be a Perfect Stranger: A Guide to Etiquette in Other People's Religious Ceremonies*, Jewish Lights, Woodstock, Vermont, 1996.
2. S. Mansur, *Delivering Care to Muslims*, Audio presentation at the 1997 King's College Conference on Death and Bereavement.
3. B. K. Turner, *Multifaith Information Manual*, Ontario Multifaith Council on Spirituality and Religion, Toronto, 1993.
4. H. Smith, *The Religions of Man*, Harper and Row, New York, 1986.
5. H. Kassis, Islam, in *Life after Death in World Religions*, H. Coward (ed.), Orbis, Maryknoll, 1997.
6. J. I. Smith, Islam, in *How Different Religions View Death and Afterlife*, C. J. Johnson and M. G. McGee (eds.), Charles, Philadelphia, 1991.

CHAPTER 10

North American Native Care of the Dying and the Grieving

Gerry R. Cox

An analysis of the dying process and the burial practices of people may give us understanding of their values and culture. Maintaining health is of primary concern for people in all cultures. Caring for the terminally ill can raise questions of the meaning of life, cause tragedy and tears, relief from pent-up emotions, and at the same time can offer those giving care immense gratification. The care of the dying by Native Americans differs from that offered by white society. In the United States, doctors and nurses are used to being in positions of power over patients and their families. Doctors and nurses also use a scientific model to treat disease that often leads to impersonal care. Mortuary practices are primarily conducted by funeral directors. Burial practices include casket companies and vault companies, personnel that the survivors typically never meet. Graves are opened and closed by backhoe operators without the families present. The practices of Native Americans are greatly different from the white cultural practices. The influence of the white culture has modified Native American practices. The current Native American practices are somewhat fragmented and confused, yet there are still basic principles that are the foundation of their care of the dying and deceased.

By studying the health practices and the burial and mortuary customs, one can learn much of the philosophy and religion of a people. The rich traditions of the 300 or so North American Native groups can be expressed through an analysis of their mortuary and burial practices. Such cultures have been present for 30,000 or more years and have left behind a record complete with rituals, artifacts, and customs. Burial practices are the one remnant that is left of all cultures.

The practices of any culture are not universal. The practices of the 300 or so tribes are not consistent from one group to another or within a single group. There are common elements of burial and mortuary practices. Depending upon the status of the person who died, the amount of public display will vary. The greater the display, the more highly valued the deceased. Public display suggests high social value. A tribal chief, a great hunter, a spiritual leader, or even a child could have high social status for one tribe while another tribe might assign greater social value to a grandfather, a storyteller, or to a holy person. The length and intensity of public grieving also tends to reflect one's social value.

Disposal methods may also reflect attitudes toward the dead. Cremation may be used as a method of sending the soul of the deceased skyward to an afterlife. It may be used to try to help the deceased on the journey out of love and respect for the deceased. Cremation may also be used to destroy the corpse so that the deceased cannot come back to inflict injury or harm upon the living. By destroying the corpse, one is done with it, and the corpse can no longer harm the living [1].

Mummification could be used to preserve the body from decay out of love for the deceased. It may aid the grieving process to know that the body of the deceased has been preserved as the living remember it. On the other hand, mummification could be used to secure personal survival for the deceased to allow them to live in an afterworld [1].

Tree burial may reflect a culture that lives among trees historically and is attempting to return to their "roots." It may simply be a product of trying to return the deceased to nature as quickly as possible by allowing animals, birds, and insects to consume the body. This reflects a naturalist philosophy. It is also possible that tree burial may be the result of a person dying in the winter when the ground was simply frozen so hard that it is nearly impossible to dig a grave until the spring thaw.

Mound builders are also quite common in North America. Some of the mounds were pits, others were foundations of houses, some were beneath houses, some were on top of the ground and covered, and still others were rocks that covered the grave that became mounds over time. The mounds may have been built to provide the deceased with the necessary provisions to make their journey to the afterworld whether in the sky or the center of the earth. It may also have been a method to keep the deceased from coming back to disturb the living.

Those who used stones to cover the grave may have done so to keep the ghost of the deceased from returning to haunt the living [2]. The rocks may also have been used to keep scavengers from ravaging the body of the deceased. It is also possible that rocks were used to mark graves. The Sioux used grave posts to mark graves. These markers may be inserted into the ground or supported with stones. The stones themselves lasted longer than the markers.

Some tribes buried people by pulling down the wickiup, hogan, or other dwelling type over the deceased. Other groups placed the body in a canoe, cave, urn, or other designed method for disposing of the body of the deceased. Some would place the body in a hole in the ground and cover it with rocks or by pulling a fallen tree over it. Many, many methods have been used.

The practice of leaving food and property for the deceased is also common. Such practices may have emerged out of fear of the corpse and the belief that the deceased might return to disturb the living if such items were not left for the deceased [2]. Such practices may have been the result of the desire to further honor the deceased by giving treasured items to be buried with the person that was greatly loved by the living. Many cultures bury items with the deceased that are intended to show the love of the living for the deceased. What is placed in the grave by the living will reflect who is in the grave. For a child, one might leave toys. In a warrior's grave, one would expect to find favorite weapons, beads, medicine bags, or paint. In a woman's grave, one might find food or tools for tanning or making pottery. In a farmer's grave, one might find food, farm implements, or seeds [3].

No analysis of mortuary and burial practices could provide a complete picture of the attitudes and values of a particular people toward dying and death. One would need to observe hundreds of funerals to uncover subtle practices that might distinguish one funeral from another even in the same culture. Each funeral will differ because of differences in the age, sex, social position, amount of disposable income, or other factors that characterize either the deceased or the survivors who provide the funeral. Other factors would also include the cause of death, the time of year in which the death occurred, or the personality of the person who died. The attitudes of the survivors or the deceased could impact the type of funeral practices that emerge as well.

NATIVE AMERICAN CULTURAL PRACTICES

Native Americans have maintained their cultural traditions through a strong kinship system. As a kinship society, much of the social life—including how one makes a living, one's religion, the social learning that comes from others, and even social relationships—is the product of one's family. For Native Americans, one's way of life and way of thinking is centered on people rather than things. One universal feature of Native American culture would be that it is people-centered. Over time, non-Natives have introduced cultural elements that have threatened this system. Early settlers and traders brought disease, politics, religion, and an economic system that threatened the survival of the kinship, people-centered societies. The later introduction of "white" education even further eroded the cultural system. While much of the culture has been lost, many Native Americans are rediscovering their "roots."

Culturally, the focus on people rather than things has lead to many cultural practices that distinguish Native American culture. Native Americans are generally quite aware of their kinship system and how they are related to others. Relatives are a part of their social circle and friendship grouping. Children spend time and have experiences with grandparents and other older relatives. One's clan or lineage is part of one's life. Each clan has duties and obligations that go with such membership. One may be called upon to be a storyteller, dancer, singer, or whatever because of one's clan or lineage. Families care for the elderly at home.

People die among their clan or family groupings. Nursing homes have emerged on some reservations and many now die in hospitals, but traditionally, Native Americans educate, respect, and work together, but they also care for the living, the dying, and the dead as family groups. Native Americans have patterns of sharing along kinship lines as well. This may include money, childcare, housing, rides, help with work, or whatever is needed. Generosity and sharing are strong cultural values. The amassing of money and possessions is not a traditional practice. Goods are to be shared and savings are to be used. The give-away ceremonies are still practiced among many groups. Public ceremonies are also organized along kinship lines. Even dying has a ceremony.

Tribal Practices in Dying

The culture of Native Americans also impacts their patterns for dying. Their relationships with the white culture have also impacted these patterns. Prejudices toward them have probably existed since before the colonists came into contact with them. Many describe them as incompetent and needing of government care and direction. Their problems with alcohol, suicide, and high rates of infant mortality and alcohol abuse among both adults and children are further reasons for negative opinions of their peoples. The traditional views of them as treacherous and murderous have persisted through the years. More recently, improved views of Native Americans have begun to emerge.

Native Americans have a different culture. The lifestyle of the tribes differs greatly, but some cultural patterns do emerge. While the white culture is future oriented, Native Americans are more focused upon the present. Time is to be enjoyed and lived, not dreaded. Calendars and time are not important in the Native cultures. One is to live life with family and friends. There is no need to hurry. Life is full when one has food to share, family and friends to enjoy, and ceremonies to attend. Enjoy the present and the future will take care of itself. Native Americans also value leisure. In the white culture, people often return to work to rest up after a vacation or holiday. Native Americans work as needed not because it is there to do. The Navajo do not distinguish between work and play. One is to have fun at whatever one does. For the Navajo, good behavior means completing one's duties to one's family, being generous to others, minding one's business, and not bragging on oneself. For the Sioux, good behavior would include respecting others, being socially sensitive, and honoring nature. How long or hard one works is not highly valued. This does not mean that Native Americans do not work hard or long hours. They might work 20 hours a day and then not show up at work the next day. Family and friends come first. If a relative or friend needs your services, that is more important than a job. Native Americans do not work for the sake of work.

Native Americans also have a strong sense of humor. Carl Gorman, who taught me the ways of the Navajo, lived and taught that one is to maintain a sense of humor during good times and sad times. Humor is different in each society, but all societies have humor. For Native Americans, all aspects of life, including death, are subjects of humor and laughter. The naturalistic philosophy of tribes generally means that when it is one's time to die, then one should die. They would not use medically futile interventions for the dying. One should die naturally without tubes and machines. One does not show love by trying to keep a person alive as long as possible. One does not allow a loved one to die with strangers.

Native Americans are also more likely to be silent and to have periods of few words. One may go on a trip with a Native American and have few words exchanged. In the white culture, those who travel together feel a social obligation to talk to fill the time. A smile or a touch is more highly valued than words in most Native American groups. One should take time for thought before expressing oneself. Spirituality is also a basic part of the Native American culture. One achieves courage and optimism from one's spiritual life and religion. Balance with nature and spirituality is essential to good health. Healing ceremonies are designed to restore such balance. Everything in life has a purpose. Even pain has a purpose. Pain causes courage to grow. One cannot be brave if one has only experienced wonderful things in one's life. One must also have respect for ceremonies. Among the Navajo, ceremonies exist for almost every event in one's life. A ceremony exists for the baby's first laugh, healing, welcome home events, birth, marriage, death, and other life events. The ceremonies teach about clan life, personal relationships, values, wholeness, and relationships. Dying is a part of life. One accepts one's fate.

Medical Care of Native Americans

The medical care of Native Americans has been fragmented and confused. As many have been forced to reservations or restricted areas maintained by the Federal government, many traditional practices have been lost. White medicine has also been introduced over time. Many Native Americans live in cities and are primary users of white medicine. While each of the approximately 300 tribes had their own beliefs and practices regarding health and illness, generally most would believe that health is the result of living in harmony or balance with nature and having the ability to survive under extremely difficult circumstances. Humans have an intimate, personal relationship with nature. The earth is alive and also has a desire to be healthy. Like humans, the earth is occasionally ill and at other times it is healthy. It, too, can be out of balance. The earth is the friend of the human. It gives food, shelter, clothing, and medicine to humans. The earth belongs to life. Life belongs to the land. The land belongs to itself. One who is in harmony with the earth will be in balance and will be healthy. Health is in the control of the individual.

Everything in life has a purpose. The land feeds and clothes humans. Every illness or pain has a purpose. One must pay the price for what one does. Each human has the power to control one's self. This spirit power is the source of illness and pain. One must pay the price for one's acts whether in the past or in the future. Science may view the cause of disease as from some bacteria or other empirically controlled cause. The Native American views illness as being the price that one pays rather than as the result of bacteria or germs or whatever.

Native Americans often feel a sense of distance from those who care for them in hospitals. They are close to the shaman and other healers. For white medical caregivers, Native Americans tend to be difficult patients. The white culture is greatly attached to science and its ways. Native Americans respond differently than white patients. A Sioux may have as many relatives as possible in the hospital room. They may want to use smoke for purification, which would set off smoke detectors. An Apache who is dying may not have any visitors so that he or she is allowed to die with dignity by being alone. The Navajo who wants to leave the hospital to have a "sing" may baffle a physician. Science is not a part of the way of life of the Native American.

Tribal Healing

The traditional healer of the Native American is the shaman. The traditional Native American culture has generally maintained the belief that the shaman is a healer. The shaman is to be knowledgeable in the ways of the earth, humans, and nature. To be the recipient of medicine power, one must live one's life in balance. There are four directions, four seasons, four ages of humans, and four kingdoms of life. One must renew the commitment to this balance every day [4]. The shaman is to determine the cause of the illness or pain and then must develop the proper treatment of the illness or pain. The special ceremonies may take from a few minutes to several days. Other shaman teach shaman. It takes years to a lifetime to learn the craft. One is never finished with the learning. The shaman tries to determine the spiritual causes of the illness as well. Holistic medicine may be an attempt to recognize the multiple causes of illnesses. Just as each life has a purpose, each illness has a purpose. The shaman attempts to determine the cause of the illness and to cure it.

To heal, the shaman does not stop with the idea that a drug or other medicine can cure. To cure, the shaman administers physical medicine, but he or she also administers spiritual medicine. The treatment is a process that heals not only the physical illness, but also administers to the spiritual needs that must be addressed to bring the person back to harmony or balance [5]. The medicine power enables the possessor of the spirit to personal contact with the invisible world of the spirits [4]. If one is meant to die, then there is little that the shaman can do. One cannot defy nature. What can be done, will be done. More than that is unnecessary and may be an affront to nature. Death is not to be feared, but life is to be appreciated for one's self and for one's loved ones.

Attitudes Toward Dying and Death

While generalizations are dangerous, the variety of cultural expressions of dying and death do have some commonalities for the various tribes. Most tribes express a willingness to surrender to death at any time with little fear. The Lakota Chief Crazy Horse was noted for his chant before going into battle that, "Today is a good day to die." Every day is a good day to die if one has lived one's life. Every day is to be lived as if it were one's last day. One must enjoy life and live fully. Just as one cannot buy land, one cannot buy life. Death is waiting. One cannot escape. One does not seek death before its time. Nor does one avoid death or try to delay its occurrence. No one is ever truly alone. The dead are not altogether powerless. There is no death, but rather a change of worlds [4]. Despite the high rates that occur among some tribes, tribes generally reject suicide. The Lakota teach that those who commit suicide will wander the earth lost and lonely.

SOUTHWESTERN TRIBAL BURIAL PRACTICES

Apache

The Apache were the last of the hostile tribes to submit to the whites and were, like the Navajo, thought to be descendents of the Athapascan-speaking peoples. While there is debate as to when and where the Apache arrived, as with the Navajo, they quickly left their mark as a fierce and warlike tribe. Like the Navajo, the Apache engaged in banditry, but unlike the Navajo, they also engaged in war as a way of life. The Jicarilla and Mescalero Apaches seem to have borrowed from the Plains Indians and lived in tipis, used braids, and wore buckskin as did the Plains Indians. The Chiricahua and other Apache groups lived in wickiups which are basically a grass and bush covering over young trees. Unlike the Navajo, the Apache did not develop arts and crafts to any extent. Their burial and mortuary practices are similar.

The Apache culture is not a simple culture. To be an Apache is not a traditional part of the culture. The word Apache was not a word used by the tribe historically. It means enemy and was used by their foes to describe them. Terrell suggests that the actual name Apache is a corruption of the word Apachu which the Spanish described as Apache [6]. Like the Navajo, the Apache are a matrilineal and matrilocal society that trace their descent through the female side and have the groom move in with his wife's people [6]. For the Apache, the grandmothers instruct their grandchildren on the proper ways of the people, and girl children are considered more valuable to the tribe than boy children are. Both receive the same physical training on foot and on horseback as they grow toward becoming adults

[6]. Unlike the Navajo who developed into a single tribe, the Apache developed into several divisions or tribal groups. The Apache are not one tribe. Their ways are not the same for all groups. The Western Apache are noted for their lack of words. As with other tribes, the Apache believe that words themselves have the power to make things happen. Prayers, poems, songs, and spells are not differentiated. All have spiritual powers to cause things to happen. One rarely sings or says poems for entertainment. Such activities are used in ceremonies. Such activities are used in time of crises and in any undertaking in one's life. When one is suffering from an illness or injury, one may be "sung over."

In describing the healing ceremonies of the Apache, Basso indicates that when one is the object of a ceremony, it is considered wrong to talk to the person [7]. The only people who are able to talk to the patient are the shaman and the relative who is in charge of the ceremony. The patient only speaks openly when he or she is asked to pray. Imagine their surprise when a nurse or physician asks the Apache patient questions about their pillow, medicine, food, health, or well being while they are receiving treatment in a hospital. Like most other tribes, the patient or the family will invite the shaman to do a ceremonial when someone is suffering from illness or injury.

The shaman may or may not accept an invitation to do a ceremonial. If the shaman accepts, then a ritual is performed. The Apache fear the dangers of witchcraft, animals that could cause misfortune, and the evil that may result from failing to properly respect the supernatural forces and supreme deity that watch over humans [8]. Disease has a cause. The agents of disease can assume the form of a snake or owl, enter our dreams, or materialize as a ghost and cause one to suffer from disease and illness or other forms of misfortune [9]. The purpose of the shaman is to counteract their evil, to exorcise the harm that might be associated with the rituals, and to manage the elaborate ceremonies such as sand paintings which, like the Navajo, are destroyed after the healing ritual [8]. For a more complete description of the healing ritual read Opler [9].

For the non-Apache who might be invited to attend a curing ceremony, the ceremony will usually begin in the early evening and continue until nearly dawn of the next day. Some ceremonies will last as long as four days. Normally close friends and relatives attend the ceremonies. This typically does not include children. The Apache seem to have a great fear of death and communicate this fear to children at an early age. The Apache also practiced methods with children that are largely not recommended today such as not allowing children to be around the dying or even viewing the dead and preventing children from associating with other children who are grieving until they have been cleansed [10]. The Apache generally feel that children are to be protected from the ravages of illness and death. When one dies, one dies alone if possible. Children would rarely be present. If ceremonies last more than one day, they are typically from dark until after midnight. There will be abundant food that will be provided by the patient's relatives. There will be numerous ritual articles that are fully described in Opler that will be used in the ceremony [9]. The shaman will sing, pray, perform various rituals to try to determine what are the sources of the illness or injury and what can be done to overcome the injury or cure the illness. The ceremonies are often quite loud. Music is associated with the supernatural and religious life in all civilizations, and it is a therapeutic tool that promotes a religious attitude that encourages spiritual development [11]. The drum is the heartbeat of the earth that creates a sound as old as the earth and beats within each of us as our heart [12]. Everyone, from the shaman to the patient to the participants, gains from the healing ceremony. If the patient dies, it was the person's time to die or that the spirits were simply too strong. If one lives or dies, it was meant to be. Suffering is a natural part of life. Each person must confront whatever destiny one faces and must eventually face death with a spirit of acceptance [13]. Most Apaches view the illness of the Spanish and white people as being too strong for the shaman and that if the shaman does not cure these diseases, the shaman is not at fault [14].

The Apache are a gay people who love to laugh and always seem to appreciate something funny and are forever joking and laughing [15]. The Apache also use clowns and dancers to keep illness away [9]. The Apache use strong communications, humor, music, art, and social support to help cure illness and injury.

The Apache believe that when a person dies his or her spirit does not go immediately to the underworld, but rather, the spirit stays for a while. Which means that those relatives who touch the body are likely to get ghost sickness and may themselves need healing ceremonies conducted for them [16]. One of the reasons given for burying the deceased is goods with the body is to prevent ghost sickness [17].

When an Apache dies, the dead person is dressed in the best clothes that are available, wrapped in a blanket, carried to the hills, thrown into a crevice in the rocks, or buried in a shallow grave [17]. For the Western Apache, ashes and pollen would be sprinkled in a circle around the grave beginning at the southwest corner to offer the soul a safe journey to heaven, after which the crevice or shallow grave would be covered to prevent coyotes or other animals from getting to the corpse [17]. The Apache would use as small of a place as possible to put the corpse, such as a place where a rock had shifted or a stump had fallen, and then they would put back the rock or stump to cover the body [17]. The Apache who pride themselves on caring for those in need such as the elderly, ill, orphans, and so forth, often leave a jug of water for the deceased to drink. This practice can be traced back to an earlier legend that the Gahan or Mountain Spirit will come to rescue the thirsty and take them to the mountains to dwell with the mountain spirits [18].

The Apache did have a wake and did cry and wail for the deceased. The Apache would also set aside a part of their fields for the dead and would not cultivate the field for a period of time to honor the deceased [19]. Like the Navajo with the hogan, the Apache would sometimes leave the body in the wickiup and push it down on top of the body [19]. The Chiricahua Apache wives and children would often cut their hair short, cover their faces with mud and ashes, and dance to keep the ghosts from capturing them after the death of a warrior [19]. The Mescalero Apache saw death as the final foe and did not perform rites upon the death of a loved one [19]. For all Apache groups, the death of a warrior aroused much grief while the death of the squaw seemed almost unnoticed except of intimate friends and relatives [19].

Like the Navajo, the Apache saw death as the enemy and expressed no great desire to be among the dead or their ghosts. Both tribes also view ghosts as being responsible for sickness and death and fear the threat of deceased relatives, and yet, because of their fear of the dead, both tribes felt a tremendous need to properly dispose of the dead to protect themselves [20].

Navajo Burial Practices

The Navajo are generally thought to be of the Athapascan family, as are the Apaches. Some questions exist as to when they arrived in the Southwest and whether or not they did cross the Bering Straits to reach North America. Perhaps, they did come from below from the underworld where there was no light from the sun or stars [18]. Like the Apache and the Sioux, the name for the tribe known as the Navajo is not what they traditionally called themselves. The word Navajo was not even in their language [6]. The word Navajo represents the Navajo word, Dineh, which means people. The name Apache also means people. The largest tribe, the Navajo, have a relatively more consistent culture than the Apache. The Navajo borrowed from the people around them. Unlike most other Southwestern tribes, the Navajo were not farmers, but rather made their living from hunting and banditry. The largest of the United States tribes today, the Navajo are also thought to be the last to settle in the Southwest. From the Pueblos, they borrowed the loom, learned to grow cotton, and to grow corn. From the Spanish, they borrowed horses, sheep, wool, and silversmithing. The Navajo would steal and capture not only material good, but people. They would marry them and borrow their culture as well [6]. Whether the Navajo moved to the Anasazi land or were descendents of the Anasazi, they choose not to inhabit their deserted big towns. Instead, they built their traditional hogans of mud, logs, bushes, and sticks [6].

Like the Apache, their approach to illness also has a spiritual basis. The Navajo believe that the Great Spirit would never put an illness on the earth without making a remedy available [20]. It is the task of the shaman to name that disease and to discover the cure for the disease. Illness and disease are caused by a person breaking a taboo, an attack of a witch, offending a ghost, or by failing to live one's life in balance.

For the Navajo, the hatqali, chanter, or shaman is the person who is to be familiar with the chants, songs, and requirements of the chants. An elderly shaman chooses one to learn the ways of the chanter. Often this will be a son, brother, or other male relative. After many years of study, one may also become a chanter. It may take as long as eight years to learn the songs and methods of painting in the sand [21]. Like the Apache and the Sioux shaman, the Navajo healer may also refuse the request for services. The chanter may refuse after learning the cause of the illness and the condition of the patient. Generally, the chanter will accept the patient. Typically, women do not serve as chanters, but some have done so. Many women know a great deal about medicine and are used by the shaman to obtain and administer medicine. If the chanter has difficulty determining the cause of the illness, a diviner may be called. After the divination is completed, the shaman may call upon a medicine woman or man to treat the person with medicine, and then the shaman will perform a song for the ill person. Sometimes, the same person will perform all three tasks. Each person who performs a task in the healing ritual will expect to receive a fee for his or her services.

The ceremonies of the Navajo are very complex and must be performed accurately to be successful. It may take as long as three or four years to learn two ceremonies [20]. Some rituals last for as long as nine days and must be recited accurately from memory. If one fails to chant even a small part of the ritual or omits a detail from a sand painting, or neglects a detail from a prayer stick, the patient will not recover. The chanter will move his hand. The practice of the motion of the hand is a gift to the chanter. Like those searching for water, the diviner knows when the hand moves in a certain way that the cause of the disease has been found. Sand paintings, star gazing, and other methods are used to discover the cause of an illness. Like the Lakota, the Navajo listen. What they hear may also tell them the cause of the illness. As with the Apache and the Lakota, the goal is to achieve harmony or balance. Generally, the Navajo have hope and optimism. Like the Apache, the Navajo are a gay people. They love to laugh and joke. Perhaps this is the source of the optimism and hope that they express. They generally believe that their ceremonies will carry them through any crisis. The Navajo are a humble people. Rarely do they take credit for their acts. Typically, they deny any special knowledge or skills, but they also typically expect praise from others for their actions. One is not to brag on oneself, but it is quite accepted and often expected for others to do so.

The Navajo have perhaps the most complex healing rituals. Charms, sand cornmeal paintings, prayer sticks, masks, and many more items are used. Ceremonies are far more traditional and unchanging. Generally, many Navajo recognize that their traditional healing rituals are not as effective against "white" diseases. Many Navajo, like other tribes, use both white medicine and their own traditional medicine to try to manage disease today.

The Navajo believe that life begins when the wind enters the body through the orifices and particularly the ears. Death occurs when the wind leaves the body through the fingers [22]. Death is the end of all good things to the people. No Navajo looks forward to life in the next world as a reward for good deeds in this life. At best, life in the afterworld is uninviting. To the living, the dead are objects of horror that must be buried with elaborate precautions to protect the living from having problems with the ghosts of the dead [22]. One must even avoid whistling after dark to avoid attracting ghosts [23]. To bury the dead, one must prepare by going through rituals. The rituals may include removing one's clothes and bathing, covering oneself with yucca leaf, using sign language to communicate, and eating only certain foods [24]. When possible, the Navajo gets a white person who may serve as a teacher or missionary to the tribe to do the burial. If that is not possible, then the Navajo may hire another Navajo who is not a relative to conduct the burial and other duties [22].

The burial practices vary immensely. Depending upon whether the deceased was an infant, elderly, or another age group, the Navajo choose two or four people to become mourners for the deceased. One of these would be a near relative or clansman of the deceased. Another is commonly from the clan of the father, wife, or husband of the deceased. One of these is chosen to direct the rite. They will bathe the body, dress the body in fine clothes, and place the right moccasin on the left foot and the left moccasin on the right foot. If the person was not removed from the hogan before death occurred, the body will be removed from the hogan through a hole made in the North side of the hogan. The door of the hogan is on the East. Depending upon the view of the spirit of the deceased, the hogan may or may not ever be used again. The mourners will carry the body to the burial site in a prescribed fashion using only sign language to communicate along the way. The mourners will bury the body in a deep hole a long way from the hogan and include the saddle, blankets, jewelry, and other treasures with the body. Traditionally, they would kill the horse at the gravesite and leave the tools used to dig the grave broken on the gravesite as well [24]. Each of the four mourners would have specific tasks. One would lead the horse carrying the possession of the one who died to the gravesite. Two would carry the body. The fourth would warn those that might meet along the way who might cross the death line to not cross the death line or the circle route taken with the body until the four days of mourning are completed [25]. Mourners are also expected to remain quiet, to not spit, to avoid turning even a stone on its side, to skip and hop on their return, to avoid stepping on a cactus or brush, and to return by a different route so that the ghost cannot follow [25].

The Navajo often bury valuable items with the body. They may even bury money, which makes grave robbing a problem [26]. To rob a grave is a serious offense. Those who rob graves take great risk of getting ghost sickness, which could kill them. Since the ghost of the deceased is at the very bottom of the grave, those who rob graves must purify themselves after robbing a grave before they can touch another person [24].

During the mourning period, mourners may kill horses or sheep, break dishes, destroy the hogan, and avoid eating and other behaviors. Family members may weep silently in another hogan, people may remain apart for four days of the mourning period. Other mourners will purify themselves with the smoke of a sage fire [22]. Should the ground be too hard during the winter weather, the body would be placed in the hogan, and the hogan would be crushed in on top of the body [22].

For the Navajo, death beliefs are filled with dreams, omens, and potents relating to death and the dead. They do not have a belief in a glorious afterlife for the soul, but rather have a vague conception of an afterlife as an ephemeral and shadowy existence with an end to all that is good [27]. Not only is death to be avoided as long as possible, but those who are dead are a threat to the living. Homes of the dead are haunted as are the ruins of the Anasazi and other ancient peoples. The Ghostway and Ghost Dance rituals are used to stave off offended ghosts [24]. All ghosts are feared. The dead are thought to be the source of all sickness and disease whether physical or mental. Holy Way Chants, Life Way Chants, Ghost Dance rituals, astrological rituals, and so forth are used to deal with malevolent ghosts. Even the hogan is constructed and blessed with an awareness of astronomical directs and concern for the traditions of the past [28].

In recent years, the Navajo have dropped many of their traditional ways of dealing with the dead. Today, the burial of the dead is surrendered to white people whenever possible. The Navajo allow missionaries to bury their dead when possible [29]. Schools have been provided with coffins or at least lumber for them, and staff members have taken responsibility for burial [22]. Since World War II, even more changes have occurred. Since white soldiers were publicly buried with honor, the Navajo gave their own dead soldiers public burial [30]. The Navajo still have a strong fear of contact with the dead [26].

Hopi Burial Practices

As a Southwestern tribe in the midst of the Navajo, the Hopi are called the peaceful ones. Though some of the Navajo may call them old women, they have also been called the Moqui or the dead. The Hopi left behind many ruins for the archeologist to study. As a pueblo people, they built and abandoned many sites and left behind their exquisite basketry and pottery. For the Hopi, the perfect individual is one who obeys the laws and conforms to the pure and perfect pattern laid down by the Creator and then becomes a Kachina when he dies and goes directly to the next universe without having to pass through all of the intermediate worlds or stages of existence [31]. The Hopi suggest that life is a process. A process of childhood, youth, adulthood, and old age that follows a path that leads to the sun [32]. They also believe that long ago people lived in the underworld where there was much rain and crops grew very well. Unfortunately, people began to quarrel as they do today so they had to journey to the upper world and wander until the Bear Clan group arrived at Shungopovi and took possession of the land [32].

Unlike the Navajo and the Apache, the Hopi do not seem to have such great fear of the ghost. The Hopi suggest that the dead return as Kachinas, intermediaries, or messengers rather than as gods, to help humankind on its evolutionary journey [31]. The famous and valuable Kachina dolls represent Kachinas, but they are not given power. They help children to know the masks and names of real Kachinas, but they are not sacred objects with spiritual powers [31]. The Hopi compare the journey of the individual to the journey of their people. One follows the path of life and, at death, the individual is allowed to return to the lowerworld through the place of emergence to the ultimate home where the souls of the dead live like those living on earth [32]. The souls of the dead often revisit the upperworld in the form of clouds represented by the masked dancers called Kachinas to bring rain and other necessities to the living [31].

Like the Navajo and the Apache, the Hopi seem to feel that excessive handling of the dead body could cause illness [33]. While all three tribes exhibit great fear of death and the dead, the Hopi remain in the house where the death took place and do not destroy the dwelling as the Apache and Navajo often do [34].

When one is dying, the young leave the house of death so that they do not become frightened or even die because of their fear, and only the brave remain with the dying [34]. The adult who chooses to stay will attend the dying and prepare the body after the person dies. A man would be wrapped in buckskin and a woman in her wedding blanket, with both being buried in whatever he or she was wearing at the time of death [34]. The Hopi do not wash or prepare the body in any way other than to wash the hair with yucca suds and to tie the hair with yucca fiber. They place the body in a sitting position with the knees and arms flexed and tied with yucca to hold them in place if necessary [34]. After the death, the father of the dead person or a man in the clan of the dead person will immediately make prayer feathers and tie one to the body's hair, one to each foot for the journey to the next world, one over the navel where the breath of a man lives, and one under each hand [34]. The face would be covered with raw cotton to signify the future existence of the deceased as a cloud. Piki bread and a small gourd of water would be placed in the pockets of the dead person to provide lunch for their journey to the next world [33]. One of the men will carry the body to the cemetery, dig a hole for the body, place the body in the hole, fill the gravesite, and place a stick on the grave to provide a ladder for the deceased to climb to the next world [34].

The Hopi believe that Masau'u is the God of Death and is in charge of the underworld where dead spirits go and that a touch of his club brings death to the living. Masau'u is in the dark, which leads the Hopi to fear the dark [33]. Traditionally, the Hopi made a great show of not mourning for their dead, but now they, like the Navajo, let the missionaries bury their dead. The Hopi also have mourning rituals [33]. Like the Anasazi, the Hopi use Kivas for rituals and bury their deceased beneath the Kivas [35]. The hole in the floor of the Kiva represents the place of emergence in the path of life [32].

Anasazi Burial Practices

The Anasazi culture is perhaps the most famous of the prehistoric tribes because of Mesa Verde National Park. It is also one of the newest prehistoric tribes with a rich cultural heritage. For over a thousand years, the Anasazi culture flourished. They developed weaving of baskets, foot coverings, utensils, clothing, and storage containers of many sizes and purposes [6]. The pit house, which ultimately evolved into the Kiva, was developed along with basketry to include the making of burial shrouds [36]. The Anasazi culture covered a great territory and numerous communities that supported hundreds of people. Many of the artifacts that were left behind still have the bright colors and exhibit the craft of their construction that belies their age of hundreds of years [36]. While no explanation exists as to what happened to these people, there is not evidence of any warfare or destruction by another culture [6].

While not much is known of their burial practices, they did leave behind artifacts that provide clues to some of their basic practices. When a death occurred, the Anasazi placed the deceased in a tight flexed position with the knees to the chest and buried them with many possessions such as beads, sandals, digging sticks, blankets, smoking pipes, and mats. The body was placed in a basket and mats were laid over the body before the grave was covered [36]. At times, the Anasazi apparently buried their dead beneath garbage piles and rockslides; though it could be that the dead fell to their deaths into the garbage piles or were crushed to death by rockslides. In other eras, there is no evidence of burials of any sort. Perhaps the dead are sealed into places that have not yet been discovered. At other times, the Anasazi sealed their dead in rooms of their houses where they still remain [37].

Like the later Hopi and Zuni tribes, the Anasazi made Kivas of two distinct types. Some were circular, while others were rectangular. Some Kivas had roofs, and other Kivas had none [35]. Since the Anasazi buried their dead where they lived and provided them with possessions for an afterlife, it would seem that they had little fear of the dead or of ghosts.

PLAINS TRIBAL BURIAL PRACTICES

Sioux Burial Practices

Like the Apache and Navajo, the name Sioux is not the name of the tribe. The word Sioux in Teton dialect would be Lakota or in Santee dialect Dakota according to Terrell [6]. There is probably more generalized knowledge of Plains tribes since they are most often portrayed in movies and television. Unlike the more sedentary tribes of the Southwest, the Plains tribes were mobile on a large scale. With the great temperature variations of the Great Plains, the inhabitants needed to adapt to all kinds of climatic changes. They were primarily dependent upon the bison as a source of food, clothing, and shelter. Other animals and plant life were also major sources of food, but the bison offered the most dramatic picture of the life of the Plains tribes. There were sedentary tribes, but the various groups that spoke the Siouan language were the hunters and nomads of film and television. The coming of the horse following the arrival of the Europeans added greatly to their prowess as warriors and hunters. A war-like tribe, they have made their name in history by fighting against the European Americans in such famous battles as "Little Big Horn" and "Wounded Knee." The former recently portrayed in Kevin Costner's film, "Dances with Wolves," and earlier portrayed in the film, "Little Big Man" which starred Dustin Hoffman.

The eight (seven main tribes and one, the Assiniboin, were outside of the loose confederation) Sioux tribes were relatively similar in their burial and mortuary practices. Like many other Western tribes, the Plains tribes believed that everything in the world around them was filled with spirits and powers that affected their lives, whether from the sun, the mountains, the buffalo, or the eagle [38].

For the Lakota, the healers were typically senior men or women who had a calling to be healers in dreams or visions that were beyond their control. A person's vision comes from the spirit world. The person may take years to complete his or her vision quest. At one level, the vision quest is a life-long activity. To determine one's role in life might require only a few weeks or months. The vision quest ceremony is much shorter, but it is an equally powerful event. For an excellent description of the ceremony, read Stolzman [39]. If one has a calling to be a healer as a herbalist, medicine person, or shaman, one may therefore be obligated to begin healing work. DeMallie and Parks indicate that once a person assumes the obligation to pursue the career, it may take years to acquire the power and reputation to move from an assistant or singer to become a healer [40]. Like the Apache and Navajo, the Lakota have to request the services of the shaman. Like the Apache and the Navajo, the Lakota shaman may refuse to provide those services. The curing rituals for the Lakota are based upon family and friends being present. Unlike the Apache, the Lakota will want the children to be present. Social support of close friends and family is expected. Friends and family surround a person who is seriously ill to provide social support and share rituals. Even if one uses white medicine, one might also have Lakota curing rituals performed. The concept of social support is encouraged as a way to help the patient to achieve balance and harmony. One's friends do not wait in a waiting room. Strangers do not administer to a patient. The sense of wholeness and harmony that is gained from the social support of many friends and family members will aid the patient to gain a better sense of self-understanding. It will also provide an awareness of balance and harmony that will also lessen the fears of the illness or injury and also lower the feelings of depression and loneliness. The main motif of the Lakota ritual is purification.

The world is full of wonders, and humans are given the privilege to live in a world that is so wonderful. The longer that a Lakota lives, the more praise that he or she is to give. The healing ceremonies of the Lakota not only seek to heal the sick, but the healing ceremonies also offer a calmness and confidence to the tribal community. Drums, singing, dancing, and prayer are basic to the Lakota culture. The traditional ceremonies were passed down through the oral tradition of the Lakota. Since many of them now have been written, there have been changes. The Lakota way of producing a singing voice is somewhat unique. Lakota music produces sounds that range from an ear-piercing sound to a very mellow sound. When the melody descends, the voice gets more rhythmic. When women sing, they often develop a trilling sound to indicate happiness or appreciation. The voices of singers are judged on range, volume, and quality. The Lakota sing about sacred ways, sacred things, and to aid others. The Lakota are a spiritual people.

The spirit world is part of everything. The Lakota see everything as being filled with spirits and powers that control or otherwise effect the lives of the people [38]. The mountains, the eagle, the buffalo, the wolf, and the fox all have spiritual powers and medicines that effect the lives and even cause the deaths of people. People are no better or worse than other living things. Whatever will be will be. The earth feeds us, clothes us, and is there for us to use and to preserve. We are just passing through. We do not own the world. The Great Spirit or Great Mystery is the essence that permeates all life [20]. You have to know who you are to feel the Great Spirit in nature. It is only through nature that one can gain communion with the Holy Mystery [20]. The sacred pipe or calumet is the most sacred of all religious objects. The pipe, like the buffalo, corn, and all things, is a gift from the holy powers that run the world [41]. By smoking, one expresses the desire to have everything in one's life expressed as prayer that ascended to the Great Spirit or Great Mystery [41]. The world is sacramental and full of gifts of God that should cause one to return one's self to that God or spirit [41]. The Black Hills are sacred because everything that the Lakota might need or desire could be found there. The Black Hills are the throb of Earth Mother, and we, as humans, are to treat all other humans as brothers and sisters in order to elevate our inner spirits [20]. How we treat others determines how we become as humans [20]. The essence of humans is contemplative to the Lakota, that humans should appreciate the splendors of creations and give a proper return to the Great Spirit who was responsible for providing such creations [41]. There are five great values for the Sioux. One is to be generous and sharing, honor nature, live a life of freedom and courage, show respect for the old ones, and to live with nature in a natural lifestyle.

Like the Apache, the Lakota did not develop a strong attachment to material goods. As a nomadic people, the Lakota did not have a permanent place that would allow them to amass worldly goods. Like the Apache, the Lakota had equality. According to Steiger, women served on councils, played an important role in the affairs of the tribe, and helped make tribal decision in spite of the fact that white leaders refused to meet with them to discuss tribal issues [20]. For the Lakota, the dignity of every person must be held sacred. As with the Apache, there are four seasons, four directions, four winds, and four ages of humans. Everything must return to the circle. The circle includes the sun rising each day and setting each night, and if left incomplete in our lives, the lack of a circle affects one's physical, mental, and spiritual self [20]. The Lakota suggest that non-Indians should listen to the earth. One should try to hear what the ground has to say. What is the essence of the spirit of the earth? What is the essence of the spirit of the water? Of the mountains? Of the air? What is each of them saying to us? The Lakota typically carry a medicine bag that contains something of meaning from each of the four elements of the world. This may include ash or burned rock representing fire, a dried plant representing water, a piece of bone or feather representing air, and a stone or rock from the earth. Each item has something to say to the person. Each person must listen and then learn. The six powers—the Father Sky, the Earth Mother, and the four directions—are all part of the mystery of the Wakan Tanka or the Great Holy. Everything is sacred and is provided to help those who are willing to listen. The Lakota, like many other tribes, accept the concept of a guardian spirit who will also help those who will listen [9]. For the Lakota, health and illness and dying are a part of life. One accepts one's fate. How one lives determines that fate.

Like the tribes previously discussed, the Sioux feared the dead and would burn the dwelling of the deceased, forbid the use of his or her name, and bury personal goods with the corpse to keep the ghost of the deceased from coming along to live with friends and relatives [42]. Yet, death in old age was not feared nor were their ghosts who were thought to remain among the living for a time after their death [36].

The Sioux took the position that death will occur to all regardless of one's achievements, fame, wisdom, bravery, or whatever and that the mortuary practices allowed the living a way of showing their reverent respect for the dead [43]. If the deceased were a young person, and particularly a child, the mourners would gash their arms and legs and engage in ritual crying [36]. When death occurred in the home, the burial would be delayed for a day and a half in the hope that the deceased might revive [43]. The body would be dressed in the finest clothes available that would be provided by a relative if the deceased had none. The body would be wrapped tightly in robes with the weapons, tools, medicines, and pipe; and then, the bundle would be placed on a scaffold for air burial with food and drink placed beneath the scaffold for the deceased [36].

Some Dakota or Sioux groups used earth burial. There is evidence that in earlier times they used mound burial [36]. During winter when scaffolds could not be built, trees were often used for burial [43]. After the body was prepared and properly wrapped, the adult members of the family began wacekiyapi or worship rite for the deceased in which men might run pegs through their arms or legs, women might slash their limbs and cut off their little fingers at the first joint. Both men and women might cut their hair and express their grief by singing, wailing, or weeping [43]. The favorite horse of the deceased would be killed beneath the scaffold of its owner and its tail tied to the scaffold. The mourning would continue for as long as a year [44]. By placing the body on a scaffold or in a tree, the Dakotas and similar tribes believed that the soul would then be free to rise into the sky if the person died of natural causes. If the person died in battle, the Dakotas would often leave the person on the plains where he was slain to allow his spirit to rise into the sky [38]. For the Dakota or Sioux, the spirits of the dead are not gone or lost to humankind, but rather continue to exist here and can be reached by the living for support and aid [40].

Burial Practices of the Cheyenne

The Cheyenne lived among the Blackfoot, Crow, Dakota, and Comanche, among others. The Cheyenne joined the Sioux and Arapahos to defeat George Armstrong Custer in 1876 at Little Big Horn [45]. Like other Plains tribes, the Cheyenne believed that a supernatural power permeates every phase of being, including peace, war, hunting, courtship, art, and music [46]. Like the other Plains tribes, the Cheyenne came to depend upon the bison. The burial practices of the Cheyenne were like those of the Arapaho, Comanche, Kiowa, Kiowa Apache, and Sioux or Dakota Tribes [43]. When the Cheyenne buried their dead in the ground, they would cover the grave with rocks, and those who passed by would place a rock or other symbolic artifact on the grave to give honor to the deceased [47]. Another slight difference in mortuary practices that separates the Cheyenne from the other Plains tribes would be that the Cheyenne would give the property not buried with the warrior who died to his widow or to the daughters. To the sons, they would give nothing, with the idea that the sons could steal their own goods from their enemy's [48].

BURIAL PRACTICES OF THE MOUNDS BUILDERS

The early history of the U.S. tribes is not completely developed. Perhaps, between 25,000 and 40,000 years ago, tribes began to occupy what is now the United States. The early Folsom discovery suggests that the early tribes were skilled hunters who destroyed mammoths, muskox, and bison, but they did not keep any records or leave any remains to allow knowledge of what kind of culture and people they were. What is available for study is the enormous number of mounds that are scattered from Southern Mexico to the Great Lakes to Florida. A great deal of controversy does, however, surround whom the mounds builders were.

One argument is that the mounds builders were a superior group when compared to ordinary Native Americans and are a vanished people who were of the Israelite tribe of Joseph, and they are the ones who built the mounds [49]. Powell suggests that there was not a single group or tribe who built the mounds and that any search for the original tribe was simply fruitless [50]. Henry C. Schoolcraft, in a masterful six volume text, suggests that there is nothing to suggest that the mounds builders had Asiatic or European origins from the artifacts left behind nor that any of the tribes who build mounds were in any way connected to each other [51]. The Angel site, the Clovis site, the Cahokia site, the Hopewell site, Moundville (Alabama), and numerous others are similar to one another, but there is no real evidence of what rituals or attitudes the people who buried their deceased practiced. Nor is their any evidence of social differentiation of those who were buried. Mounds range from rooms constructed for burial as in the Angel site to burial in a trash heap in Arizona. While there are thousands of mounds all across the United States, much of what was buried has rotted and disappeared leaving behind only things made of stone, copper, shell, and bones [51]. What little information that does exist suggests that the peoples who built mounds must have had a farming culture and that they were able to support a large population. It is possible that North American tribes began farming as early as 9,000 to 11,000 years ago [44]. Mounds range in size from small hills to hundreds of acres. They range in shapes from small mounds of dirt to a pyramid shape [6].

Mounds were constructed with flat stones, dirt, poles, twigs, grass, mud coatings, mud plaster, slab lids, and whatever else that could be used including garbage [3]. The mounds have included gifts and supplies for the deceased to use on their journey [51]. Rather than being a culture of mound builders, it may be that what occurred was simply that various tribes disposed of their dead in similar ways. Some tribes built pyramids while others built humps. Typically, most tribes have offered goods and gifts to the deceased. The mound builders may have offered such gifts and simply placed the body on the ground. After the body was covered, it may have created a mound over time. A lack of digging tools or whatever could explain their practices.

NORTH AMERICAN NATIVE CARE OF
THE DYING AND GRIEVING

The basis of the care of the dying by Native Americans lies in nature and healing rituals. The use of medicine by Native Americans was a major part of their healing or caring practices for the ill and dying. According to Hightower, over 200 drugs that are now used by white medicine have their origins from Native Americans [52]. Native American healing arts have included sweat baths, rituals, and herb medicines. Nature is the basis of the healing. Even the medicines are natural. Rituals are used when picking the plants, processing the plants for use, and when administering the medicines to patients. The health care of the white culture also includes medicine, but it does not include rituals. When white medicine allows the use of the shaman and healers with their rituals, the healing or serenity of dying is enhanced. Quite often, the Native American perceives his or her illness to be caused by something other than what the white physician has diagnosed. The hospitals are unfamiliar. The patient is often forced to wait, often alone, for long periods of time without any explanation or reason being given to them. Physicians and caregivers at white institutions are often demanding and impatient. This often results in the Native American patient reacting by silence, fear, or simply leaving the hospital or institution providing care. White medicine is typically not explained to the patient. It is refused, not taken, or simply discarded when the caregivers are no longer present. White medicine appears to be unnatural when it is administered in bottles, capsules, or syringes.

The staff of the hospital may feel just as estranged as the Native American who comes to use their services. Hospital staff often resent the large number of Native Americans who enter the patient's room. They also often come when it is not visiting time and seemingly stay forever. They may also want to burn items to make the room sacred. The cleansing smoke may set off alarms and sprinklers. Their methods of bathing, their refusal to wear hospital gowns, and their loud singing make it quite difficult for the staff to accept them. The lack of visitors for the dying Apache also puzzles them.

Native Americans generally accept death. It is inevitable. It is not the fault of the shaman or caregiver. It was the person's time to die or the spirits were stronger than the shaman was. Death by suicide is viewed differently. Native American culture places much value on children. Prayers and rituals were performed to give health and life to children [53]. My own study of suicide among 14 tribes suggests that ethnic renewal will lower suicide rates among Native Americans. Consistently, those responding to questions about suicide reported that loneliness, isolation, peer pressure, difficulty, depression, and bad spirits drove people to suicide. They also consistently indicated that those who commit suicide would wander the earth as lost lonely spirits who will never rest in peace. They also indicated that suicides could be avoided by following traditional ways—prayer, rituals, and remaining spiritual. Each life has a purpose. One may have a vision quest to find that purpose. Suicide prevents one from living the life that was intended. Similarly, euthanasia may prevent one from following his or her vision quest. When it is one's time to die, then one will die. One should not prevent death if it is time, nor should one cause another or oneself to die before his or her time. When death does occur, specific rituals and practices are to be followed to dispose of the dead.

There is evidence that U.S. tribes used all known methods of disposal of the dead ranging from burial both in the ground and in the air, cremation, and mummification. It is also probable that the cause of death, where the death occurred, the age of the deceased, the sex of the deceased, and the social status of the deceased impacted the mortuary and burial practices of the tribe. We do lack sufficient information about how such factors influence burial practices. Evidence tends to show a general pattern that many tribes exhibit a fear of the dead. It is also likely that climate, weather, availability of materials to dispose of the body, and religious beliefs were major determinants as to how bodies of the dead were disposed. Burial practices also seemed to remain stable for a remarkably long period of time in most tribes [54]. Almost universally, tribes provide provisions for a spirit journey, whether for a single burial or for a group burial [3]. If nothing else is known, it is clear that tribal groups did not abandon their dead. They provided them with ceremonies and dignified disposal. Native Americans provide social support through the tribe or clan of the individual in the dying and burial process. That same social support system sustains the bereaved after the disposal of the dead. The grief process includes the ceremony of the funeral, the burial, and the give-away ceremony. Extreme emotions are usually managed by these ceremonies. The spiritual nature of the living and the dead permeate the entire process.

REFERENCES

1. B. Malinowski, *Magic, Science, and Religion and Other Essays*, Doubleday, Garden City, New York, 1925.
2. J. G. Fraser, On Certain Burial Customs as Illustrative of Primitive Theory of the Soul, *Royal Anthropological Institue of Great Britain and Ireland, 15*, pp. 64-104, 1886.
3. M. J. Atkinson, *Indians of the Southwest*, Naylor, San Antonio, Texas, 1935.
4. B. Steiger, *Medicine Power: The American Indian's Revival of his Spiritual Heritage*, Doubleday, Garden City, New York, 1974.
5. J. Highwater, *Indian America*, McKay, New York, 1975.
6. J. U. Terrell, *The American Indian Almanac*, Barnes and Noble, New York, 1971.
7. K. H. Basso, To Give Up On Words: Silence in the Western Apache Culture, *Southwestern Journal of Anthropology, 26*:3, pp. 213-230, 1970.
8. J. Sherman, *Indian Tribes of North America*, Crescent, New York, 1996.
9. M. E. Opler, *An Apache Life-Way: The Economic, Social, and Religious Institutions of the Chiricahua Indians*, University of Chicago Press, Chicago, 1941.
10. V. E. V. Tiller, *The Jicarilla Apache Tribe: A History, 1846-1970*, University of Nebraska, Lincoln, Nebraska, 1983.
11. M. J. Lewis and J. Hughes, A Comparison of the Effects of Sacred and Secular Music on Elderly People, *Journal of Psychology, 131*:1, pp. 45-55, 1997.
12. F. R. Gustafson, *Dancing Between Two Worlds: Jung and the Native American Soul*, Paulist Press, New York, 1997.
13. C. F. Starkloff, *The People of the Center: American Indian Religion and Christianity*, Seabury Press, New York, 1974.
14. H. H. Stoeckel, *Survival of the Spirit*, University of Nevada, Reno, Nevada, 1993.
15. G. Goodwin, *The Social Organization of the Western Apache*, University of Chicago Press, Chicago, 1942.
16. J. L. Haley, *Apaches: A History and Cultural Portrait*, Doubleday, Garden City, New York, 1981.
17. J. C. Cremony, *Life Among the Apaches: 1849-1864*, Roman and Company, San Francisco, 1951.
18. B. Dutton and C. Olin, *Myths and Legends of the Indians of the Southwest: Navajo, Pima, Apache*, Bellerophon Books, Santa Barbara, California, 1979.

19. T. E. Mails, *The People Called Apache*, Prentice-Hall, Englewood Cliffs, New Jersey, 1974.

20. B. Steiger, *Indian Medicine Power*, Whitford Press, West Chester, Pennsylvania, 1984.

21. E. Shorris, *The Death of the Great Spirit: An Elegy for the American Indian*, Crescent, New York, 1971.

22. D. Leighton and C. Kluckhohn, *Children of the People: The Navajo Individual and His Development*, Harvard University Press, Cambridge, 1948.

23. Franciscan Fathers, *An Ethnological Dictionary of the Navaho Language*, The Franciscan Fathers, St. Michaels, Arizona, 1910.

24. C. Frisbie and D. P. McAllester (eds.), *Navajo Blessing Way Singer: The Autobiography of Frank Mitchell, 1881-1967*, University of Arizona, Tucson, Arizona, 1978.

25. G. A. Reichard, *Social Life of the Navajo Indians*, Columbia University Press, New York, 1928.

26. R. W. Young, *The Navajo Yearbook*, Arizona Navajo Agency, Window Rock, Arizona, 1961.

27. R. W. Habenstein and W. M. Lamers, *Funeral Customs the World Over*, Bulfin, Milwaukee, 1963.

28. J. G. Monroe and R. A. Williamson, *They Dance in the Sky: Native American Star Myth*, Houghton Mifflin, Boston, 1987.

29. E. C. Vogt, Navajo, in *Perspectives in American Indian Cultural Change*, E. H. Spicer (ed.), University of Chicago Press, Chicago, 1961.

30. R. M. Underhill, *The Navajo*, University of Oklahoma Press, Norman, Oklahoma, 1956.

31. F. Waters, *Book of the Hopi*, Viking, New York, 1963.

32. L. Thompson, *Culture in Crisis: A Study of the Hopi Indians*, Harper, New York, 1950.

33. V. E. V. Tiller, *The Hopi Indians of Old Oraibi: Change and Continuity*, University of Michigan, Ann Arbor, Michigan, 1972.

34. E. Beaglehole and P. Beaglehole, *Hopi of the Second Mesa*, Millwood, New York, 1976.

35. J. W. Fewkes, *Preliminary Report of a Visit to the Navaho National Monument Arizona*, U.S. Government Printing Office, Washington, D.C., 1911.

36. R. F. Spencer, J. D. Jennings, C. E. Dibble, E. Johnson, A. R. King, T. Stern, K. M. Stewart, O. C. Stewart, and W. J. Wallace, *The Native Americans*, Harper and Row, New York, 1965.

37. S. E. Fletcher, *The American Indiana*, Grossett and Dunlap, New York, 1954.

38. B. Copps, *The Indians*, Time-Life, New York, 1973.

39. W. Stolzman, *How to Take Part in Dakota Ceremonies*, Tipi Press, Chamberlain, South Dakota, 1995.

40. R. J. DeMallie and D. R. Parks, *Sioux Indian Religion: Tradition and Innovation*, University of Oklahoma Press, Norman, Oklahoma, 1987.

41. D. L. Carmody and J. T. Carmody, *Native American Religions: An Introduction*, Paulist Press, New York, 1993.

42. O. Lafarge, *A Pictorial History of the American Indian*, Crown Publishers, New York, 1956.

43. R. B. Hassrick, *The Sioux: Life and Customs of a Warrior Society*, University of Oklahoma Press, Norman, Oklahoma, 1964.

44. J. W. Powers, *Indians of the Southern Plains*, Capricorn, New York, 1971.

45. H. E. Driver, *Indians of North America*, University of Chicago Press, Chicago, 1969.
46. G. A. Dorsey, *The Cheyenne*, Rio Grande Press, Glorieta, New Mexico, 1971.
47. M. Sandoz, *Cheyenne Autumn*, Hastings House, New York, 1953.
48. K. N. Llewellyn and E. A. Hoebel, *The Cheyenne Way: Conflict and Case Law in Primitive Jurisprudence*, University of Oklahoma Press, Norman, Oklahoma, 1941.
49. R. Silverberg, *Mound Builders of Ancient America: The Archaeology of a Myth*, New York Graphic Society, Greenwich, Connecticut, 1968.
50. J. W. Powell, On Limitations to Use of Some Anthropological Data, in *Smithsonian Institution Bureau of Ethnology First Annual Report, 1879-1880*, U.S. Government Printing Office, Washington, D.C., 1940.
51. F. H. H. Roberts, Jr., *Archaeological Remains in the Whitewater District Eastern Arizona*, U.S. Government Printing Office, Washington, D.C., 1940.
52. J. Hightower, *Indian America*, David McKay, New York, 1975.
53. F. W. Voget, *They Call Me Agnes: A Crow Narrative Based on the Life of Agnes Yellowtail Deernose*, University of Oklahoma Press, Norman, Oklahoma, 1995.
54. E. W. Voegelin, *Mortuary Customs of the Shawnee and Other Eastern Tribes*, Indiana Historical Society, Indianapolis, Indiana, 1944.

CHAPTER 11

The Wheel of Life: The Concept of Death and Bereavement in the Pagan Community

Rev. Mia Reeves

HISTORY OF PAGANISM

When speaking of the pagans of a community it is necessary to realize that there are many different sects of paganism. There is Asatru, the heathens, who follow the Nordic pantheon. There are the Kemetics, who emulate the ancient Egyptians in their beliefs. There is Goddess worship, which honors various Goddesses and their laws. There is Wicca, a religion with its base in ancient nature worship, which is divided into many different traditions, including Gardnerian, Alexandrian, Dianic, Faery, Celtic, Eclectic, and solitary practitioners. There are many more types of pagans, but they all have a core system of belief surrounding the concept of life and death.

In order to comprehend the views of each, understanding the original inception of the pagan belief system is an invaluable asset.

The word *pagan* has its roots in *paganus*—of the country. Those who were born and lived in the Western world outside of the hub of Roman law and/or influence of the teachings of The Bible in the British Isles were a simple folk whose religious beliefs were founded in the natural world that surrounded them. They celebrated Festivals and Holidays that corresponded with the solstices and equinoxes, and the time of planting, harvest, and the turning of the seasons. They were lead by a priestess and priest who conducted these rituals and supported those of the community [1].

They lived fully. They took delight and pleasure in all that life had to offer. Sexuality was not imbued with the negativity that it has taken on today with the morals of the Victorian era coloring the natural act of copulation. At

Beltane—May Day—the villagers celebrated the planting by lighting bonfires, having joyous celebrations, and ending the ritual by pairing off and retiring to the woods to enact the sanctity of the "Great Rite"—symbolic of the consummation of the union between the Maiden Goddess and the God of the Greenwood which brings fertility to the world.

Midsummer was the celebration of the harvest and the birth of the Sun King. His birth after He fathered Himself represents the growth and gathering of the crops that provided sustenance and life to the villagers who celebrated this holiday.

The Sun King's reign is short lived however—at Mabon, the final harvest, he is sacrificed to ensure the return of the sun. This is the final holiday of the year for the pagans.

Samhain was the beginning of the year for the pagan, and on this solemn night the veil between the worlds was considered to be at its thinnest. The ancestors were honored, and those who had gone before them in the prior year were celebrated and remembered. The serpent was not a representation of evil, but of regeneration—it shed its skin as a pagan's unique spirit shed its body in preparation of the next life [2].

The pagans accepted this circle of life. Their religion exemplified their belief that the Wheel turned not only for the Mother Earth, but for each of them as well. They believed in reincarnation, and knew that they would return time and time again to the earth in human form, and that they had set foot there many times before. Life was sacred to the pagans; they respected the life force and gift of life that they were given by their deities. The most honored rite that could be enacted was the giving of life to the Gods in hopes to entreat them for a fruitful harvest.

Despite the myths and tales that surround their belief practices, pagans sacrificed life forces only under extreme circumstances. Animals were sacrificed before humans were, with prayers and thanks to their noble spirits being offered. Only in extreme circumstances were humans sacrificed—such as if there were a drought or if the crops were failing.

The circle of life was accepted and expected by those who worshiped the nature pantheon. They believed in reincarnation, and that they spent the time waiting for their next incarnation in the Summerlands, a beautiful natural area abundant with food and drink. Here they rested from the experience of their prior lives, readying themselves for their next one. They chose their new body and those who would bear them in their quest to learn the lessons necessary and to deal with karma acquired in past lives.

Life was sacred. It was a gift of the Gods, and not taken lightly. They were a joyous, passionate people who lived their existences to the fullest. The life force was considered a power, and there was no greater honor than to give one's life in the sacrifice representing the death of the Sun King, in order to sustain the village and assist the Mother Earth in giving her bounty.

Death happened; it was natural. Their grief rituals were not mournful, pain-wracked ceremonies. The High Priestess, family, and village would join with the soul making their transition, not fearful of death but singing, chanting, and praying as they sat with the person facing their movement into the Summerlands. After the person passed, friends and relatives would have a supper consisting of the deceased's favorite meals, so that the soul could enjoy the fruits of the earth one last time before moving on [1].

In the funeral itself, the family and friends did not express themselves by wailing or grieving; this would frighten and confuse the departed spirit, who could still be with them. As those who left this incarnation moved toward the Summerlands, the priestess kept up a constant dialogue with the departed, comforting and guiding them to the new plane of existence. Sometimes the spirit was confused and had difficulty finding its way home, and the priestess' discourse was helpful in dispelling this fear and confusion.

The women's bodies were buried, while the men were hung in sacks in the trees for the Bird Goddess. The pagans felt that the body without the soul was a mere vessel, and it should be returned to the Earth Mother from whence it came [1].

The Vikings/Nordic people had a similar rich view of life. They believed in karmic law in that their afterlife offered both a paradise and place of punishment, and one's behavior in life determined to which of Hel's realms one was relegated. Those who were chosen by a specific Goddess or God went to reside in their hall; the most familiar of these was Thor's hall of Valhalla, set aside for those valiant in battle [3]. The more familiar of the other Goddesses and Gods were Odin, Frigga, Tyr, Sif, Frey, Freyja, Heimdal, and Balder [4].

The Vikings believed that they were not only the worshipers of the Gods, but also "spiritually and physically" related to them. They followed a high code of honor, found within the Nine Noble Virtues and the book of the *Poetic Edda* called "Havamal." The Nine Noble Virtues were those of Courage, Truth, Honor, Fidelity, Discipline, Hospitality, Industriousness, Self-Reliance, and Perseverance. The Havamal provides rules of conduct as well, through its teachings [4]. They also had a system of Nordic runes which not only comprised their alphabet but also were symbolic in their order and their shape.

To the Nordic people who followed this rich religion, death was not seen as the total ending of existence, as did the earth worshipers. They saw that nature evidenced the constant renewal of life after death. They had a varying manner of burial for those who had made their transitions.

The first was a funeral pyre. It has been discovered in actual archeological sites the presence of human sacrifice (a wife or devoted servant typically) and the sacrifice of numerous animals. The person who had died was also supplied with all the needed tools for existence in the afterlife.

The second form of burial was internment in the earth. The site was usually shaped like a boat, and these mounds were made large enough to accommodate those sacrifices and implements which would accompany the dead on their journey into the next realm [4].

Kemetic was the term which the practitioners of the faith of Ancient Egypt called themselves. It was a monalatryous religion, in that they believed in one source of the Divine represented by many different aspects. What might appear to the layman as a polytheistic belief structure was rather something much more involved, combining elements of both polytheism and monotheism [5].

The Egyptians believed in an afterlife and, much as did the Nordic people, interred tools and sacrificial victims along with the deceased. They believed in resurrection and that the corruption of the body would affect them in the future. Thus, the need for the preparation of the corpse in the elaborate mummification process was a way of ensuring eternal life for those who could afford this preparation.

Many other pagan religions existed, each with their own rich belief structures and views of the afterlife. One factor typified all of these faiths—they believed that the spirit did not cease to exist once the body had died. It is also fair to state that most pagan religions realized the concept of reincarnation and life eternally renewing itself from watching the Earth move from her dormant to fertile period, and then back again, in a never-ending Wheel of Life.

TODAY'S PAGAN

As stated earlier, there are many different paths that pagans take in today's society. They follow much of the ancient laws and beliefs of the pantheons which they have chosen.

The most familiar to those outside of the pagan community is that of Wicca, which is the term used for those who follow the pagan path of Earth worship. What is not commonly understood, however, is that Wicca itself has many different sects and belief systems.

There are tenets accepted by every path of Wicca. Without exception, the Wiccan follows the Rede, a poem scribed by Doreen Valiente in the mid-twentieth century, which has the basic premise of "do as you will, save it harm none." They believe in a pantheon consisting of the Triple Goddess of the Moon and the Dual God of Nature. The names by which they call these deities differ not only from sect to sect, but from Coven to Coven; however, they are, for the most part, different names for the same Goddess and God. The differences between each path involves such names, varying laws concerning how an initiate may be accepted into a Coven and other worshiping Circle.

Each Deity represents the facets of the life cycle—from birth to death, all are intertwined [6]. The Goddesses and Gods of birth and sexual passion are also often associated with death, because "death is the gateway to another life" [7].

Those who follow the religion of Asatru believe in the Nordic pantheon of Odin, Freya, Thor, etc., as did the ancient Vikings who worshiped the same Gods. Asatru returned as a religion in the 1970s, and today, like Wicca, it is recognized by both the United States and Canadian government as valid. The name of "Asatru" means "those of the Aesir," or those of the Norse Gods [8].

They hold fast to the tenets of the Nine Noble Virtues and those found in the *Poetic Eddas*. Their faith recognizes a number of rituals, the most known of which are the "blot" and the "sumbel."

The blot is a sacrifice, and this entails a ritual sacrifice of a consecrated liquid to the Goddess or God being worshiped. Those who worship commune with the particular Deity being honored by drinking some, then pouring out the remainder as a libation. Typically, the liquid is alcoholic, such as cider, ale, or mead.

The Sumbel is a ritualized toast. There are three rounds of toasting: the first is dedicated to the various Goddesses and Gods, beginning with Odin. This is followed by a toast to the venerated ancestors, and culminates by an open third round [8].

When honoring those who make their transitions, formal acts of libations and toasts are included in the Asatrus' rituals.

The Kemetic still follow that which their predecessors believed, emulating their worship and honoring their Goddesses and Gods, in the form of one Deity, Netjer, who was the sum of all of the Goddesses and Gods.

It is divided into three main categories of devotion: the formal worship service (the "State" ritual), the devotional practice of its followers, and ancestral devotion. The State rituals are conservative rites practiced as close to the Ancient Egyptian manner of worship as possible. An example of this would be the *Rite of the House of the Morning*, which is a daily devotional to the sunrise, greeting the returning sun, which also includes invocations and praises to Netjer.

The practice of daily devotion is one that all followers, laymen and priests, must follow. The cornerstone of the "Kemetic Orthodox faith is found in the universal rite called the *Senut* (shrine)." Every devotee performs a set of prayers every day in their household shrine, where they both worship and communicate with Netjer.

Finally, there is the worship of ancestral devotion. The dead, *Akhu*, are obviously closer to Netjer than are those living in this plane of existence; in remembering and revering their beloved ancestors and others who are no longer with them, the dead continue to live forever. Offerings are left to the ancestors so that not only are they venerated, but they will look kindly on and protect the living [5].

It is obvious that today the practice of mummification and entombing those who make their transitions is no longer feasible. Still, the Kemetics honor their ancestors, venerating them even after death, remembering all that they represented.

Goddess worshipers are exactly that—those who follow the Will of the Goddess. Although they typically believe in a dual pantheon like the Wiccans above, their belief structure differs in that it is focused on the worship of the Goddess of the Ten Thousand Names. They call forth Her as Kali, Kuan Yin, Dianna, Aradia, and a myriad of others from the pantheons of various religions.

There are those who would argue that the Wiccans who follow the Diana tradition are solely Goddess worshipers, but as they follow the other laws and tenets of Wicca, this has no verity. Typically, a Dianic Wiccan only follows the Goddess in Her triple moon aspect of Maiden, Mother/Warrior, and Wise Woman/Crone. The names for each of these aspects may vary from Coven to Coven, but often they are Selene, Diana, or Artemis and Hecate, respectively.

DEATH

Although the religions that the pagans follow offer a view of the afterlife that is based on meritorious behavior and often pleasant and beautiful, there is many times the natural apprehension as the pagan approaches her or his transition. The fear of death that is found in those who follow the pagan path is often one developed by a Western concept with which most have been raised. Western religions, most notably Christianity, have a vision of the afterlife that contains not only a paradise but a place of torment and punishment for those who have not performed the necessary behavior in order to avoid this hell. For some of those who have embraced the pagan path after leaving such an organized religion, there remains a residual fear that perhaps they have erred in their beliefs and will be punished for them. The religions of the Book (i.e., Judaism, Christianity, and Islam) insist that their way is the only way, and those who deviate from this path are damned.

However, most come to terms with their fear of death, realizing the dichotomy that is evidenced by a belief shaded by fear and punishment. Should this be true, one of valor who leads an exemplary life, such as Ghandi or the Dalai Lama, is condemned to eternal torment. To one who believes in a Divine Spirit of compassion, this makes no sense. Pagans believe that we learn from our behavior in this life and either return to learn again or celebrate that which we have learned. Karmic laws (what you put out into the universe returns to you threefold) is not only dealt with after death, but also during present life. There is no hell, no place of eternal torment in many of the belief structures; and if a place of punishment exists, it is for those whose deeds on this plane merit such a punishment. Where there is light there is darkness, and this is a part of the natural order of things. The Mother who brings forth the harvest is also upheaved by earthquakes that can kill millions. There is no evil or good in either example; it simply is.

With this mentality in mind, the pagan prepares for death with less fear than perhaps a sadness in leaving this plane. If they have developed strong attachments, it is important for them to release them before making their transitions. There sometimes is the reluctance to release this life, as the patient may have found it sweet and long to retain contact with this plane.

Ritual is an integral part of the pagan belief system. They hold rituals for their holidays, for their Esbats, for their ceremonies such as handfasting (marriage) and croning (celebrating the end of menses of a woman), and for private ceremonies. From as simple a ritual as burning a candle while praying to a full-blown ritual involving a grove of celebrants with a High Priestess and Priest enacting a scripted ceremony, ritual becomes one of the manners in which the pagan connects to the numinous.

As such, there are grief rituals and the easing of transitions for those who are preparing to end their existence on this plane. When in the hospital, the patient should always have a fellow pagan there, someone familiar with whom they share either a friendship or a Sisterhood/Brotherhood. The patient should never be left alone, but should be spoken to, constantly, even if in a coma. If the body cannot react, certainly the spirit can. In this manner they are prepared to join with the Goddess and God, dispelling their attachment to this plane [1].

There are often different tools used to achieve this goal. Certain incenses, specific colored candles, music, and guided meditations are some of these. It is imperative that the patient, who has become accustomed to reacting favorably to these stimuli, be allowed to experience them in the setting in which they prepare for their transition. Rituals that assist those who love those who are about to depart should also be allowed. Grieving is a natural part of death, on both sides, and by allowing those involved with the passing to demonstrate and alleviate their grief is imperative [9]. The Asatru may wish to perform a Blot and Sumbel, the Kemetics share in a devotional prayer, or the earth worshipers call down the moon in a ritual to connect with the Mother. All of these must be allowed for the patient, for they will not only feel comfortable with the familiarity of these rituals, but know that they soon will be before the Goddesses and/or Gods of their belief (the Kemetic with Netjer).

In Wicca, there is a chant: "We all come from the Goddess, and to her we shall return, like a drop of rain flowing to the ocean." It is this mentality, the concept of uniting with the Goddesses and Gods of their personal beliefs, that must be stressed to the person preparing for joining with the Divine Spirit.

Two things of import: if the patient is a Dianic Wiccan or a Goddess worshiper, it is typical for them to be attended only by women [1]. Those who offer care to them in the hospital should be female, from the doctor to the interns. There is a difference between male and female energy, and for those who follow the Goddess path, this difference is integral to their sense of peace and comfort. This, of course, is left to the discretion of the patient, so that if she so wishes her entire family may be included as she prepares for her transition. However, initially she should be approached by females in order to honor her chosen path.

Secondly, there may be opposition from the family of the patient. If they are of a different belief structure, they may object to the patient being honored in a pagan manner. It is likely that they will wish the patient to be treated as if they are of the faith practiced by the family member(s). It is possible that they will refuse admittance to the members of the patient's Coven, Sisterhood, or Brotherhood, separating the patient from those with whom they feel a need to connect and assist in the coming transition.

It is important not to allow these well-meaning people to upset the patient or to bring their negative energy around them. If at all possible, they should be kept from the patient if she so desires. If they are unable to make such a decision (i.e., they are in a coma), this negativity should be disallowed [1]. As many of the pagan religions are not accepted by today's society, it is difficult for the patient's wishes to be respected by those who do not believe in their paths. No matter their faith, their beliefs should be treated with the respect that they deserve.

It is understandable that the loving family members fear for the soul of the patient, and will want to "save" them from the path that they have chosen. Just as it absolutely would be unacceptable for a Catholic priest to administer Catholic last rites to a Jewish patient simply because the family felt that this was better for their loved one, those of a pagan path should be treated with the same dignity and respect. Their beliefs may not be completely understood or accepted by those who are related to them, but their beliefs in no way lack the verity of their family's beliefs.

In conclusion, when a pagan is preparing for their transition, they typically will wish to be surrounded by those who honor them, those with whom they have celebrated the Goddesses and Gods of their beliefs. They will wish to contemplate their transitions in an atmosphere of peace, with the familiarity of the rituals and prayers that are part of their religion.

To quote a pagan woman with whom I am familiar: "I do know that when I pass I would like to be surrounded by friends and family. I would love for there to be music and I would love for all of us to build an altar together honoring the life I have just lived" [10]. For, as in the culture of the Celts, "it is felt that no one is truly gone until you stop telling their story" [10].

In the pagan's view, the story of those who are loved never ends.

REFERENCES

1. Z. Budapest, *The Holy Book of Women's Mysteries*, Wingbow Press, Oakland, California, 1989.
2. M. Pinoi, Death and the Modern Pagan, www.grailmedia.com.
3. T. Todd, Interview May 14, 2001, About.com Guide to Alternative Religions.
4. Asatru, www.ravennorth.com, 2001.
5. What is Kemetic Orthodoxy?, www.kemetic.org, The House of Netjer, 2001.
6. Starhawk, Samhain, www.belefnet.com.

7. M. Pinoi, Death and the Modern Pagan, www.grailmedia.com.
8. T. Todd, Religion and Faith Basics—Asatru, int. 3/28/01, About.com, Guide to Alternative Religions
9. Starhawk, *The Pagan Book of Living and Dying*, Harper, San Francisco, California, 1996.
10. C. Wykoff, Interview May 16, 2001, Interfaith Minister and Artistic Director of Earth Honoring Ritual Performing Group *Circle of Soul.*

BIBLIOGRAPHY

Adler, M., *Drawing Down the Moon,* Penguin/Arkana, New York, 1979.
Chadwick, N., *The Celts*, Penguin Books, New York, 1971.
Diana, Interview with Three Major Contributors to *The Pagan Book of Living and Dying*— Starhawk, www.reclaiming.org.
Ferrar, J. and Stewart, M. R., *The Witches' Bible*, Phoenix, Custer, Washington, 1996.
www.paganwiccan.about.com, Okelle.
Sulyma-Massoni, C., A Rite of Passage, Witches' League for Public Awareness, www.celticrow.com.

CHAPTER 12

Some Concluding Observations

John D. Morgan

I begin each of my courses with a slide that says that the study of death is life-enhancing. In accepting the limits of our financial resources, the limits of our time or energy, we budget to get the most from what we have. But our culture continues to allow us to think that we can always pull out of our pocket another five years of life, another ten years of a relationship. As Robert Kastenbaum has noted,

> Basically, one could have subtracted dying, death, and grief from human experience and it would have made little difference to the studies, texts, and courses promulgated by the social and behavioural sciences until the last few years—and even today, it is possible for future scholars and practitioners to complete their formal education with only the wispiest of thanatological encounters [1, p. 79].

One cannot talk about death and religion without mentioning spirituality. We have learned much from philosophical and theological traditions about the topic of spirituality. However, I think far more important is the lesson that we learn from the disadvantaged in the world: the dying, the grieving, and those who are dismissed by one or another prejudice in society; from those who at the bottom of the cultural heap. They too teach us about spirituality.

A few years ago I was invited by a colleague to address his class about death and spirituality. I began the class with the remark that being confused about spirituality is, in a sense, the way it ought to be. The question of spirituality flows from the most basic questions we as humans ask: "What do I know?" "What must I do?" "For what can I hope?" "Who am I?"

> The *spiritual* is a dimension of our humanness. Most dimensions of our humanness are not uniquely human. . . . [We share them with other creatures.] Spirituality is experienced at the meeting point, or as some would say, the

merging point, between our self and that which we usually feel is not our self
[2, pp. 52-53, *passim*]

Spirituality is the organization of consciousness [3, p. 540]; not some super-naturally oriented package of ideas. It is a focus on what we, our very natural bodies and brains, in this most natural world, *can become* [3, p. 540].

For Becker "Spirituality is not a simple reflex of hunger and fear, it is an expression of the will to live, the burning desire of the creature to count, to make a difference on the planet because he has lived, has emerged on it, has worked, suffered, and died" [4, p. 3]. Each choice that we make, whether it is simple as deciding between a 29 cent throwaway pen or a $200 precise writing instrument, entails value commitments. These value commitments are results of the spiritual nature of the person.

I believe that the following will be helpful in the analysis of spirituality. Barely skimming the surface of the history of thought, we see many definitions of what it is to be a person. These definitions range from "spiritual substance" [5], to "will to power" [6], and includes such awarenesses as the person as a moral creator [7], the person as a problem solver [8], the person as a network of relationships [9], the person as worker [10], the person as freedom [11], the person as sexual [12], the person as part of the Absolute [13], the person as redeemed [13], the person as destined to do the will of God [13].

Each of these views are intrinsically understandable. Each can be intelligently defended. Each make a certain kind of sense. We find ourselves agreeing with many of these positions in whole or in part. Yet, our agreement is a "yes, but!" We agree, more or less, not fully. The diversity of viewpoints teaches us the greatest lesson of spirituality: the person is a self-creator, a being who decides in one way or another what kind of being s/he will be. Our spirituality gives each of us the particular integration of these identifying characteristics. We thus arrive at a more formal definition of spirituality. *Spirituality refers to the ability of the human person to choose the relative importance of the physical, social, emotional, religious, and intellectual stimuli that influence him or her and thereby engage in a continuing process of meaning making.*

All conscious human activity is a form of spirituality; however, what is commonly spoken of as spirituality is what might be called "self-aware spirituality," that is an awareness of oneself as a unique center of knowledge and valuation. This spirituality is a two-edged sword. It is our agony and our ecstasy. Because of it we are aware of our radical otherness, what Ortega y Gasset called our radical solitude [14, p. 126]. As we mature spiritually we become more aware that we are not *just* a product of nature or of nurture. We become aware that we are self-creations. This self creation demands terrible responsibility and the loneliness that comes with responsibility.

Yet at the same time, in our self-aware spirituality our ego boundaries become permeable. We are aware of the connection of the self with other persons, with the environment, with our God. We become aware of a higher order of the universe, a meaning in the universe, in which we participate but which we do not control. We become aware of the sacredness of every moment. We become very conscious of the limits of time, and of our *vocation*. Each of us is a spiritual being who knows that s/he is alone in the universe. We have a need to make sense out of our lives and we know that this is the one chance that we have to be the person that we could be.

Since the person is a meaning seeking being, spiritual pain is produced when one has the sense that his/her life is meaningless. No one can tell another where to find meaning, we can only support one another in the process of meaning creation. We offer each other social support, that is, asking another "How are you?" and staying long enough to get the answer [15].

The great traditions that we have seen in this volume illustrate again and again that the human person is more than a physical object. The traditions agree that the person is on a path, a self made path, creating him or her self. The language may differ, but they agree on the idea of self creation. Finally, the great traditions indicate that we are not alone. Each of use a part of a larger whole and finds happiness in that larger whole.

Spirituality is fundamental to the human person. Spirituality shows itself primary as a continual quest for meaning. The dying and bereaved teach us that the processes in which they move occur because of the meanings that they have found in their own lives and the lives of their loved ones. Thus, dying and grieving as spiritual journeys perhaps best summed up in the phrase of Herman Feifel, "To die—this is the human condition; to live decently and well—this is man's privilege" [16, p. 12].

REFERENCES

1. R. Kastenbaum, Reconstructing Death in Postmodern Society. *Omega, 27*:1, pp. 75-89,1993.
2. D. Klass, Spirituality, Protestantism, and Death, in *Death and Spirituality*, K. J. Doka and J. D. Morgan (eds.), Baywood, Amityville, New York, pp. 51-74, 1993.
3. P. Hefner, The Spiritual Task of Religion in Culture: An Evolutionary Perspective, *Zygon: Journal of Religion and Science, 33*:4, pp. 535-544, 1998.
4. E. Becker, *Escape from Evil*, Collier Macmillan, New York, 1975.
5. T. Aquinas, Summa Theologiae, I, q. 75, A. 2, in *Introduction to Saint Thomas Aquinas*, A. C. Pegis (ed.), The Modern Library, New York, 1948.
6. J. J. Snyder, Fredrich Nietzsche: The Human Person as Will to Power, in *Images of the Human: The Philosophy of the Human Person in a Religious Context*, H. Brown, D. L. Hudecki, L. A. Kennedy, and J. J. Snyder (eds.), Loyola, Chicago, pp. 331-366, 1995.
7. I. Kant, *Foundations of the Metaphysics of Morals*, L. W. Beck (trans.), Bobbs-Merrill, Indianapolis, 1959.

8. W. James, The Sentiment of Rationality, in *Essays in Pragmatism*, A. Castell (ed.), Hefner, New York, 1948.

9. G. Marcel, *Being and Having: An Existentialist Diary*, Harper Torchbooks, New York, 1989.

10. M. T. Ryan, Karl Marx: The Human Person as Worker, in *Images of the Human: The Philosophy of the Human Person in a Religious Context*, H. Brown, D. L. Hudecki, L. A. Kennedy, and J. J. Snyder (eds.), Loyola, Chicago, pp. 251-294, 1995.

11. J.-P. Sartre, Existentialism, in *Existentialism and Human Emotions*, J.-P. Sartre (ed.), Citadel, Secaucus, New Jersey, pp. 9-51, 1957.

12. D. W. Hudson, Sigmund Freud: The Human Person as Sexual, in *Images of the Human: The Philosophy of the Human Person in a Religious Context*, H. Brown, D. L. Hudecki, L. A. Kennedy, and J. J. Snyder (eds.), Loyola, Chicago, pp. 367-396, 1995.

13. H. Smith, *The Religions of Man*, Harper and Row, New York, 1986.

14. J. Ortega y Gasset, In Search of Goethe from Within, in *The Dehumanization of Art and Other Writings on Art and Culture*, J. Ortega y Gasset (ed.), Doubleday, Garden City, New York, pp. 121-160, 1956.

15. F. D. Ritchie, *Learning From the Experts*, Lecture given at the 1995 King's College Conference on Death and Bereavement.

16. H. Feifel, The Meaning of Death in American Society, in *Death Education: Preparation for Living*, B. R. Green and D. P. Irish, Schenkman, Cambridge, Massachusetts, pp. 3-12, 1971.

Contributors

Gerry R. Cox, Ph.D., is a professor of sociology and associate with the Center for Death Education & Bioethics at the University of Wisconsin-La Crosse. He is a member of the International Work Group on Death, Dying and Bereavement, as well as co-editor of *Illness, Crisis, and Loss* with B. Bendiksen. He has taught death and dying courses, trained hospice volunteers, facilitated bereavement groups, and has lectured and conducted workshops. He has edited, co-edited, and authored seven books and over 40 articles and chapters in books and journals including *Death, Dying & Bioethics* (with B. Bendiksen).

John T. Chirban, Ph.D., is a professor of theology at Holy Cross Greek Orthodox Seminary in Brookline, Massachusetts and adjunct professor of psychology at Harvard University Medical School.

Judith Hauptman, MA, Ph.D., has taught at the Jewish Theological Seminary of America since 1973. Dr. Hauptman received a degree in Talmud from the Seminary College of Jewish Studies at JTS (now Albert A. List College) and a degree in economics from Barnard College and earned an MA and a PhD in Talmud from JTS. After serving as the Rabbi Philip R. Alstat Professor of Talmud, Dr. Hauptman recently became the first to hold the E. Billi Ivry Chair of Talmud and Rabbinic Culture. A popular lecturer and prolific writer, Dr. Hauptman has published extensively.

Leslie Kawamura, Ph.D., is presently professor of Buddhism in the Department of Religious Studies at the University of Calgary. He has been instrumental in establishing the Asian Studies Major with minors in both East Asia and South Asian Studies. He serves as the Chair of the Asian Studies Group at the University and on many committees related to globalization and internationalization of the University. He has read papers in England, Hungary, Switzerland, Japan, and Austria, and has published articles in many International Journals. His major area of research is Yogacara Buddhism (Psychological school of Buddhism) and he has translated Buddhist texts from Sanskrit, Tibetan, Classical Chinese, and Japanese. He has a varied interest in Religious Studies, extending from the science of religion to palliative care. He often serves as a chaplain in the local Hospital, especially for trauma cases.

Dennis Klass, Ph.D., is a professor at Webster University in St. Louis, Missouri. He has been interested in death, dying, and bereavement since 1968 when he was a graduate assistant in the famous Death and Dying Seminar led by Elisabeth Kübler-Ross at the University of Chicago. Dr. Klass is the author of two previous books and over 40 articles and book chapters on death and grief and the psychology of religions.

Peter Albert Koop, Ph.D., is Emeritus Professor of Economics at King's College, University of Western Ontario. Dr. Koop combines his specialization in social justice issues with his interest in the history of Mennonites in North America.

Pittu Laungani, is Emeritus Professor of Psychology at South Bank University, London, England. He is a specialist in cross cultural counseling and cross cultural views of death and bereavement.

Edward Jeremy Miller earned a Ph.D. and S.T.D. from the University of Louvain, Belgium. He is Professor of Religious Studies at Gwynedd-Mercy College in suburban Philadelphia and had previously been professor of Roman Catholic theology at Emory University, Atlanta, in the Candler School of Theology. His many publications are mainly in the areas of medieval studies, constructive theology, and areas relating to John Henry Newman. He is currently working on a book connecting the educational philosophy of Cardinal Newman to the Ex Corde Ecclesiae discussions concerning Catholic higher education in the United States.

Brian Morgan, B.F.A., lives in New York City and works as a freelance writer and researcher.

John D. Morgan, Ph.D., is Emeritus Professor of Philosophy at King's College, University of Western Ontario, London, Canada. He is the founder and coordinator of the King's College Centre for Education about Death and Bereavement, and the Series Editor of *Death, Value and Meaning* for Baywood.

Mia Reeves, B.A., is a free-lance minister and therapist in New York.

Ronald Trojcak, Ph.D., after beginning his undergraduate education at the University of Illinois as a music major, was ordained a Roman priest in 1962, having attended what is now called the University of St. Mary of the Lake, Mundelein, Illinois. After six years as a parish priest he attended McCormick Theological Seminary in Chicago (Th.M. degree). He received his Ph.D. in theology from the University of St. Michael's College, Toronto, Ontario. He has been on the faculty of King's College, London, Ontario since 1972 until the present, with one year stints at St. Dominics Seminary, Lusoka, Zambia, and Rush College, Holly Springs, Mississippi.

Index

DEATH AND BEREAVEMENT AROUND THE WORLD

edited by John D. Morgan and Pittu Laungani

Volume 1
Major Religious Traditions

Volume 2
Death and Bereavement in the Americas

Volume 3
Death and Bereavement in Europe

Volume 4
Death and Bereavement in Asia, Australia and New Zealand

Volume 5
Essays Reflecting on the Discoveries of the Earlier Volumes